HEROES AND TOILERS

Studies of the Weatherhead East Asian Institute, Columbia University
A Center for Korean Research Book

STUDIES OF THE WEATHERHEAD EAST ASIAN INSTITUTE, COLUMBIA UNIVERSITY

The Studies of the Weatherhead East Asian Institute of Columbia University were inaugurated in 1962 to bring to a wider public the results of significant new research on modern and contemporary East Asia.

For a complete list see page 263.

Heroes and Toilers

WORK AS LIFE IN POSTWAR
NORTH KOREA, 1953–1961

Cheehyung Harrison Kim

Columbia University Press
New York

This work was supported by the Core University Program for Korean Studies through the Ministry of Education of the Republic of Korea and the Korean Studies Promotion Service of the Academy of Korean Studies (AKS-2016-OLU-2250006).

Columbia University Press
Publishers Since 1893
New York   Chichester, West Sussex
cup.columbia.edu

Library of Congress Cataloging-in-Publication Data
Names: Kim, Cheehyung Harrison, author.
Title: Heroes and toilers : work as life in postwar North Korea, 1953–1961 /
Cheehyung Harrison Kim.
Description: New York : Columbia University Press, [2018] | Series: Studies of the
Weatherhead East Asian Institute, Columbia University | Includes bibliographical
references and index.
Identifiers: LCCN 2018016927 (print) | LCCN 2018034682 (ebook) |
ISBN 9780231546096 (e-book) | ISBN 9780231185301 (cloth : alk. paper)
Subjects: LCSH: Work—Korea (North)—History—20th century.
Classification: LCC BF481 (ebook) | LCC BF481 .K45 2018 (print) |
DDC 951.9304/3—dc23
LC record available at https://lccn.loc.gov/2018016927

Cover design: Lisa Hamm
Cover image: Photograph courtesy of the Hŭngnam Fertilizer Factory Museum.

For Areum

Contents

Acknowledgments

The ideas in this book began to come together some time ago. Many people have shaped them. To start, I thank the monk Cheorung for those alpine lessons in metaphysics. During the Dallas years, Nikki Sutker Bender, Julian Gudgeon, David Ginchansky, Cory Sutker, Dan and Tony Rucker, Jon Stanley, Mike Leddy, Reb Glazer Greene, Mike Quinn, and Shay Ometz were sources of laughter and adventure.

During the University of Texas years, John Robinette, Andrea Foy, Sean Boldt, Bibbin Gill-Griffin, Ajay Kapoor, Ken Potochnic, Cheryl Mayoff Navarrete, Nathan Beach, David Kimling, Jeff Stevens, Alex Hilburn, and Meaghan Samuels made Austin evenings blissful. From that moment, Jason Griffin has been with me on peregrinations across continents and in consciousness. During the Cleveland years, I felt the merriest camaraderie from Kate Masley and Tara Luffy Moore.

During the utopian years at Columbia University, Charles Kim, Hwisang Cho, Sun-Chul Kim, Hayes Moore, Anne Ishii, Jenny Wang Medina, Andy Rodekohr, Jimin Kim, Eleanor Hyun, Se-Mi Oh, Jisoo Kim, Alyssa Park, Joy Kim, Jessica Ko, Daham Chong, Bongjoo Shim, Sara Kile, Chad Diehl, Jonathan Twombly, Sixiang Wang, Miryong Shim, Carl Lau, Eric Han, Janet Lee, Brian Hwang, Sandra Peters, Hee-Sook Shin, Yukino Nakashima, Elizabeth Woyke, Myung Soo Kim, and Hosub Hwang kept me filled with ideals, dreams, and courage.

Beyond academia, Wolsan and Yulsan Liem, Eunhye Kim, Hye-Jung Park, Hyun Lee, Juyeon Rhee, Young Choe, Injoo Whang, Yong Un Yuk, Loyda Colon, J. T. Takagi, Hosu Kim, Sukjong Hong, and Sukmin Yoon showed me how good it feels to be part of a progressive community. From South Korea's counterpart, Kim Dong-kyu, Kim Aehwa, Ju Jaejun, Lee Changgeun, Kim Ji-Hyun, Min Dong-Wook, Lee Young-Soo, Jang Soo Kyung, Oh Jongryul, and Lee Jonghoe shared their exhilaration and inspiration from fighting the good fight.

During the Seoul research years, Kim Yong Woo, Oh Seung Eun, Yeom Woon-Ok, Hong Yang-Hee, Michael Kim, Sang-Hyun Kim, Hong Sung-hee, Min Gayoung, Ha YoungJun, Yun Hae-Dong, Kim Changhyun, Lee Seung-Won, Jeong Myeon, Kwon Hyeoung-Jin, Lee Dongheon, Lee San-grok, Kim Sung-Min, Lee Changnam, Shim Jaekyom, Lee Wonkeun, Cho Hunsang, Ryu Hojin, and Jeong Daehoon welcomed me into their magnanimous academic communities. Thanks also go to the good people running the North Korean Information Center at the National Library of Korea.

At Duke University during the postdoc years, Hae-Young Kim, Aimee Kwon, Leo Ching, Eunyoung Kim, Mindy Marcus, Hwansoo Kim, Carlos Rojas, Junehee Kwon, Simon Partner, Guo-Juin Hong, Jocelyn Olcott, and Eric Ferreri gave genuine advice, opened their unbelievable resources, and invited me to amazing house parties. While on my trip to North Korea, the guide team of Chŏng Yonghŭi, Kim Hyŏnok, and Ri Yujong were gracious, patient, and broad-minded during many hours of conversation.

At the University of Missouri, I found unpretentious and engaged collegiality in John Wigger, Robert Smale, Catherine Rymph, Jeff Pasley, Dominic Yang, Melinda Lockwood, Jenny Morton, Lynn Summers, Patty Eggleston, Daniel Domingues, Nancy Taube, Linda Reeder, Keona Ervin, Jerry Frank, John Frymire, Lois Huneycutt, Ilyana Karthas, Victor McFarland, Michelle Morris, Johnathan Sperber, Sheena Greitens, Seungkwon You, Je-Kook Chung, Clara Choi, Sang Hun Chun, Nicoya Gomes, Lesley Sapp, Tiffanesha Williams, Japheth Knopp, Dae-Young Kim, Mansoo Yu, and Ilhoi Yoo. I am especially thankful to Sang Kim of the Asian Affairs Center for his extraordinary leadership and unwavering confidence in my work. My Missouri years were constantly joyful because of Sarah Park Kim, Jerry Lee, Soyon An, Sarah Song Southworth, Zach Southworth, Jamie Lee, and Dongwon Shin.

At the University of Hawai'i at Mānoa, Shana Brown, Young-a Park, Sang-Hyop Lee, Ned Shultz, David Hanlon, Wensheng Wang, Suzanna

Reiss, David Chappell, Susan Carlson, Julie Motooka, Chris Bae, Jennie Jin, Noe Arista, John Rosa, Myungji Yang, Tae-Ung Baik, Hugh Kang, Hagen Koo, Yong-Ho Choe, Mercy Labuguen, Kortne Oshiro-Chin, and Jude Yang welcomed me to the academic community I have been searching for.

In North Korean studies, I am lucky and reassured to be trudging together with Dafna Zur, Immanuel Kim, Dima Mironenko, Ruth Barraclough, and Owen Miller. In Korean and Asian studies at large, through conferences, talks, and workshops, Andre Schmid, Jun Yoo, Paul Chang, Nan Kim, Todd Henry, Jin-kyung Lee, Carter Eckert, Vladimir Tikhonov, Aaron Moore, Sandra Fahy, Tani Barlow, Iñigo Adriasola, Janet Poole, Sunyoung Park, Suzy Kim, Carl Young, Adam Cathcart, Eunsung Cho, Steven Pieragastini, Covell Meyskens, Janice Kim, Travis Workman, Namhee Lee, and Andrea Longobardi provided crucial remarks on parts of the manuscript.

In the process of transforming the manuscript into a book, Ross Yelsey at Weatherhead provided steadfast guidance. Caelyn Cobb and Miriam Grossman at Columbia University Press shared their sharp and sophisticated prose sensibility. From the manuscript reviewers, I received essential interjections. To Annie Barva, who copyedited the manuscript, I am most grateful.

My giants Charles Armstrong, Cha Mun Seok, Hyun Ok Park, Jie-Hyun Lim, Khang Jeongseog, Alf Lüdtke, Theodore Hughes, Paik Won-dam, JaHyun Kim Haboush, Melbourne Tapper, James Pfeiffer, Rachel Chapman, Mahmood Mamdani, Eugenia Lean, and Bruce Cumings changed my academic life with the indulgence of their time, critical wisdom, and radical syllabi. In particular, Cha Mun Seok and Khang Jeong-seog kept my fire going with their unrivaled intellectual dexterity and authentic personalities. Special among the giants is my teacher and friend Charles Armstrong. He pushed me to take off. When I landed, a pioneer had already been there. His brilliance, humor, and adventurous spirit have been paramount to my academic journey. Long may you run, Charles.

Boundless support came from Oh Hwaja, Kim Younghwa, Kim Chang-seob, and Cha Geunhui—the family I gained through my partner, Areum. The high expectations held by Sooja, my mother, and Sangdae, my father, were in the end useful. Eeh-Hyung, my brother, and Lisa Banks kept me a tad off the straight and narrow with their poetic interventions. Stella and Daria, my kids, younger than this study, deserve my gratitude for the hugs and the misrecognition of me as the tallest person on earth. Finally, I thank Areum, my partner, for creating the map and for our inimitable life together.

The research for the book was carried out with the funding support of Columbia University's Department of East Asian Languages and Cultures, Columbia University's Weatherhead East Asian Institute, the U.S. Department of Education's Jacob K. Javits Fellowship Program, Duke University's Department of Asian and Middle Eastern Studies, the University of Missouri's Department of History, the University of Missouri's Asian Affairs Center, the University of Missouri's Research Council, the National Research Foundation of Korea's Humanities Korea Fellowship Program, and the American Council of Learned Society's New Faculty Fellowship Program. At the University of Hawai'i at Mānoa, this work was supported by the Core University Program for Korean Studies through the Ministry of Education of the Republic of Korea and Korean Studies Promotion Service of the Academy of Korean Studies (AKS-2015-OLU-2250005), the National Research Foundation of Korea Grant funded by the Korean Government (NRF-2017S1A6A3A01079727), and a grant from the Min Kwan-Shik Faculty Enhancement Fund at the University of Hawai'i Center for Korean Studies.

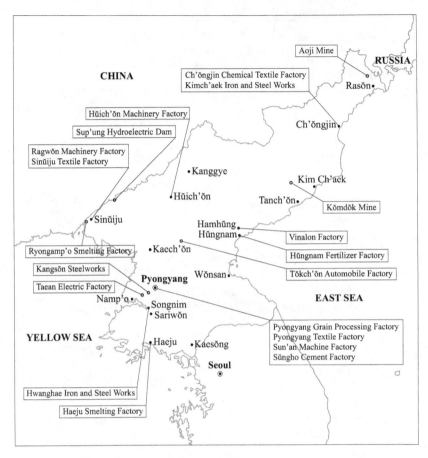

Map 0.1 Major industrial sites of postwar North Korea.
Source: Map by Areum Sophia Kim.

HEROES AND TOILERS

INTRODUCTION

Postwar North Korea

The Era of Work

Machinery is the surest means of lengthening the working day.
—KARL MARX, *CAPITAL*

One evening in June 1960, metalworker Chŏn Charyŏn poured a bucket of water over his head and, holding a large hammer, entered a steel smokestack. The 45-meter-long (49-yard) smokestack was on its side, on the ground, and some parts had become red hot from hours of burning wood underneath it. It was an old smokestack from another factory, full of dents. The banging of Chŏn Charyŏn's hammer rang from the inside as he began to flatten out the dents. The intense heat singed his uniform and melted his boots, but he hammered on. Earlier in the day an order had been given to the metalworkers to repair the smokestack and install it at the Boiler Shop of the Vinalon Factory, currently under construction.[1] At first, the metalworkers were of the opinion that building a new smokestack was costlier but easier than salvaging an old one, but when Chŏn Charyŏn stood up and said, "How can we call ourselves the metalworkers of this era if we can't handle one old smokestack?" they knew a decision was made.[2] Chŏn had been born a servant and would have most likely died a servant if not for the changes since the founding of North Korea. Now a citizen of a socialist country, he was an honorable worker participating in building a new world, an important part of which at the moment was the completion of the Vinalon Factory, which would relieve the shortage of clothing.[3] A year later, with the factory construction complete, Chŏn Charyŏn, once bound for a life of servitude, received

[1]

the title "labor hero" given out by the highest law-making organ, the Supreme People's Assembly.

Chŏn Charyŏn's story holds the central questions of this study. What does it mean to work? What does it mean to be a labor hero? How is the state or the nation tied to the activity of work? What do Chŏn's background and the situation of the smokestack say about the disposition of labor heroes? Is there a dimension of ordinariness—everydayness—within Chŏn's extraordinary act? What about the dangerous situation he throws himself into? What kind of work setting allows—promotes, perhaps—such a dangerous act? What does his story say about the socialist economic plan? How does the plan dictate the production process? What is the connection between the plan and Chŏn's heroic but entirely individual and random act? Is there a realm of practice in socialist production where the plan does not reach? If so, what does that say about the role of individual choice within the plan? Is there an ideological dimension in Chŏn's belief in building a new world? Is it conceivable to formulate an ideology of work in which a dangerous work situation is overlooked while the work is glorified? How is this work ideology related to productivity? Is an ideology of work unique to socialist production, or is it a general feature of industrial work observed throughout the world?

Chŏn Charyŏn was one of twenty-three workers nationally recognized as labor heroes for their efforts during the construction of the Vinalon Factory. His story fits into the typical hero-worker discourse ubiquitous and instrumental in North Korea's history (and, of course, in the histories of other socialist countries), but it was in the decade following the Korean War that the hero-worker discourse became an essential part of North Korea's production regime, by which I mean the coming together of the ruling party, policy- and law-making organs, trade unions, and cultural and artistic organizations—all with the single aim of increasing production.

The postwar period, considered in this work as lasting from 1953 to 1961, is characterized by five interconnected historical moments. The first is postwar reconstruction from 1953 to 1956, which formally raised the agricultural and industrial economy to prewar levels. This moment includes the Three-Year Plan, 1954–1956, which entailed the restoration of major industrial sites and the acceptance of large-scale foreign assistance. The second moment is industrial expansion and agricultural cooperativization from 1957 to 1961, which prioritized heavy industry over consumer goods and transformed the entire farming population into agricultural wageworkers. The

Five-Year Plan was implemented during this moment and officially lasted four years, from 1957 to 1960. A major reason for the early completion of the plan was the claim that by 1960 the foundation for a state-led socialist economy had been established, most significantly through the complete nationalization of industrial and agricultural production.

The third moment is the control of the political world by Kim Il Sung (Kim Ilsŏng) and his faction of former partisans of Manchuria. By the Fourth Congress of the Korean Workers' Party in September 1961, the partisan faction was the dominant political group in the party, the legislature, and the military. This moment includes the August Factional Incident of 1956, which at first shook Kim Il Sung's power base but consequently strengthened it by resulting in a systematic removal of competing political groups. The fourth moment is the subordination of trade unions and factory management under party control. The General Federation of Trade Unions of North Korea, the highest governing body of unions, declared in early 1959 that its purpose was to carry out the party's aims. By the end of 1961, following Kim Il Sung's famed visit to the Taean Electric Factory, the party's Central Committee was the most authoritative voice in production management. Last, the fifth moment is the expansion of mass movements, the purposes of which were to increase production and productivity and to promote innovations from the workers' workplaces. Like labor heroes, mass movements are a constant feature in North Korea's history, but it was during the postwar decade that they expanded greatly as an everyday practice of the population and as a prevalent theme in arts and literature.

In terms of periodization, the period I discuss is not the era of Juche (*chuch'e*), the philosophy and ideology of, at least formally, self-reliance and self-determination attributed to Kim Il Sung. The Juche era took root in the late 1960s and officially began in the early 1970s with the adoption of a Juche-based constitution in December 1972.[4] Nor is the period I discuss the era of Kim Il Sung's absolute power and religious-like glorification. Although his authority in the party, the Supreme People's Assembly, and the military became great, the period I cover, 1953 to 1961, is characterized by the dominance by Kim's political faction, not necessarily by Kim Il Sung. Rival political groups, with their own leading figures, existed in North Korea until the late 1950s, and excessive adulation of leadership was openly discouraged for years in socialist countries after Nikita Khrushchev's criticism of Joseph Stalin's immense individual power in February 1956.

The era of Kim Il Sung's unassailable authority and veneration would begin in the following decade, though their inception is indeed found in the postwar era. Rather, this postwar period can be called the *era of work*, when state apparatuses were pulled together to send the people to the factories and farms, to make them stay there, and to make their work productive and meaningful.

The Claims

The investigation in these pages moves along a chain of four claims. First, the state's pursuit of unity and progress after the Korean War was most concretely practiced through work—work identified as an honorable, dutiful, and joyful activity. Work—specifically, industrial work—was elevated to an ideological and ethical category, like the nation, thereby dissimulating the practices of subjugation and exploitation inherent in all industrial work. Industrial work as an organizing practice and as ideological ground for national unity was uniquely manifested in postwar North Korea. The famous example is the Ch'ŏllima Work Team Movement, which began in 1959, mobilized millions of workers, and functioned as a lasting cultural trope. At the same time, work as an economic and political activity essential to the governing of the ruling class is a universally observed practice in the modern era, though perhaps more intensely practiced in state socialist and postcolonial countries. It is easy to conjure up violence and indoctrination as methods of rule in these countries, a view common in the case of North Korea largely because of its peculiar presence in world media, but such a picture speaks more to Cold War ideological imaginations than to actual state practice. Unjust imprisonment and punishment have undoubtedly occurred (and still occur) in North Korea, but the historical picture is more complex, particularly in the postwar period. The state deployed violence mostly on high-profile elites, people such as Pak Hŏnyŏng, the foreign minister whose execution in 1955 symbolized the debacle of the Korean War. Violence monopolized and deployed by the state may be severe in state socialist countries such as North Korea, but it is no less severe in so-called liberal countries such as South Korea. Indoctrination (otherwise known by that awful word *brainwashing*), too, is a common universal practice of nation-states. All industrial work, whether carried out in a socialist country or a nonsocialist country, requires the ideological education of the worker to willingly accept and repeat the often harsh process of production.

Second, for work to be purposeful and valuable, it had to be executed daily: the potential of work as a surplus-producing activity was realized in everyday life. In short, work had to be *repeated*. In postwar North Korea, where industrial growth was essential, the merger between work and everyday life became ever more important. From building childcare centers to emphasizing work attendance, the discourse and practice of industrialization found a dimension of concreteness in everyday life. In other words, the concrete space in which the ideological force of work took effect was everyday life. For production to occur and reoccur and for governing to be consequential, the state had to seize everyday life—everyday life operating as modes of production and administration. The quotidian field took on an ethical and ideological utility conceived and implemented by the North Korean state. Everydayness became the language of industrial work and state management. Although ideology is a popular way of explaining North Korea, both for the world outside it and for its own ruling class, I do not subscribe to the view that North Korea possesses a particular ideology more powerful than other ideologies elsewhere. Nor do I think that ideology as it is commonly understood—as a mind-altering device with a corresponding reality of subjugation—possesses much explanatory usefulness. Rather, I readily evoke the ideological category because what can be seen as uniquely ideological in North Korea can reveal the workings of ideology in general. For example, the ideological trait in the activity of work is *everydayness*. And within everydayness, the ideological force is *repetition*. In the pursuit of rapid industrial growth, the North Korean state heavily stressed order and consistency in postwar life, both at work and at home. Mass movements are again key examples, with their emphasis on the repetition of disciplined work. Equally important was the built environment—housing, daycare centers, and workers' break rooms—which, at least in principle, helped the workers return to the factories in a consistent manner. I mention repetition and everydayness to suggest that ideology operates in mundane ways. The ideological hold is found not so much in monuments and parades but in wages and apartments. Such a connection has relevance to the mechanism of ideology in general—in all places, not just in North Korea. The influence of ideology hence takes effect in the everyday, as in the case of workers' repetitive participation in the work of factories.

Third, in the setting of the state's plan to industrialize the country and to imbue the nation with the spirit of work as an honorable and dutiful activity, the people of North Korea responded diversely and dialectically. Some, such as Chŏn Charyŏn, the metalworker, rose to the occasion and became nationally recognized, attaining material and political benefits in the process, whereas others were less obliging, even incorrigible and resistive—coming to work late, frequently switching jobs, fighting with coworkers, and participating in the black market. Most people, however, followed the state's call so as to secure their livelihood, resolve conflict, and find some level of enjoyment and happiness. Their world was undeniably framed by the historical situation of the global political economy, but within it they created their own everyday rhythm, constantly reconfiguring the state plan to accommodate their circumstances. They were historical actors simultaneously participating in and distancing themselves from various authorities, whether the authority was a union chief or an overachieving coworker. Central to the inquiry on lived experience is therefore the relationship between domination and agency, a relationship discussed often simplistically in the case of North Korea. The presumption is that the North Korean state has maintained power by suppressing its people and that this suppression, whether ideological or physical, is so strong—so complete—that resistance against the state has not and does not happen. North Korea's postwar period is seen as a moment when domination was the very reason for its rapid economic growth and national unity. To argue the existence of people's agency separate from state power, however, is just as flawed. Instead, ambiguity should be elevated as the condition of practice—ambiguity in the relationship between domination and agency, where domination and agency are in practice dependent on each other. The lived experience entails an undifferentiating process in which the division between domination and agency becomes undetectable. Life is experienced as a whole, even while within demanding state apparatuses. One specific consideration is the practice of choice. This theme is prodigiously observed in the cultural materials of the postwar era. The people's actions in postwar North Korea were not about blindly following orders but about making choices, confronting oppositions, and forging their own reality. For the socialist plan to be realized, it depended on individual choices and negotiations among committed members of the state, even when this dependency meant that the result regularly diverged from the original goal. Choice and program shared the same space in everyday life.

The recognition of this relationship is a confirmation of resistance as a plural field of interactions. Organized protests are powerful, but they are a rare kind of resistance, sometimes not the best option. In places such as North Korea, everyday forms of resistance leading to small changes were everywhere and vital to historical actors in remaking their world.

Fourth, North Korea's postwar industrialization, while expanding the authority of the state and the nation, was a process of further integration with capitalism. The expansion of the nation occurred as communities and classes broke down in the aftermath of the Korean War, creating a national culture centered on the communal image of the state and its leadership. The expansion of the state occurred to consolidate the economic, political, and military domains under a single legal authority. This consolidation was especially important in the domain of production. Through nationalization of industries and collectivization of farms, all by 1958, the state emerged as the sole authority in capturing surplus value (which comes only from unpaid labor). The state ownership of production and circulation is considered a mark of socialism—extensive and permanent state control as an alternative system to private control in capitalism. My position, however, is that the permanent authority of the state in industrial production re-created the exploitative conditions of capitalism, especially as the state became the mediating agent in the exchange of labor power for wage. This position is based on the premise that socialism, as it existed in the twentieth century, could not skip over the historical stage of capitalism. Rather than private firms, the state played the role of appropriating surplus value and accumulating capital. Socialism as a system based on useful labor and equal sharing of surplus became lost as the state, the ruling party, and civic and labor organizations came to share the same purpose and ideological message. A key moment in socialism's dissolution in North Korea was February 1959, when the General Federation of Trade Unions openly accepted the party's goals as the unions' goals. Here, the notion of a single global political economy is relevant not only because the border between socialist and capitalist blocs remained porous in many ways but also because both sides saw industrialism as the primary road toward national culture and wealth. Industrialism in various postcolonial nation-states, including those espousing socialism, required large-scale factories, massive input of natural resources, low-skill machine operation, and, above all, consistent and abundant labor power compensated by wage. The universal practice of industrialism denotes the frailty of the designations *capitalism* and *socialism*.

Industrialism, then, is the political-economic realm where capital thrives in both socialism and capitalism. To identify the state's involvement in the history of socialism, various labels are used, including *existing socialism*, *socialism of the twentieth century*, *communism*, and *state socialism*, among which I prefer to use *state socialism*.

Everyday Life, Industrialism, Work

In the history of state socialism, the everyday is conceived as a discursive and practical space of state power, instrumental in the construction of a socialist civilization. It was Leon Trotsky who said, "Greater attention must be paid to the facts of everyday life."[5] This includes nonproductive activities of leisure: "The working class state," stated Trotsky, "is neither a spiritual order nor a monastery. . . . The longing for amusement, distraction, sightseeing, and laughter is the most legitimate desire of human nature. We are able, and indeed obliged, to give the satisfaction of this desire a higher artistic quality, at the same time making amusement a weapon of collective education."[6] In postwar North Korea, everyday life was an aspect of idealized totality formally connecting people's needs with state needs—a style of control insisting on totality not through coercion but through individual self-determination in relation to the nation-state. This feature of state power was and is noticeable in North Korea. As the historian Suzy Kim shows, the revolutionary period before the Korean War was fundamentally centered on the creation of a new socialist everyday that "fused individual and collective interests into one."[7]

North Korea's everyday life was at the same time about more than state power. As Kim's study further shows, the revolutionary forging of the everyday was part of a socialist modernity that was seeking to "liberate people from the adverse effects of capitalism toward the full achievement of human potential and emancipation through new forms of community."[8] For instance, when the people were called on to enter the factory setting, North Korea's Youth League emphasized the practice of arriving at work early to have time for reading.[9] What is notable about socialist modernity, then, as Kim asserts, is its critique of capitalism from the position of collective life, "putting society above the logic of capital."[10] This was a project of creating a reality radically different from both the colonial past and the capitalist market presently prevailing in countries such as South Korea and its patron, the United States.

North Korea's postwar situation, however, irreparably disrupted the project of creating a different modernity. As industrialism became the most prominent motive in life and work, it was impossible to shield the people from the exploitative conditions of capitalist industrial production, which emerged despite the rationality of state socialism. This is not to say that state socialism failed to create its own reality. Rather, the recognition of industrial practice is a chance to redefine state socialism. The philosopher Kojin Karatani is my starting point. In putting aside the base–superstructure model in which the state and nation are ideological outcomes of the economic base, Karatani sees the state and nation as active entities colluding with the commodity system (the old "base"), each operating as a distinct mode of exchange. The state, for instance, practices the exchange mode of "plunder and redistribution" (taxation for welfare), and the mode of exchange for the nation is "reciprocity" (gifts for obligations). The commodity system, in contrast, is dependent on the exchange among free beings through an equalizing medium (money for work). The three exchange modes are always present as a combination in every historical formation.[11]

When the commodity system is the dominant mode of exchange over the state and nation, the historical formation is capitalism, in which production relies primarily on labor power as a commodity—that is, wage labor.[12] This does not mean the state and nation go away. On the contrary, the commodity system depends on the state and nation to overcome its limitations and to transform itself into something seemingly natural ("free" labor). For Karatani, recognizing that the world since the eighteenth century has been at the stage of capitalism—with the twentieth century's late capitalism defined by state management of capital and by the welfare state—is a necessary step in formulating a critique of capital's global expansion.[13] Despite their inspiring and transformative effects, the socialist revolutions of the twentieth century—in particular those in postcolonial countries such as North Korea—chiefly entailed state ownership of industries. A major obstacle to the realization of socialism starts from this moment because state ownership can never abolish the fundamental capitalist problem of labor-power commodity (wage labor), where the proletariat becomes the wageworkers of the state.[14] In North Korea, wage labor became the predominant form of work from 1958, when the cooperativization of all farmland, completed by October that year, concluded the nationalization of production, which had begun with large industries in 1946 and continued with small enterprises in 1955. The type of wage considered most appropriate in socialism was piecework wage. The North Korean state viewed it as a wage system justly compensating the quantifiable results of labor (see chapter 2).[15] What is problematic is that piecework wage was also the quintessential method of payment in industrial capitalism, extensively practiced in factories and inherently exploitative because the workers could be driven to increase the speed and intensity of their work for more pay. Furthermore, in North Korea there were different rates for piecework according to the type of work: dangerous and difficult work received a higher minimum rate. Piecework in North Korea was thus individualized, competitive, and hierarchical.

The impossibility that state ownership can abolish capital, Karatani emphasizes, is a notion already stressed by Karl Marx, whose call for seizing state power was not for the sake of state ownership but for the sake of abolishing the relation between capital and the wage–labor classes.[16] The seizure of state power by the working class, as is well known, was always a temporary action: the end of class rule was to be followed by the withering of the state. But, of course, the revolutions espoused by socialism did not abolish the labor-power commodity and instead put in place a system of permanent state control over production and circulation, which was another kind of class rule. The historical ramification is that the socialists who seized power in places such as North Korea ended up playing the role played elsewhere by the bourgeoisie or the absolute monarchy.[17] The appearance of Kim Il Sung on the political scene and the continuation of the Kim family leadership were, therefore, not idiosyncratic aspects of a peculiar form of authoritarianism but necessary practices in the development of capitalism, necessary in the process of aligning capital with the nation and state. In other words, the Kim family and the ruling class loyal to the family functioned much like the bourgeois class in organizing the accumulation of surplus. To state this more clearly: state socialism is a category of capitalist formation in which the state is the active mediator of capital.

How is the industrial labor process specifically related to exploitation? Marx's work is a good place to look. Industrial labor is foremost about machinery, which, "like every other component of constant capital, creates no new value."[18] Any and all new value comes from the worker—that is, the worker's labor power. As Marx observed, machine-related work increases the production of surplus value in various ways. First, it depreciates the value of the labor-power commodity (the workers) by cheapening all the commodities entering into production. Second, it raises the social value of the article produced as machine work becomes labor of a higher degree. Third, it diminishes the number of workers in a factory. Fourth, it prolongs the working day to compensate for the decrease in the number of workers. And finally, it increases the intensity of labor as the worker gains experience with the machine.[19] Each method is also a point of exploitation, which can be defined as a condition arising from the ratio of value produced by the worker for livelihood and the value produced by the same worker appropriated by the ownership. The prolongation of the working day in industrial labor is a perplexing feature: the machine-produced commodity increases the social value of the commodity to the extent that the large surplus margin becomes a powerful motive for the owner to demand longer hours from fewer workers. Marx expresses the problem as such: "Hence that remarkable phenomenon in the history of modern industry, that machinery sweeps away every moral and natural restriction on the length of the working day. Hence too the economic paradox that the most powerful instrument for reducing labor-time suffers a dialectical inversion and becomes the most unfailing means for turning the whole lifetime of the worker and his family into labor-time at capital's disposal."[20] The fading of moral and natural restrictions on work has the disastrous effect of reconfiguring *work as life*—the transformation of life into labor power, which occurs at a large scale during industrialization.

The notion of intensity is particularly relevant for this study because it has to do with speed, efficiency, and, the most troublesome concept, productivity. Marx says that even when the working day is legally limited, the problem of intensity remains an acute form of exploitation: machinery "serves as a means of systematically getting more work done within a given period of time, or in other words, constantly exploiting labor-power more intensively."[21] This process is not necessarily coercion; it is ostensibly ordinary. As machine work becomes routinized, the worker's growing experience naturally leads to an increase in speed and intensity of labor, with the worker in the process receiving a greater quantity of machines to operate.[22] What can be gathered from Marx is that in capitalist production the seemingly progressive elements such as improvements in technology and workers' experience are the very grounds of exploitation because efficiency and productivity translate to more surplus captured by the ownership. The pertinent example of industrial exploitation in postwar North Korea is the practice of mass-production campaigns, epitomized by the Ch'ŏllima Work Team Movement of 1959. These campaigns produced extraordinary economic results, galvanized the nation, and provided credibility to the state, but from the position of capitalist expansion they were simultaneously practices of collusion among capital, nation, and state to create, from the postwar context of poverty and destruction, a situation wherein surplus production became possible.

Staying on the topic of machines a little longer is useful. Machines are actually a problem. The sociologist Michael Burawoy puts the question directly: "Can socialism operate with capitalist machines, or do the machines impose constraints on relations of and in production that make socialism impossible?" Burawoy's answer is a pessimistic one because "capitalist relations in production are shaped by capitalist relations of production."[23] The features of the capitalist production process—typified by fragmented work, separation of manual and mental activities, the obscuring and securing of surplus value, and hierarchy and inequality among workers—are carried to each production site. Hence, Burawoy's position is that the "type of machine that is designed to increase efficiency under capitalism is the very machine that enhances control; efficiency becomes domination."[24] In the mid–twentieth century, state socialist countries that implemented industrialization had no choice but to implement the industrial process developed from capitalism. The techniques and procedures related to machines were born out of industrial capitalism and thus made to support the capitalist relations of production.

North Korea's industrial history attests to this picture. Postliberation nation building and postwar reconstruction were reliant on the thousands of industrial sites originally built by Japanese capitalist enterprises during the colonial period (1910–1945). The major enterprises in colonial Korea built by great Japanese firms became, without reservation, North Korea's emblematic factories. Hwanghae Iron and Steel Works, located in Kyŏimp'o at the mouth of the Taedong River, close to Pyongyang, is such a factory. It was first built by the Mitsubishi Company in 1914 and later managed by the Nihon Iron and Steel Company.[25] In the aftermath of the Korean War, Hwanghae Iron and Steel Works, heavily damaged by bombings, became a symbolic site of reconstruction and recovery (see chapter 4). At least formally and nominally, Hwanghae Steel was to be reborn as a state-owned enterprise of a sovereign nation, partaking in international socialist trade based on solidarity and need and contributing to the process of transforming the mode of production in the name of socialism. But, of course, it was the same factory originally built to support the capitalist imperial projects of Japan, which meant that the relations in production on the shop floor came from hierarchical wage labor. Yun Sejung's novel *Yonggwangno nŭn sumshinda* (The furnace is breathing, 1960),[26] about steelworkers striving to restart a blast furnace, is based on the lives of women and men at Hwanghae Steel who transformed the war-damaged factory into one of the most productive steel factories in North Korea. The novel idealizes the socialist production system and reminds the reader of the revolutionary mission embodied in hard work, but it is also rich with details of the shop floor, revealing the everyday struggles of the workers.

In my claim that the capitalist production process, defined by commodified and hierarchical labor, was at the core of North Korea's postwar industrial economy, I am not denying difference. The varying combinations of capital, state, and nation gave rise to distinct historical realities in North Korea and South Korea. What is pivotal here is not to consider historical reality as a kind of superstructure determined by an economic base. Rather, capital, state, and nation are all active modes of exchange, and each provides its own relationship with people and nature, albeit constantly in collusion with other modes. This relationship is also always transnational. The differences between North Korea and South Korea are therefore less about alternative realities than about global Cold War propaganda— seemingly contrasting cultural production based on particular artistic and literary formulations, on the one hand, and superficially divergent practices of representing national sovereignty and the ruling class, on the other. So it could be said that whereas South Korea's postwar national community was dependent primarily on the market logic of crisis, endorsed by a development-oriented welfare state, and influenced by American cultural production, North Korea's postwar national community was based largely on the appearance of interaction among the production logic of industrialism, the state acting as the sole mediator of economic forces and nationhood, and the culture of militarism originating in the Soviet Union.

More precisely, the differences are equivalents. Within the social formation of capitalism, the state socialism of North Korea and the state capitalism of South Korea are equivalent practices aiming for the same objectives of surplus accumulation, labor discipline, and national unity. A brief list illustrates these equivalents. The symbol of Kim Il Sung and his family as the unifying identity of the nation, essential for accumulation, finds an equivalent in South Korea's capitalist conglomerates using patriotic sentiment to consolidate the population as producers-consumers. South Korea's obsession with developing toward advanced-nation status finds an equivalent in North Korea's preoccupation with national/territorial unification, both trajectories concealing enormous amounts of exploitation and inequality in each country. The passing of power from Kim Il Sung to Kim Jong Il and now to Kim Jong Un finds an equivalent in South Korean conglomerates' maintaining their symbolic power by keeping the corporate leadership within the founding families. The notion of cyclic market crises driving privatization and austerity in South Korea finds an equivalent in North Korea's notion of constant threat from imperialist countries, which legitimates the antidemocratic culture of militarism in education, leisure, and work. The move in South Korea toward greater control over workers by suppressing labor unions and propagating antiunion ideas finds an equivalent in North Korea's politics of sovereignty, which justifies the construction of enemies who threaten national sovereignty. And the ubiquitous propaganda in North Korea produced by the party and state finds an equivalent in the advertisements that inundate everyday life in South Korea, rendering the entire population targets of corporate marketing.

It is in such a light that I find the sociologist Hyun Ok Park's recent work relevant to my study. Park's notion of a "market utopia" as the source for democracy and freedom shapes the book's elegant and groundbreaking thesis that "capital has already unified Korea in a transnational form." Unification here is not about territorial integration but is "driven by the exchange of capital, labor, and ideas across the borders of Korean communities." In this shift, Park observes the politics of unification as a "flight from history to idealism," where peace is achievable through trade and liberty through regime change and where "individuals are juridical subjects engaging in market exchange." An important aspect about market utopia is thus its concealment of history: "The notion of market exchange as the foundation of peace and freedom obscures the historical present. That is, it obscures not only the crisis of industrial capitalism and its consequent development of a new relationship between the state, finance capital, and industrial capital in South Korea but also changes in North Korea."[27] This obscuring of history by the market—resulting in history's repetition through the form of crisis—is what Park refers to as the "capitalist unconscious." Moreover, the "changes in North Korea" are transformations taking place for the past sixty years through the presence of commodity exchange.

North Korea has already accepted market logic as the rationale of labor and accumulation. Indeed, pertinent to my study is Park's assessment that the "actual socialist economy depended on the vertiginous implications of the bureaucratization of the state and the continued commodity production and regulation of labor." Park's notion of crisis is especially salient; she locates the new form of Korean ethnic sovereignty within capitalist crisis. To be sure, this crisis is articulated in terms of not only economic factors "but also the very problematic of history and everyday experience arising from capitalist accumulation and its politico-cultural mediation."[28] Although Park reserves the concept of crisis for the context of South Korea (and state capitalism), I read in her work the recognition of an equivalent in North Korea (and state socialism) in the concept of revolution. Whereas the aim of crisis is to promote accumulation, the aim of revolution is to continuously develop productive forces. In this framework, Park sees Juche ideology as "part and parcel of North Korea's distinctive formula of permanent revolution."[29] The permanent vigilance of revolutionary life, as espoused by revolutionaries from Mao Zedong to Kim Il Sung, was the socialist answer to the historical problem of instability arising from the interaction among capital, nation, and state. The condition of capital's unification of contemporary Korea is therefore the result of two distinct but equivalent historical processes of crisis and accumulation in the two nation-states. And in my view, this process in North Korea began during the postwar era of industrialization.

As much as I aim to locate North Korea within the transnational context of capitalist expansion, I am equally devoted in these pages to exploring how the people lived and worked within the distinct historical reality of state socialism. Work and everyday life constitute the double core of this story. My intent is to recognize the diversity in the act of living, conceived as everyday practices within a hegemonic system. Practice foremost entails historical actors evaluating their situation, making choices, and acting sensibly within a larger hegemonic system. For me, the outcome of practice, whether success or failure, is not as important as its details. I am certain that people, even while living under oppressive conditions, are rational, resilient, and creative.

In mid-2018, the North Korean state seems to be stable for the future. The Seventh Korean Workers' Party Congress, held in Pyongyang in May 2016 after more than three decades of hiatus (the Sixth Congress was in October 1980), formalized the new leadership structure and broadcast to the world the continuation of its style of socialism. The state-level meetings between North Korea, South Korea, and the United States are creating some prospects toward peace and partnerships. Although the state maintains the authoritarian system established during the Kim Il Sung era, the population has become more uneven than ever. Increases in trade, information, and consumption in the past decade have led to unprecedented accumulation for the wealthy class, who have access to the best goods and services available on the global market, even as inequality grows prodigiously according to occupation, family status, and place of residence. The border between North Korea and China is porous, an area where ordinary people can make a living in extralegal trade or in the transnational labor market, which often pulls men into hazardous work and women into sex work. Meanwhile, distorted socialism lives on in North Korea as spectacle— murals, monuments, and mania, all of which transform into media items and memes that the outside world consumes with a sense of its exotic and disdainful otherness. At the heart of all this is the insidious troika of capital, nation, and state. By situating North Korea historically, I am saying that its problems are humanity's problems, not because North Korea is some kind of threat to "freedom" or "democracy" or "our way of life" but because it holds all the problems that humanity faces together in this world. North Korea exists, as does the United States and South Korea, within the single structure that causes the same problems throughout the globe. I am also saying that socialism beyond capital has yet to arrive and remains a choice for humanity's common progress.

Note on Translation and Definition of the Term *Work*

The words *work* and *labor* denote the human activity of transforming an object or idea for use or exchange. *Work* connotes the qualitative form of such activity, and *labor* its quantitative form ("honest work" versus "wage labor"). The categories break down in application, however. For example, the term *working class* refers mainly to the economic characteristic of the laboring people, and the name "Labor Day" is a qualitative treatment of work as a public holiday. Consistency in definition becomes more difficult with translation. From English to Korean, *work* can be translated as both "*nodong*" and "*kŭllo*," the latter of which has the connotation of "diligent work." *Labor*, however, is almost always translated as "*nodong*." From Korean to English, *nodong* is usually translated as "labor," although *nodongja*—"one who labors"—is translated less as "laborer" than as "worker." In sum, work as a qualitative activity in the realm of usefulness is equivalent to both *nodong* and *kŭllo*, and labor as a quantitative activity in the realm of value production is mainly equivalent to *nodong*. Although the terms *labor* and *work* are interchangeable in use, in both English and Korean each has a certain signification to which this study tries to be consistent, using *work* to refer to a qualitative activity and *labor* to refer to a quantitative activity.

Plan of the Book

Chapter 1 presents the historical meaning of work in North Korea. When and how work became imbued with the sense of duty, sacredness, and happiness are the key questions of the chapter. The North Korean state emphasized hard work from its beginning. Hwang Changyŏp's book *Sahoe palchŏnsa* (The history of societal development, 1956)[30] draws an elegant sketch of why physical work is an honorable activity in socialism. Thinking about work in North Korea also leads to what work has meant in human history, including the ideas of Aristotle, Adam Smith, Karl Marx, and Vladimir Lenin. In his notion of work and labor, Marx did not think of labor as a sacred and joyous activity in and of itself. An essential feature of communism, for Marx, was the return of labor into life: labor was honorable insofar as life was honorable. Work as a source of happiness and a collective duty in socialism came from the philosophy of Lenin. Socialist work is a variation of the liberal idea of work envisioned by Adam Smith and shaped in the context of industrial revolution. Lenin redefined this liberal notion of work under state socialism as a revolutionary process necessary for emancipation.

Chapter 2 considers work as various forms of practice—production within socialism, organization through unions, and object of management by the state and party. Socialist work management was developed in Stalin's Soviet Union, where work and politics came to share the same ideological space. In the case of North Korea, a useful starting point is the

Korean War. The situation of war allowed legal changes that made switching jobs or quitting work difficult, mobilized women as the most important source of wartime labor, and launched the major project of relocating factories into safer areas so production could continue. Influenced by the extralegal practice of wartime labor, work in the postwar period came to be coordinated by a regime of production made up of the state, party, unions, and agencies of propaganda. During this period, the one-person management system (*yuil kwallije*), with the factory director in charge of production, which had been the favored management system since 1948, gave way to a party-dominated management system, the Taean Work System. In addition, an important characteristic of the production regime during this period was its effort to increase productivity not through coercion but through wage motivation (especially piecework wage) and the calibration of workload, work time, and work space.

Chapter 3 is about the production of everyday life as modes of production and administration. Everyday life was remade in the context of establishing the economic foundations for state socialism. This remaking required foremost the monopoly of politics and production by a single authority—the authority of Kim Il Sung and his faction of former partisans of Manchuria. Controlling production entailed, first, the post–Korean War recovery of the damaged but still considerable industrial system; second, the proletarianization of all producers, especially farmers, into wage-workers; and, third, the complete nationalization of production, including the collectivization of agriculture, to ensure no surplus remained in the private domain. Political control entailed the systematic removal of competing political groups by Kim Il Sung and his partisan faction. Political purges began during the war, with the persecution of Soviet Koreans, such as Hŏ Kai, and the former South Korean Workers' Party members, the most infamous case being the arrest and execution of the revolutionary Pak Hŏnyŏng. The Yan'an group, made up of Chinese Koreans who participated in the Chinese Revolution, was removed from the Korean Workers' Party and the state following the August Factional Incident of 1956, during which Kim Il Sung's power and policies were seriously challenged. In this chapter, the remaking of everyday life is approached, first, from the ideological dimension of the notion of repetitive work; second, from the mass movements that took place in all sectors of industry to increase production and productivity, with the Ch'ŏllima Work Team Movement of 1959 as a representative campaign; and, third, from the construction of totality between living and working, where social needs and state needs are simultaneously satisfied. Repetitive work, mass movements, and totality between life and work merged in the space of everyday life.

Chapter 4 is a detailed exploration of North Korea's everyday work in the decade following the Korean War. The chapter presents what it must have been like to live and work in North Korea during this period. The chapter centers on various themes, including *choice, resistance, appropriation, representation, aesthetics*, and *contention*. They are analyzed through textual and visual materials such as fiction, poetry, painting, film, and memoir. One such work of fiction is the novel *The Furnace Is Breathing* by Yun Sejung, the analysis of which reveals a contentious world of work in relation to the central plan. This chapter shows that North Korea's citizen-workers did not quietly submit to the demands of socialist industrialism. Within the fervor of socialist transformation, the rhythm of everyday life was sometimes in line with and sometimes in opposition to the demands of the state. What determined this rhythm was a confluence of state power and the quest for individual happiness, a confluence played out in everyday space.

Chapter 5 concerns the Vinalon Factory and its main product. In the early 1960s, the synthetic fiber vinalon became North Korea's national fiber, a product symbolizing the independence and ingenuity of its state-led socialism, from the raw materials needed to make it (the abundant coal and limestone) to the person who invented it (the colonial Korean chemist Ri Sŭnggi, scouted by North Korea in 1950). The Vinalon Factory near Hamhŭng City—a factory originally built by a Japanese chemical company and a city rebuilt with the assistance of East Germany—also became a national emblem of its own as a factory arising solely from the toil of the North Korean people. As this chapter shows, the history of vinalon is a transnational convergence of the colonial industrial system, the postliberation efforts of state building, the dynamics of multinational postwar reconstruction, and the Kim Il Sung government's monopoly of production and politics. At the same time, "Vinalon City," as the enormous factory was called, was immutably localized as part of everyday ideology: the completion of the factory was possible with the help of thousands of volunteer workers who possessed no special skills, and the workers who turned vinalon into clothes also wore them. It was in everyday life that vinalon exerted its ideological force.

The conclusion provides final remarks about North Korea's relationship with industrialism and, using North Korea as a case, offers reflections on global problems of labor exploitation and state authoritarianism. It was not a personal penchant for power but the state's preoccupation with industrialism that justified industrial work as the ethical and ideological standard for the population. Social life came to be defined by the production regime, and work became the grounds for state power. Moreover, the aim of labor became not only usefulness but also the abstract realization of the nation as framed by the state. Everyday work was thus the means of domination. This story is echoed in many other countries, not only the poor, authoritarian, and postcolonial countries but also the so-called advanced and liberal countries. A useful critique of North Korea requires a critique of industrial labor and the state's direct involvement in exploitative work. Such a critique also reveals universal problems existing throughout the world. One way of considering real change thus begins with the negation of work as it is practiced in capitalism—a double movement of resistance against the capital-commodity economy and the hegemonic state that begins with small changes in one's own everyday reality.

CHAPTER 1

The Historical Concept of Work

Eager to begin work, always resolute as early spring.

—PAEK SŎK, "IRŬN POM" (EARLY SPRING)

T he concept of work in North Korea is a concept with deep historical roots. During the stretch from the mid-1950s to the early 1960s, the North Korean state sought national recovery from the Korean War and laid the economic foundation for state socialism. Work, in the process, became subsumed under ideology—under state and party control legitimating the appropriation of surplus value, the value created only from unpaid labor. In the effort to rebuild the economy after a devastating war, the North Korean state and the Korean Workers' Party attempted to organize the labor power of workers and farmers into a single labor regime directly controlled by the hegemonic state. Put differently, the party–state alliance during this period tried to make its own interest of increasing productivity and surplus into the interest of collective labor.

North Korea's leadership always considered work important, even before the founding of the Democratic People's Republic of Korea (DPRK). "Every single one of you must carry out the struggle of labor to increase production. Everyone will need to become hero workers," Kim Il Sung said to workers at the Hŭngnam Fertilizer Factory in April 1946.[1] From the beginning (and to this day), the workers were asked to work *hard*—for the nation, for the party, for socialism. The concept of work presented here is thus largely an elite concept. To consider work as a mode of domination is to see how it was conceived by the authority—from the state, the party, and the trade unions all the way to the factory managers and shop-floor

leaders. The ethical world envisioned by the ruling class was defined foremost by work as an ethical and ideological practice. Doing an honest day's
work was the first step in becoming a good citizen, an idea North Korea's
ruling class shared not only with other socialist allies but also with capitalist rivals.

This chapter begins with a comparison to two earlier moments: the postliberation period (1945–1950) and the Korean War (1950–1953). In the former, state formation was both a political project to garner support for the
newly emerging Workers' Party and an economic project to organize the
labor power of disparate classes and to centralize their surplus. In the latter, the need to maintain a costly and protracted war transformed the North
Korean economy into a type of war communism, which justified the sus-
pension of workers' rights established during the postliberation period.
Keeping the workers producing was just as important as fighting the war
itself. The comparison points out that the idea of productivity merged with
North Korea's socialism early on, and a major determinant in the merger
was the logic of industrialism central to modernization all over the world.
The last third of this chapter offers an analysis of how happiness is tied to
work in socialism. Work as a source of joy is considered in relation to Marx's
conception of division of labor. Marx did not conceive labor in and of itself
as a joyous activity and emphasized the radical task of socialism to absorb
labor back into life. Rather, the cheerful view of work originates from
nineteenth-century Europe's liberal tradition, which had already internal-
ized the ethical notion of work arising from Protestant Christianity's
embrace of capitalism in the sixteenth century. How such a religious and
liberal notion of work found its way into the socialism of the twentieth
century is most palpably answered in the works of Vladimir Lenin. It was
Lenin who prescribed physical labor as the duty and joy of a new revolutionary world.

Liberation and the Mission to Produce

Upon arriving at a wide street in Pyongyang in 1948, the left-leaning South
Korean journalist On Nakchung noticed something different about the
people in the city.[2] It was late spring, with a nice breeze, but he could not
find a single "scamp looking for a place to kill time," as he normally would
in Seoul during this time of year. "Everyone," he wrote, "is walking

actively, all dressed alike in workers' clothing." On Nakchung saw the difference in the sameness of the people, the sameness he imagined to be purposefulness. "The bloodthirsty eyes of people in Seoul burn on top of their lethargic body," his scathing comparison continued, "but the eyes of the people in Pyongyang—what are they fixed on?"

> Is it the profit of gold gained by bribing the bureaucrats? Is it the greed of stealing an office and using the position for one's benefit? Is it the desperate trade of selling the crumbs of imperialists? Is it power? Is it money? Is it sex? Is it wine? No! None of it. The people of North Korea today have only one goal. It is the completion of the 1948 People's Economic Plan. Everyone—man, woman, the old, the young—is now racing toward the goal. In Pyongyang, I saw the fire and exuberance of North Korea, something difficult to understand for anyone from South Korea.[3]

The difference On observed was present in the ordinary landscape of the city. The economic plan had descended upon the nascent country and changed its rules. No one seemed outside the boundaries of the plan, and the plan had taken on the face of the worker. That breezy spring day, On noticed something extraordinary in the most ordinary space: the plan had swallowed up everyday life and with it the everyday being.

The takeover of everyday life had been occurring for a few years, most notably due to extensive reforms. First, the land reform of 1946 was completed in just a little more than three weeks (March 5–March 31). Officially proposed by the Peasant League (a new farmers' organization), legally sanctioned by the North Korean Provisional People's Committee (the first legislative organ), and jointly planned with the Soviet Civil Administration (the occupying government of the Soviet Union), the land reform of 1946 confiscated land from the Japanese government and nationals, people who had extensively benefited from Japan, landlords with more than 5 chŏngbo of land (around 12 acres, at 2.45 acres per chŏngbo, or 5 hectares), absentee landlords, large tenant farmers, and religious organizations.[4] The confiscated land, which amounted to a million chŏngbo, was distributed to landless peasants (60.3 percent), peasants with less than 5 chŏngbo (34.6 percent), agricultural laborers (2.2 percent), landlords who moved to other areas (1.0 percent), and various people's organizations (1.9 percent).[5] For the 724,522 households receiving land for free, especially the 62.5 percent who had never owned any land,[6] the land reform was the first sweet taste of socialism.

Second, legal reforms advanced working life with basic labor rights. The Labor Laws on North Korea's Regular and White-Collar Workers, announced on June 24, 1946, legalized, among other things, (1) the eight-hour workday; (2) the shortening of dangerous work to seven hours; (3) the ban on labor for people younger than fourteen years old; (4) wage and labor contracts; (5) gender equality in wage; (6) paid time off after child-birth; (7) a workers' social welfare system; and (8) collective bargaining.[7] The Laws on North Korea's Gender Equality, passed on July 30, 1946, legal-ized gender equality in elections, wage, insurance, education, marriage, divorce, property ownership, and inheritance rights.

Third, industrial reforms began with the announcement of the Laws on the Nationalization of Industries, Transportation, Communications, and Banking on August 10, 1946. These laws eventually nationalized 1,034 fac-tories and enterprises in North Korea. The first step in nationalization was the North Korean Provisional People's Committee's confiscation, without compensation, of about 90 percent of enterprises in North Korea, owned mostly by the Japanese government and Japanese corporations. The 1,034 factories and enterprises were in the following sectors: mining (196), steel (19), coal (178), nonferrous metallurgy (11), machines (108), chemicals (12), consumer goods (346), construction materials (66), electric power (21), and lumber (77).[8] The factories actually in operation, however, were fewer, at 828, mostly in the machines, chemical, construction material, consumer goods, and lumber industries.[9] The nationalization of small private enter-prises owned and operated by North Koreans occurred in steps. The coop-erativization of handicraft enterprises began in 1947, and the nationalization of small enterprises began in 1955. In October 1958, North Korea com-pleted the cooperativization and nationalization of all private enterprises.

The people On Nakchung saw in Pyongyang in the spring of 1948 had experienced and participated in the changes brought on by the reforms. In a matter of a few years, the world they had previously known indeed changed, and, more importantly, they were asked to fulfill the state's mis-sion. "We no longer work for imperialists or exploiters, but for ourselves. This is why all workers . . . must take on a new perspective on labor and make an effort to produce a little more and a little better," Kim Il Sung said at a rally in Pyongyang on the day the nationalization law was announced.[10] The call for everyone to produce had immediate results. The

North Korean state reported that between 1946 and 1949 the total industrial output grew 337 percent, at a rate of about 50 percent annually.[11] These
figures should be questioned, as any country's statistics about growth should
be questioned, but what is undeniable is the overall economic growth in
North Korea during this period, especially from the postwar period to the
early 1960s.

Outcomes on the ground, however, varied greatly by sector. For
example, at the end of the first quarter in 1947, whereas some enterprises
were far surpassing their goals, such as the Pyongyang Grain Factory
(with flour production at 145 percent of the previous year) and the Sinŭiju
Textile Factory (with cotton fabric production at 145 percent of the previous year), other enterprises were irreparably lagging behind, such as
the Kangsŏn Steelworks (7.7 percent), Ryongamp'o Smelting Factory
(2.0 percent), and the Haeju Smelting Factory (8.9 percent).[12] Even the
most advanced enterprises were struggling. At the end of the third quarter of 1947, the Hwanghae Iron and Steel Works—an emblematic steel
factory of North Korea—was at only 70 percent of its production goal and
facing problems with fuel supplies, the piecework remuneration system,
and worker attrition.[13]

It is not my primary objective to point out the irregularities of North
Korea's production regime so much as it is to connect the production regime
with everyday life in order to see how the everyday was taken over by a
systematic drive to increase productivity—to see how the workers actually took on a "new perspective on labor" (as Kim Il Sung had called for).
The latter happened with the transformation of work into an ideological
category—work as a hegemonic process in which the everyday character
of work becomes essential for the reproduction of the condition for production. In general, the reproduction of labor power occurred *outside* the labor
process. If we look at Hwanghae Iron and Steel Works, of the six directives
the party provided to the factory to raise productivity, the very first directive deals with issues outside the setting of production: "For the workers'
preparation for the coming winter, housing repairs and supplementary
food items shall be immediately provided."[14] The third directive states,
"To prevent workers from changing jobs, wage equality shall be abol-
ished, cultural projects shall be widely organized, nurseries shall be
improved upon, and newly hired workers shall be encouraged to take pleasure in labor."[15] The attention to everyday life was hence an effort from
outside the labor process to alleviate the inconsistent levels of productivity.

A world ordered through work, where happiness is found in toil—this world began immediately after liberation on the path toward state building. The ideal state had an ideal being, someone who toiled away quietly and consistently, like the protagonist in Kim Sango's poem "Kisa" (The engineer, 1949):

Don't look for him near a desk.
Most likely, he won't be there.
Next to a furnace whose fire is weak, or near a roller,
You will see him, among the workers.[16]

Wartime Work

On February 22, 1952, twenty months into the Korean War and seven months after the start of cease-fire negotiations, the Ministry of Education transferred its authority over technical schools to the Ministry of Industry as part of a measure to increase the supply of reserve labor power during the war.[17] Technical schools were relocated to safe areas in the northern part of the country, and all students were given scholarships and rations. In a short amount of time, these schools produced a large number of reserve technicians: radio operators, drivers and mechanics, and nurses were quickly trained and deployed to battle zones.[18] In preparation for postwar reconstruction, students were sent abroad to the Soviet Union, China, and other socialist states to be trained in mining, metallurgy, machinery, chemistry, construction, and light industry.[19] In the dire setting of war, the otherwise masked connection between education and production became apparent. The war was an effective setting for high productivity. War communism created its own kind of labor regime. "Production must continue to increase," Kim Il Sung said a few days after the war began: "Since the eruption of the war, people have not worked hard because they are anxious. This has to stop. To win the war, everyone must work more and produce more. Shells are consumed as cannons are fired, and war supplies are consumed as troops march forward. The demands of the frontline cannot be met unless production is constantly increased."[20]

Productive labor was essential to the invasion of the South. The ever-greater need for centralized appropriation of surplus gave rise to a wartime production regime operating with its particular measures, including

(1) legal changes to regulate labor and mobilize new workers, (2) non-productive means of surplus accumulation, and (3) the relocation of factories. These wartime measures highlight various practices outside the labor process to accumulate surplus. The difficulty of everyday production brought on by the war led to extraproductive ways to appropriate surplus, including campaigns to reduce consumption and the enactment of the national lottery.

Suspending Rights, Mobilizing Workers

Immediately after crossing the Thirty-Eighth Parallel, North Korea's wartime government, the Military Committee, implemented an array of laws and decrees related to work. These measures had the consequences of, first, suspending fundamental labor rights established by earlier reforms and, second, criminalizing unruly work behavior. The first effort in constructing a wartime labor regime began on July 6, 1950, with the announcement "On Wartime Labor."[21] Although the state claimed that trade unions had originally proposed this order, it functioned to increase production precisely by controlling organized labor.[22] The order allowed the extension of working days and hours, strict control over labor mobility, and the strengthening of labor regulations.[23] From the end of July 1950, through the order "On Wartime Compulsory Mobilization," mandatory work became permitted if the state deemed it necessary.[24] This decision stipulated, first, that all men between the ages of eighteen and fifty-five living in certain areas could not relocate without the state's permission; second, that the same group of men must participate in production and recovery projects necessary for the war; and, third, that those who violate the first and second articles would be severely punished.[25] Despite the losses brought on by the war, the total number of manual and office workers at the end of 1953 was greater than the number before the war.[26]

Trade unions were especially restrained, with drastic curtailing of labor rights. Basic union rights, such as collective bargaining, were suspended as factory managers, the party, and the union federation collaborated to pursue wartime mobilization.[27] With top union officers in collusion with the state, the war government removed the independence of the unions established in the liberation period, relegating them to serve as another channel for propaganda and mobilization. This trend would continue in the postwar period. North Korea's early democratic reforms based primarily on radical land and labor reforms became suspended in the situation of war.

The movement of soldiers and workers to the frontline, which made consistent return to workplaces difficult, required the mobilization of workers throughout North Korea. The workers remaining at factories were asked to produce more in place of those at the frontline: they were required to perform three to four more hours of work per day and to work on non-work days.[28] One cause of the labor shortage and job attrition was military recruitment outside the official draft system. For example, from June 25 to August 15, 1950, the state mobilized 849,000 young adults as a "volunteer army," of which 230,000 were women; Kim Il Sung University alone recruited 2,800 in one day (June 27), and 80 percent of all young adults in Sunch'ŏn County of South P'yŏngan Province were recruited into the army.[29] Another equally significant cause of the labor shortage was workers choosing not to work in this dire environment. For instance, 76 percent of all workers hired by the Bureau of Electric Power in 1952 quit before the end of the year, and in the same year the Department of Light Industry reported 400,000 cases of unexcused absences and sick days, while production was 15 percent under and wage payment 15 percent over the state plan.[30]

The most crucial source of labor power during the war was women. They were called upon to fill the gap created by military recruitment, casualties, and job attrition—to helm the idling machines. To be sure, women served on the battlefield as radio operators, medics, scouts, and even combat soldiers. One of the most famous women combat soldiers was Ham Sunnyŏ, who, with four others, is claimed to have destroyed a US military vehicle, killed five US soldiers, and obtained their plans.[31] However, because most women remained outside the combat situation, they became the new industrial workers. The Military Committee called on them to quickly acquire industrial skills and to produce at a higher level than the men they replaced because although the total number of workers decreased, the factories' production goals usually did not change. Filling the labor vacancies were women whose family members and neighbors were on the battlefield, women dispatched from the Korean Workers' Party and state agencies, and women recruited by the Federation of Women's Organizations.[32] A month after the war began, some 2,300 women had entered the factories.[33] It was reported that steel and textile factories in North Hamgyŏng

Province built more childcare facilities and restrooms to accommodate the new women workers.[34] Women contributed to the wartime production system in other ways, too: raising funds and collecting supplies through donations; supporting the frontline by taking care of other people's children and writing letters; and volunteering in the rebuilding of train tracks, roads, and bridges.[35] By March 1953, 12,990 women had received awards for their wartime work.[36]

Nonproductive Production of Surplus

The demand for higher productivity during the war accompanied the demand to reduce consumption. This was a nonproductive means of accumulating surplus—surplus coming directly from daily life, while pushing the people to live with less. Calling for an increase in the production of food, coal, and steel, the Military Committee asked the people to cut down on consumption. *Saving, reducing, abstaining*—these were important practices for wartime livelihood. The rhetoric of anticonsumption became widespread during the war. For the *nomenklatura*, Kim Il Sung talked about cutting the number of banquets, reducing automobile use, and even "wearing the same shoes for twenty more days" before throwing them out.[37] "Struggle for food production is struggle for the fatherland!" was the slogan given to the farmers in the campaign to increase food production while reducing the farmers' own food consumption.[38] Even soldiers were asked to save: "Shells shall be strictly conserved, and in particular, the use of 122-mm shell should never exceed its designated use limit," Kim Il Sung cautioned.[39]

Another way to lower consumption while accumulating surplus was the direct extraction of cash. Although the amount, the frequency, and the winners are not clear, the Fatherland Restoration Lottery Drawing Committee was established on November 25, 1951,[40] with the first payout on December 2.[41] In addition, war bonds—named People's Economic Development Bonds—were sold twice, in June and December 1951.[42] The lottery and bonds had the dual function of accumulating surplus in the form of cash and reducing people's ability to consume. Cash was particularly necessary during this period—to purchase military supplies from other countries and to start repaying the loan of US$30 million that North Korea had received from the Soviet Union in 1949.[43] In the context of war in which production was unstable, the lottery and bonds were efficient and yet non-productive means of state appropriation of surplus.

At War and Work

The wartime production regime involved the relocation of production sites (*sogae*)—the tremendous project of dismantling vital factories, evacuating them to safe locations, often underground or in caves, and reassembling them to resume production. At the end of the 1940s, North Korea had a relatively significant industrial base compared to that of South Korea because it had been restored from the one built and abandoned by Japanese capitalist corporations and the colonial government. In 1948, there were a hundred functioning factories and a mining network spanning more than 3 kilometers (almost 2 miles) (see table 1.1).[44] Each factory was in turn composed of up to a dozen production facilities, with a total of about a thousand working facilities.

The total number of employed industrial workers before the war was around 200,000. Some factories were quite large and productive: the

TABLE 1.1

Number of Facilities and Workers by Industrial Sector, North Korea, 1948

Industrial Sector	Number of Operating Factories	Number of Workers
Mining	Mines totaling 3,260 meters	134,663
Chemical	12	21,146
Light (consumer goods)	44	15,906
Steel	9	14,519
Construction material	16	5,500
Machine manufacturing	13	5,285
Nonferrous metal	6	4,806
Total	**100**	**201,825**

Source: Figures compiled from Kimura Mitsuhiko and Abe Keiji, *Chŏnjaengi mandŭn nara: Pukhan ŭi kunsa kongŏphwa* (The country made by war: The military industrialization of North Korea), trans. Cha Munsŏk and Pak Chŏngjin (Seoul: Mizi, 2009), 252–288.

chemical complex at Hŭngnam, with three factories, was once the largest of its kind in the world, both in production and in the number of workers, employing 42,000 workers at its height during the colonial period.[45] Some factories, however, were difficult to manage, with productivity rates far lower than the rates during the colonial period: the vital cement factories at Sŭnghori, Madong, Ch'ŏnnaeri, Haeju, and Komusan, with a combined production capacity of 1.8 million tons a year, produced only 287,000 tons of cement in 1948.[46] But, no matter, all factories were invaluable in the eye of the state, for North Korea had neither the technology nor the time to rebuild such an industrial base. These factories had to be preserved at all cost.

The order for factory relocation was issued a few weeks after United Nations forces landed at Inch'ŏn on September 15, 1950, when the tide of war turned against North Korea for the first time. The Korean People's Army, which had claimed to have liberated Seoul on June 28 and occupied 90 percent of South Korean territory by the end of July, was pushed back up north, and Pyongyang was occupied by United Nations forces on October 19. "The relocation project is a difficult and complex project with a vast amount of workload," Kim Il Sung said on September 27, "and requires utmost secrecy and swiftness."[47] The details of the order included relocating essential equipment to safe areas, concealing the facilities that could not be relocated, and transporting state granaries to secure areas to assure "not one grain gets into the hands of the enemy."[48] The main agencies in charge of the projects were the Ministry of Mining and Manufacturing and the Ministry of Industry. Under the direction of the Mining and Manufacturing Ministry, the Sup'ung area in North P'yŏngan Province (along the Amnok River, northeast of Sinŭiju) became the wartime center of grenade manufacturing, vehicle maintenance, and electric-power production.[49]

Under the direction of the Ministry of Industry, key equipment from chemical factories at Hŭngnam (South Hamgyŏng Province on the eastern coast), metalwork factories at Munp'yŏng (south of Hŭngnam), mines at Munch'ŏn (Kangwon Province in the East), and chemical factories at Namp'o (southwest of Pyongyang) were relocated, along with hundreds of engineers and skilled workers.[50] The workers of Factory Number 65 became legendary for relocating a weapons manufacturing factory in a single night—more than 80 kilometers (50 miles) under enemy fire—and resuming production the next day.[51]

War did not stop production. Instead, it created its own kind of production regime, defined by legal changes reversing the democratic labor laws established in the prewar period; labor mobilization imposing a greater workload than before, especially on women, because they had to take on the double duty of taking care of the family and providing for the frontline; campaigns of reducing consumption through conserving and abstaining; the extraction of cash through the lottery and bonds; and the relocation of vital factories and personnel to safe areas to resume production. The three years of war was a watershed moment in North Korea's political economy. From the smoke and rubble, the state consolidated its authority over the economy and the national community.

In discussing the lasting effects of the Korean War, I think it is helpful to think about it in relation to the "state of exception" concept. The language of constant danger and threat became permanent during the war and remained in place after it. Laws and rights came be to flexible according to what the government deemed necessary for self-preservation, as in the wartime orders suspending labor rights. Socialism was talked about in the sense of the exceptional state. This is to say not only that war created its own special law but also that war revealed a political space beyond the juridical order. Giorgio Agamben sees the state of exception as defining the threshold of law. What a government considers to be a necessary and exceptional situation is an ambiguous and uncertain zone, a "threshold where fact and law seem to become undecidable."[52] Political certainty in the state of exception is, in fact, a condition of ambiguity—ambiguity framed by law.

In his New Year's address of 1953, Kim Tubong, leader of the Chinese Korean political group and chair of the Supreme People's Assembly's Standing Committee (and thus head of state), spoke about North Korea's working class during the war. As the war approached its third year, and as destruction continued while cease-fire negotiations lingered on, Kim Tubong stressed, "Our working class, despite the bombings of factories and irregular supply of materials, has reliably supplied weapons and ammunition demanded by the frontline."[53] In this seemingly benign statement is the connection between the working class and production, a connection shaped by the necessities of war. The extreme reality of wartime labor allows the government to reconstitute the juridical limits of the working condition. Kim Tubong also called for the working class to "increase production, save resources, cherish state properties, and strictly follow wartime labor regulations," while claiming that the "socialist camp has expanded and become stronger in the past year." What is more, he reported that the wartime government had exempted farmers from paying taxation in-kind, increased food rations for the families of factory and office workers, and provided students with uniforms, shoes, and housing.[54] North Korea's wartime situation, in which labor laws were suspended while goods were still provided for the population, is a reminder of Agamben's state of exception, which "appears as the opening of a fictitious lacuna in the order for the purpose of safeguarding the existence of the norm."[55] The appearance of normal socialism is a legally authorized situation of exception. Such a norm, which lies beyond the juridical boundary, is a space of ambiguity, an indeterminate political space in which the force of nationalism is the highest call. Agamben says the state of exception is a "creation of the democratic-revolutionary tradition and not the absolutist one" and is "one of the essential practices of contemporary states, including so-called democratic ones."[56] The war's legacy in creating a lasting state of exception in North Korea had particular features and causes, but they make sense and are instructive insofar as they are recognized as part of modern history.

Work as a Historical Concept

Happiness in Work

In 1956, Hwang Changyŏp (1923–2010), chair of the Philosophy Department at Kim Il Sung University, published *Sahoe palchŏnsa* (The history of societal development). It was an orthodox text in the tradition of Marx and Engels's historical materialism. In line with the classic theory, Hwang wrote that human development began when anthropoids started using tools of labor to shape their environment. "Labor created humankind," Hwang stated, "and by labor, we mean the point at which we began to use the labor tools we created for ourselves." Tools were more than just an extension of the body; they were a *means of production*, and by changing *how* people produced things, tools enabled people to change the world. Hwang called tools, experience, and habits involved in making various things *labor power*. For production to occur, however, labor power is not sufficient; it must come together with other labor powers, which Hwang called *relations of production*. For Hwang, labor power and relations of production affect each other: relations of production are determined by labor power, and labor power is developed or suppressed by relations of production.[57]

Sahoe palchŏnsa had a revolutionary purpose: to define the totality between means of production, labor power, and relations of production in the course of human history. During the capitalist phase of history, it suggested, because the means of production is owned privately by individuals (capitalists), the relations of production are necessarily an exploitative one, as one side (the workers) sells its labor power to the other side (capitalists). The value created from the products, just like the means of production, is also kept privately after the minimum amount of value is given back to the workers for their survival. In the process, because the capitalists appear as if they are in charge of the entire production—what to make and how to make it—the labor of the capitalists is perceived to be a higher form of labor. The capitalists' mental labor appears worthier, more honorable than the workers' physical labor. Capitalism is thus distinguished by privately owned means of producing surplus value, the separation between conception and execution of production, and the lowly status of workers.

This condition changes in socialism because "all means of production are collectively owned through nationalization." The collective ownership of means of production changes the nature of relations of production, from exploitation to solidarity. As Hwang put it, "In a socialist society, those who fall behind catch up with those ahead, and those who are ahead pull up those who are behind. . . . [T]he base of human relations is the 'love for your comrades.'" The relations of production based on solidarity eventually give rise to a new kind of labor because the individual works according to his or her ability and receives according to how much he or she has worked. The antagonism of the labor process found in capitalism disappears because production occurs in the interest of all. "This is why in a socialist society, the working people . . . work with a happy spirit," Hwang wrote. What is interesting in this logic is that once the means of production is collectively owned, labor becomes a joyful activity: "Workers and farmers . . . work for their own happiness and the prosperity of the entire society. The attitude toward work changes fundamentally: physical labor, which was thought to be base in a class society, is recognized to be an honorable and worthy activity. . . . At the same time labor becomes an honorable activity, it becomes a sacred task of all people."[58]

Sahoe palchŏnsa thus presented a conventional historical materialist story of how the oppressed class becomes the dominant class and how everything

about the oppressed class becomes authentic and beautiful, including physical labor, which is transformed from a demeaning human activity to a
sacred and joyful activity. This story's message is that a shift in the relations of production from capitalism to socialism gives rise to a new culture, a new rationality, and a new aesthetics of labor.

Kim Il Sung shared with Hwang the enthusiasm for work. "One important issue in the construction of socialism and communism," Kim Il Sung
said, "is educating the workers to love labor and to voluntarily participate
in work." Like Hwang's, Kim's sense of the primacy of work was based on
the view of work as the origin of wealth and happiness: "Only from a goal-
oriented labor process can wealth be created, labor tools continuously
improved, productivity increased, and society advanced." Revolution was
arduous work in disguise: "The love for labor is one of the most important
characteristics for a communist. Therefore, whether people have the cor-
rect attitude toward labor or not is an important sign of whether they can
become revolutionaries or not. . . . Those who do not work and do not like
to work can never become revolutionaries. People who do not like to work
are backward people, useless in our society."[59]

The notion of labor as a joyous activity necessary for revolution was
entrenched in North Korea's socialism, as it was in all state socialist countries of the twentieth century. "Dance and song flow out from the labor
and life of our people," Kim Il Sung said.[60] There is little doubt labor is a
fundamental human activity, but does socialist (collective) means of production naturally generate happiness in work? To answer this question, I
turn to one obvious place, the works of Marx, especially his writing on
historical materialism.

Marx's Notion of Work

The concept of historical materialism occupies a small space in Marx's vast
writing, but its impact on history has been immense. It has unleashed a
radical vision of the role of human beings, a new vision of history giving
reason to revolutionary struggles and to the existence of state socialism.
The German Ideology is the most representative text on historical materialism. In it, Marx outlines the stages of human history according to its mode
of production, which is determined by relations of production and ownership of means of production. History unfolds in stages, from the most

Figure 1.1 Happiness is to be found in work. Workers of the Gas Synthesis Shop at the Hŭngnam Fertilizer Factory, 1960s.
Source: Photograph courtesy of the Hŭngnam Fertilizer Factory Museum.

primitive to the most advanced. The stages are well known: primitive communism, Asiatic mode of production, slavery, feudalism, capitalism, imperialism, socialism, and communism. The specific mode of production in each stage inevitably breaks down through struggle, and another stage is reached—until communism is reached, where the mode of production has no inherent antagonism.

The historical development through a particular mode of production has the immediate consequence of *division of labor*. The first step in division of labor is the appearance of the division of material and mental labor, which is based on the contradiction between types of labor, not to mention the antagonistic relations between individuals, because, Marx writes, "intellectual and material activity—enjoyment and labor, production and consumption—devolve on different individuals." The contradiction between labor types inevitably results in unequal distribution of labor:

someone gains the control over the distribution of labor power. In short, labor becomes power over individuals. In the course of history, to labor means to be subjugated under labor, until, of course, the stage of communism is reached: "the communist revolution . . . *does away with labor*."[61]

In Marx's thought, it is difficult to see how labor is an honorable activity. In fact, it is quite the opposite: it is an activity that antagonizes human beings with each other. In capitalism, the demeaning quality of labor becomes more acute: "The exercise of labor power . . . is the worker's own life-activity, the manifestation of his own life. And this life-activity he sells to another person in order to secure the necessary means of subsistence. Thus his life-activity is . . . only a means to enable him to exist. He works in order to live. He does not even reckon labor as part of his life." [62] Work under capitalism is an activity carried out solely to survive. How labor can be a sacred activity is not to be found in Marx. Even in the fully realized communist mode of production, it is not labor that is respected, but life itself as labor as such goes away (*revolution does away with labor*). This distinction is imperative: labor has no value on its own outside life, and communism brings labor back into it. Under communism, work becomes honorable because life once again becomes honorable.

Shlomo Avineri emphasizes such a feature in Marx's notion of labor. A person's creative ability causes the historical emergence of labor, Avineri says, while highlighting that Marx considered some socialists as missing the point "when they postulate labor as the end of human life." Avineri also notes how modern labor contributes to the fragmentation of life: "In present day society, [labor] does not develop man but emasculates him. Instead of adding dimensions of creativity to man and widening his humanity, the process of labor in present day society degrades man into a commodity, and the product of his labor . . . becomes man's master."[63] Viewing labor as an end itself, therefore, has the effect of upholding the fragmenting process of work. To see labor as the defining goal of life is to subscribe to the ideology of work. Marx, however, according to Avineri's assessment, sees labor as a part of a person's process of self-becoming, as a person's one specific attribute. In Marx's thought, as Avineri observes, true communism ought to be the social and historical reality of self-becoming, the return of personhood to oneself as a social being.[64] Many state socialist countries of the twentieth century, including North Korea, did not stop the fragmenting process of modern labor and, in fact, promoted such labor as the supreme human activity.

The terms *work* and *labor* are similar, but a distinction between them can be made. The difference lies in the value form created. Strictly speaking, as Friedrich Engels explains, work creates use-value in a product for utility, whereas labor creates exchange-value to be circulated as a commodity: "Labor which creates use-value and is qualitatively determined is called 'work' as opposed to labor; labor which creates [exchange-]value and is only measured quantitatively is called 'labor.' "[65] However, because a product contains both labor and work, and because the application of these two terms in language is hardly precise, they are used interchangeably.

Although disparaging of modern labor, Marx was absolutely affirmative about the workers: their labor brings them together as a universal class, with a revolutionary potential to overcome the antagonistic conditions of labor. Marx thus honored the workers, not the work. At a meeting of the General Council of the First International in June 1865, he delivered the now essential report *Value, Price, and Profit*, in which he explains how profit derives not from market exchange but from unpaid labor—profit as the ratio of paid and unpaid labor—that is, as a degree of exploitation. In the report, however, in arguing how exploitative capitalist labor really is, Marx uses the word *exploitation* only once and as a side note: "The rate of profit is . . . the real ratio between paid and unpaid labor, the real degree of the exploitation—you must allow me this French word—of labor."[66] This subtle clarification by Marx was an act of respect: not even he had the right to say to workers, "You are an exploited class of people subjugated under the labor process in which you foolishly take pride." No matter how socially demeaning the work may be, the worker can usually find a bit of happiness and self-respect in the job, a tenacious characteristic Marx respected. Thus, in Marx three views on work can be distinguished: work and labor under capitalism as activities of subjugation; communism as the return of labor back into life; and the worker as a being capable of overcoming his or her condition of labor. So, as emphasized earlier, Marx did not see labor as a joyous and sacred activity in and of itself. Such a notion instead has a liberal origin grounded in religious ethics.

Work as Burden, Ethic, and Value

The meaning of work went through significant historical changes. During the period of Homeric Greece, eighth century BCE, elites and commoners alike shared physical labor; even gods and goddesses are portrayed as performing work.[67] The respect for physical work in this period was due to the importance of small-scale cultures based on the family, religion, and decentralized political authority.[68] The thought of work as a burden, especially by the elites, arose a few centuries later, around the fifth century BCE, with the development of city-states, trade, and slavery.[69] As Herbert Applebaum writes, "Abstention from work [was] the precondition for the good life, with the *good life* defined as the life of leisure to develop mind and body."[70] Aristotle was the representative voice regarding this period's notion of work. He said, "Happiness is . . . to involve leisure; for we do business"—that is, work—"in order that we may have leisure." Leisure was necessary because it enabled contemplation, the highest form of human activity leading to happiness. "Life of the intellect is divine in comparison with human life," Aristotle wrote.[71] The conception of work as burden, left to be carried out by commoners, thus had an early beginning.[72]

The modern work ethic—in which work is an honorable and dutiful act—began in the early sixteenth century in conjunction with John Calvin's Protestantism, in which the notion of a *calling* (the believer's task set forth by the Christian God) emphasized disciplined life and hard work. Max Weber's study on Protestantism shows that Christians in certain areas of northern Europe embraced capitalism (already existing), giving religious approval of the pursuit of profit.[73] On the one hand, the Protestant work ethic emphasized hard work, business enterprise, thrift, and success. On the other, it contributed to the radical ideology of early socialism, such as that of the Levelers and Diggers, involving respect for workers, common ownership of land, and equal redistribution of goods and services.[74]

The concept of labor as a value-producing activity and as a commodity became prominent in the eighteenth century. This concept is best represented in Adam Smith's labor theory of value. *Wealth of Nations* explained how Smith saw productive work as the foundation of society and division of labor as necessary in increasing productivity.[75] His work also introduced the benefits of simple skills, the use of machinery, and the idea of a society based on self-interest and minimum government interference.[76] In the nineteenth century, Smith's economic principles became the foundation of liberalism, in which the rationality of profit and loss took on a supreme position. As Applebaum writes, "[A] calculating ethos of profit and loss was rapidly replacing the traditional, religious principles of community, family, and individuals as ends in themselves. Work and workers were now a means to an end."[77] With capitalist industrialization occurring in various parts of the world, the liberalism of the nineteenth century justified the commodification of human labor as the process by which labor becomes efficient and profitable. Industrialization completed the process of separating labor from life. As Karl Polanyi postulates, under the condition of liberalism and industrialization the things once integrated with collective life—land, labor, and money—became disembedded from the community and subordinated to the market, with the consequence that land, labor, and money were transformed into fictitious commodities.[78]

Lenin and Socialist Work

The modern sense of industrial work is traceable to the Calvinist notion of labor as an honorable, sacred activity, combined with the liberal notion of labor as a value-producing activity. As a commodity that generates profit, work must be consistently reproduced. The need for consistent reproduction of work—work for work's sake—was now the essential aspect of modern work. But such a notion of work still had no room in socialism as outlined by Marx (other than as critique). In the early twentieth century, however, the modern concept of work, forged from industrialism, found an immutable place in socialism, and at its center was the philosophy of Lenin. For him, the task of erasing bourgeois defects in production required a reconfiguration of labor in relation to the newly emerging community.[79] Lenin stated:

> Communist labor in the narrower and stricter sense of the term is labor performed gratis for the benefit of society, . . . not for the purpose of obtaining a right to certain products, not according to previously established and legally fixed quotas, but voluntary labor, irrespective of quotas; it is labor performed without expectation of reward, without reward as a condition, labor performed because it has become a habit to work for the common good, and because of a conscious realization (that has become a habit) of the necessity of working for the common good—labor as the requirement of a healthy organism.[80]

With Lenin, the modern socialist sense of labor took root. In communism, labor is extraindividual and no longer private. The aim of labor is the greater good of the community, even if such labor begets no private returns in the form of wage or in-kind transfers ("performed gratis for the benefit of society"). And it must be naturally reproduced as a "habit" for the common good. Furthermore, Lenin's notion of work designates it as a consciously realized duty of society. In this respect, as Jay B. Sorenson points out, Lenin's idea of work is closer to Calvin's than to Marx's.[81]

Sorenson brings up another crucial aspect of Lenin's idea of work: work as compulsory. Lenin introduced the idea of coercion into the concept of socialist work, in which, as Sorenson puts it, labor is a product of "compulsion, not a result of motivation for individual pleasure."[82] Lenin distinguished work under socialism from work under communism, the latter of which would be wholly voluntary and performed only for the common good. And until the stage of communism is reached, Lenin emphasized in *The State and Revolution*, all citizens must be converted into workers of "*one huge syndicate, the whole state.*" Lenin called such a type of work "factory discipline," where the "whole society will have become a single . . . factory with equality of work and equality of pay."[83]

Lenin created a synthesis of several disparate notions of work: not only from Marx (in which work is a creative human activity) but also from Calvin and Smith with their ideas of work as a dutiful and value-creating activity. Work in a socialist country was to be an obligatory (compulsory) activity for everyone. It was to be an activity carried out for the common good and common happiness. For Marx, labor was an arduous and alienating activity from which human beings had to be liberated, so that labor and life could be merged. For Lenin, liberation from labor was a premature goal in the stage of socialism; liberation was instead to be sought *within* labor, as a collective effort, where happiness is to be found in toil. Lenin's idea took hold in the Soviet Union and in all other socialist states of the twentieth century, including North Korea. Hwang Changyŏp's treatise *Sahoe palchŏnsa* is to be read within this framework, where the ideas of Calvin, Smith, and Marx converge under the revolutionary vision of Lenin.

The great irony about socialist work as formulated by Lenin was its resemblance to capitalist work: both were born from the belly of industrialism. Socialist work was no more or no less difficult than its capitalist counterpart. One could be just as happy or miserable working in a capitalist factory as one could be in a socialist factory. It was industrialism that demanded difficult work, and it was industrialism that became the foundation of socialist economy. In the attempt to construct a communist reality, the socialism of the twentieth century re-created the very world in which work was alienating and agonizing. In short, socialism created what the political scientist Ch'a Munsŏk calls the "utopia of antilabor": "Industrialism positioned itself as a discourse symbolizing the progress of human history from all aspects." Industrialism was not a system belonging to a certain mode of production but a "modern obsession" indiscriminately penetrating the political and economic systems of capitalism and socialism.[84] The socialist concept of work was forged from industrialism and made into orthodoxy by Lenin's words. In North Korea, as industrialism assumed the appearance of socialism, work became an honorable activity—a sacred duty for all individuals who possessed the capacity to work.[85]

In *Joy in Work*, first published in 1927, Henri De Man considered in detail the possible hindrances to the enjoyment of work. Among them are (1) "detail work," which makes work "unmeaning" in its fragmentation of the labor process; (2) "repetitive work," which leads to monotony of motion, reduction of workers' initiative, and the slackening of attention; (3) "chronic fatigue" of the body and psychology through not only over-exertion but also voluntary organizational work; and (4) "piecework," which tends to speed up the worker unduly, gives more advantage to the employer, jeopardizes working-class solidarity, impairs quality of production, and increases the worker's insecurity.[86] In postwar North Korea, these hindrances to enjoyable work, however, were not easy to do away with, for they were entrenched within the industrial labor process. For the ordinary worker, a factory job meant detailed, repetitive, and difficult work compensated through piecework wage. For the ordinary worker everywhere, a job was not something he or she enjoyed; it was something he or she endured.

From the perspective of De Man, the concept of work implemented in postwar North Korea was bound to create the conditions for unhappy work. This was done not through deception: the leadership made plain in propaganda and on the shop floor the type of work demanded of the North Korean workers. The workers were asked—were obligated—to work hard for a long time with little in return, to endure fatigue and give up leisure time for voluntary labor. North Korea's historical reality should not be simplified: it was a product of radical legal measures, economic pressures, political struggles, ideological forces, and (albeit problematic) rational individual choices. However, it is hard not to see the drive toward industrialism as straining the possibilities of communally useful production and equally redistributed surplus. The largely peasant population was rapidly transformed into industrial workers, whose work was less about usefulness than about surplus for industrial growth. Working to produce surplus became the fundamental role of work, and legal, ideological, political, and educational apparatuses were transformed with this calling.

CHAPTER 2

Work as State Practice

When you choose to live in this world, your being is not your own [人在江湖
身不由己 (injaegangho sinbulyugi)].

—OLD EAST ASIAN SAYING

I n the postwar years, North Korea's production regime brought
together the government, the Korean Workers' Party, unions, factory
management, and cultural organizations with the aim of increasing
productivity. In the process, work became a field of various practices of
the regime. In this chapter, I explore how the production regime imposed
discipline on labor unions, how the factory-management system (*kongjang
kwallije*) dealt with the growing authority of the Korean Workers' Party,
and how work on the shop floor was calibrated and monetized for the purpose of industrial efficacy. One side of thinking about North Korea's work
as practice is to recognize factory work as a site of party politics and ideological education, aimed at both unions and individual workers. Another
side is to consider factory work as an object of calculation, where industrial
efficacy was managed by calibrating workload, work time, and work space
as well as by monetizing work through various types of wage. Both sides
were equally important in North Korea's postwar situation, and both
sides speak to the universal aspects of industrialism, which further contex-
tualizes North Korea within modern history.

By the late 1950s, the demand on everyone to become model workers
had created a labor process defined by competitive and intensive work. On
the one hand, such a work environment regularly induced high and sometimes extraordinary rates of production. There was, for example, the legendary textile worker Yi Hwasun, who alone handled seventy-two weaving

machines and produced more than a million meters (about a million yards) of fabric a year. On the other hand, competition was accompanied by shortages of workers and resources and led to the phenomenon of antiproductivity, a situation on the shop floor where workers intentionally tried to be unproductive.[1] The high expectation to produce represented both the state capacity to influence collective labor and the state's own anxiety in the face of material shortage and workers' own sense of autonomy.

Like all other state socialist countries, the North Korean state was besotted by the promises of industrialism (a condition also found in the so-called capitalist world) and hence demanded discipline and sacrifice from the population. Labor became duty, and productivity became the measure of human character. The need to increase productivity—to pump out more surplus from each worker—made competition a hallmark of the labor process: alienated labor became the formal condition of production. The recurring shortage of resources and uneven material returns for the population, including a nationwide food crisis in 1955, however, led to the state's increasing emphasis on the ideological side of work. Work became an activity whose end goal was the regeneration of work itself. That is to say, work became an activity of subordination. The ideological role of work found its presence in work management as the party became the most authoritative voice in the labor process in the late 1950s.

Factory management in state socialism, including North Korea's, is a troika system consisting of party officials, operation specialists, and union representatives. Depending on the historical moment, one group tended to dominate the other two, with the party historically being the most powerful organ.[2] In the decade after the Korean War, factory management in North Korea saw a transition from management headed by the factory director (*chibaein*) to management led by the party. While the troika structure remained in place, a system of "one-person management" (*yuil kwallije*), with the factory director in charge, was replaced in the late 1950s by a type of management known as the Taean Work System (Taean ŭi Saŏp Ch'egye) led by factory party officials.

In postwar North Korea, work management was excessively represented by aspects of the moral (as was true in other state socialist countries). That is, the factors influencing work and production were portrayed largely by abstract, interior categories such as devotion, responsibility, and patriotism. Although one role of management was indeed to incite the workers to work harder and better, equally important for management were the practices of calibration and monetization of work. The postwar situation was a prime setting for North Korea's production regime to recalculate the standards of workload, work time, and work space. The collective work experience gained during the Korean War—that is, the exceptional and extralegal work experience of war communism—was the grounds on which new labor standards were formulated. At the same time, the postwar situation was the beginning of the application of a wage system to all types of work. In general, office workers received fixed wages (*chŏngaek imgŭm*), which were based on labor time, and manual workers received piecework wages (*togŭp imgŭm*), which were based on the number of goods produced. The piecework wage was touted as the most appropriate type of wage in the industrial work of socialism because a worker received according to the quantity actually produced. Such a rationality, however, was also found in capitalism, and, in fact, Marx had viewed the piecework wage as a quintessential wage type used in capitalist exploitation.

The two sides of work as the practice of the production regime—an interior category of the individual and a calculative category of standards and wages—are transnational characteristics observable not only in other state socialist countries but also in capitalist countries. They are characteristics of modern industrialism, appearing uniquely within the historical context of the nation-state. The global state socialist economy is, then, one major manifestation of modern industrialism rooted in capitalism. The role of the state as a strong mediating agent, relative to the market and nation, is the key feature of state socialism. The components of capitalism, especially its industrial components, do not go away, and in fact the contradictions of state socialism (hierarchical wage labor, state-to-state inequality) point to the continuous function of capital. The same argument applies to capitalism: the state and nation necessarily participate in capitalism, although the state has a lesser role than it has in state socialism. The differences between socialism and capitalism are experientially real, however, because different capacities of the state give rise to distinct historical formations.

Production Under State Socialism

Work is approached in this section from the setting of production process, value creation, surplus seizure, and centralized planning. Karl Marx and Adam Smith shared a similarity in their view of work as a singularly important human activity, though from different positions—as an extension of a person's creative ability in Marx's view and as the ultimate source of wealth in Smith's.[3] In everyday life, too, it is plain to see how people live is tied to how people produce. Work and its constellations define a particular way of living. In other words, the question of work under socialism is the question "What is socialism?" The initial, circular answer would be: socialism is foremost *production under socialism*. Within the universal context of capitalism, the strong role of the state in twentieth-century socialism created a distinctive historical reality, especially in the realm of work and production. The differences in the historical form, however, are not absolute differences. Instead, the differences are what can be called *equivalents*, which arise as distinct experiences but have the same aim of advancing capitalism.

In his study of the state socialist political economy, János Kornai writes that its defining feature is shortage—shortage in production, distribution, and resources.[4] The shortage is attributed to the behavior of socialist firms with respect to goal, supply, and demand. Comparing state-owned firms (SOF) under socialism and private firms (PF) under capitalism, Kornai says: (1) whereas the PF's interest is profit, the SOF's interest is recognition from superior organizations; (2) whereas the PF has hard budget constraints, the SOF has soft budget constraints; (3) whereas the PF is unsure of demand, the SOF is sure of demand; and (4) whereas supply inputs are constrained in the PF, the supply inputs are stockpiled in the SOF.[5] Central to Kornai's observation is the notion that shortage arises because the socialist state's central plan can never know real consumer needs and because the plan sets as the goal of production the satisfaction of the plan. For Kornai, state socialism's failure to provide a high living standard all over the world came not only from mismanagement but also from the inherent problems in its economic system.

Kornai's classic work *The Socialist System* (1992) is significant for pointing out the shortcomings of nonmarket efforts in state socialism. The application of terms such as *supply*, *demand*, and *profit* is especially relevant in providing a picture of a massive state bureaucracy dictating the economic needs of a population. Where I diverge from Kornai, however, starts with the observation that all the shortcomings of the state socialist system are also found in the so-called capitalist system, without exception. In this respect, Kornai's comparison seems to be between an ideal capitalist system and a real socialist system: how capitalism ought to operate is compared to how the state socialist economy actually operates. In an ideal situation, the plan and the market would have equivalent effective and ineffective aspects in determining needs and production. A more precise comparison is to be found in Michael Burawoy's study *The Politics of Production* (1985).

Burawoy starts the discussion of the political space of production in actually existing socialism by comparing what would be the ideal versions of capitalism and socialism. Burawoy's focal point of comparison is surplus, the "difference between what is appropriated and what is distributed back to the direct producers in the form of wages, benefits, and subsidies." In capitalism, surplus is appropriated privately and is the direct value of unpaid labor time, whereas in socialism surplus is appropriated centrally by the state. In capitalism, the market determines the inputs and outputs, but in socialism the plan guides the inputs and outputs, with plan targets determined between distributor sites and production sites. The uncertainties of the market in capitalism result in profit motive and lead to waste, whereas the uncertainties of the plan in socialism result in plan fetishism and lead to overlooking what is needed. Competition in capitalism is analogous to plan bargaining in socialism, which determines reachable and sustainable goals as well as the resources for inputs.[6]

Within the labor process, too, capitalism and socialism have ideal equivalents. Capitalism has strong pressures to increase surplus by increasing productivity, work intensity, and technological efficiency, while lowering wages and rendering the number of employees adjustable. In socialism, the central plan, which is never sure of production capacity, pressures enterprises to change the productivity, the machinery, the technology, and even the product.[7] Uncertainties thus exist in both systems, states Burawoy: "The anarchy of the capitalist market finds its analogue in the anarchy of the socialist plan. Under capitalism demand constraints make themselves felt through the absorption and expulsion of *labor power*. Under state socialism, supply constraints generate continual reorganization of the *labor process*. The fluidity of task structure and the continual need to redistribute workers among machines make it very difficult to deskill production—to separate conception and execution."[8] The key equivalent difference in the two systems is the presence of anarchy: anarchy of the market in capitalism and anarchy of the plan in socialism. Anarchy is the principal cause of changes to the labor process and production in both systems. In state socialism, anarchy of the plan—the impossibility that the state can definitively determine societal needs—brings uncertainty to the labor process and requires continuous innovations and improvisations in production. In postwar North Korea, the need for improvisation in spite of the plan had the effect of making the work experience gained on the shop floor and individual achievement two vital parts of production. Worker attrition and relocation, which shortened work experience, hence became serious and lasting problems for the management of work in North Korea.

Organizing Labor for Production

A year after liberation, in 1946, North Korea was still predominantly a place of small farmers: peasants composed 74.1 percent of a population totaling 9.3 million, whereas manual workers made up only 12.5 percent and office workers only 6.2 percent of the total population.[9] The number of employed wageworkers was 260,000; South Korea had almost three times that number.[10] The peasant demographic in North Korea drastically changed in the next ten years, however, as private agriculture became collective agriculture and as farmers became wageworkers in factories and cooperative farms. The working class was created through the proletarianization of peasants. From 1949 to 1960, the percentage of manual workers increased from 19 percent to 38 percent, and the percentage of office workers went from 7 percent to 14 percent. In contrast, peasants disappeared as a demographic category starting in 1959, and in their place 44 percent of the total population became agricultural cooperative workers.[11] There were 1.4 million employed wageworkers at the end of 1960 in a total population of 10.8 million.[12] The creation of new workers was an urgent task of the state, involving intense ideological education and admittance of peasants into the Korean Workers' Party in large numbers. While stressing class consciousness and workers' solidarity, these efforts emphasized loyalty to the party, state, and leadership above all else.[13]

One of the first modern labor-related organizations in Korea was Chosŏn Research Society on Labor Issues, formed on February 7, 1920. The members were not workers themselves, and unionization was not an immediate goal, but the members were nevertheless interested in labor problems arising from capitalism. Based on the experience of this organization, the Chosŏn Workers' Mutual Aid Society was founded on April 11, with 678 initial members. This organization operated a night school for workers starting in October 1920, establishing three classes in the Chongno,

Yongsan, and Tongdaemun areas of Seoul. In July 1921, the organization established a consumers' cooperative in Seoul's Kwansu District, providing food and necessities to its 2,000 plus members for a low weekly fee. At its height, the Mutual Aid Society had 17,259 members with fifteen branches throughout Korea, including Pyongyang, Kaesŏng, and Kwangju. On October 15, 1922, the organization dissolved due to problems related to the larger factional conflict within Korea's socialist movement—that is, the conflict between the Shanghai, Seoul, and Irkutsk factions.[14]

The successor to the Workers' Mutual Aid Society was the Chosŏn Workers' League, formed three days after the breakup of the Mutual Aid Society. The league participated in and mobilized numerous strikes in the early 1920s, during a period when Korean workers earned 50 percent of the wage earned by Japanese workers. Some important strikes involving the Workers' League include the shoe manufacturers' strike in December 1922 (with 150 workers and members); the strike of women workers from Seoul's rubber factories in June–July 1923 (with 300 workers and members); and the sock makers' strike, also in June–July 1923, in which eleven factories participated, resulting in a wage increase and the reinstatement of workers.[15] On April 20, 1924, the Workers' League dissolved with the creation of a nationwide labor-peasant organization.

Whether the Mutual Aid Society and the Workers' League are the beginnings of Korea's labor movement is debatable because they were formed and their activities took place under colonial rule, with permission from imperial Japan's Government-General of Korea. This is especially true after 1919, when colonial policy became more militant and coercive, finally resulting in coercive labor and military mobilizations beginning in the 1930s. Strictly speaking, independent trade unions were not openly active until liberation. In early November 1945, representatives of unions operating underground gathered in Seoul and formed the National Council of Chosŏn Labor Unions, eventually gaining 574,475 members, a quarter of which were women workers.[16] On November 30, the unions in the northern half of Korea formed the North Korea Headquarters of the National Council of Chosŏn Labor Unions, which paved the way for North Korea's own union structure.[17]

In the first half of 1946, two changes further separated North Korea's unions from South Korea's. First was the establishment of North Korea's own federation structure on March 30, 1946, the General Federation of Labor Unions of North Korea; and second was the permanent change on May 25 of "Labor" to "Trade" (*chigŏp*) in the name to mark the inclusion of all types of work—so that the federation became the General Federation of Trade Unions of North Korea (GFTUNK).[18] The GFTUNK's initial aims were to observe the state's labor laws, to carry out mass campaigns, to increase production, and to support the nation-building efforts.[19] According to the American journalist Anna Louise Strong, who visited North Korea in 1947, the GFTUNK had 17 industrial unions and 3,507 trade unions, comprising a total of 380,000 members. In her report, Strong notes that the mining industry had the most number of unionized workers, with 52,000, followed by the transportation industry and the chemical industry, each with 45,000 union members.[20] Finally, on January 23, 1951, during the Korean War, the central committee of the GFTUNK proclaimed that an independent federation would represent all the workers on the Korean Peninsula and decided to drop "North" from its name, resulting in the General Federation of Trade Unions of Korea (GFTUK).[21]

From early on, North Korea's organized labor faced difficulty in union independence. Because the working class was thought to be formally in control of state power, unions were conceived as a subordinate of the state, functioning to regulate the workers for the purpose of productivity and industrialization. The question of union autonomy was famously debated twice in North Korea's history. The first debate was in 1947, when the Labor minister O Kisŏp criticized the party for setting unrealistic goals, for trying to industrialize too rapidly, and for the harmful effects of "production increase" campaigns aimed at the workers. The second debate was in 1956, when the chair of the GFTUK, Sŏ Hwi, attempted to expand the federation's authority. He is supposed to have said: "The party cannot lead the Trade Federation. There are more union members than party members, so the Trade Federation is the larger organization. All party members are also members of the Trade Federation, so the party must be led by the Trade Federation."[22] In both debates, neither O Kisŏp nor Sŏ Hwi fought for the right of unions to independently represent the workers against industries and the state. Rather, their intention was to increase the authority of the GFTUK with respect to the party. From the perspective of the state, however, O Kisŏp and Sŏ Hwi promoted extreme unionism and thus had to be removed from their positions. The stance of Kim Il Sung was that in socialism, where all industries are state owned, unlike in capitalism, the interest of industries and the interest of the working class are the same.[23] In February 1959, Ri Hyosun became the chair of the GFTUK, and at the general meeting in November the GFTUK declared socialist education (not workers' representation) as its top priority. This was the moment when labor formally came to be under the control of the state.[24]

Factory Management

One-Person Management

The most influential source of economic management in state socialist countries of the twentieth century was the Soviet Union's management experience. More specifically, it was the management system established toward the end of Stalin's rule, during the period of the Soviet Union's much publicized economic growth. The emulation of factory management according to High Stalinism (1946–1950) had to do with the general domination by the Soviet system itself, but it also had to do with the Soviet Union's actual economic achievements after World War II. In the state socialist economy, growth was generally seen as directly proportional to the number of workers. Between 1945 and 1950, the total number of workers in the Soviet Union increased by 43 percent (12 million new workers), and the number of workers in the manufacturing, construction, and transportation sectors saw increases of 49 percent, 70 percent, and 63 percent, respectively, demonstrating the highest growth in the country since the First Five-Year Plan (1928–1932).[25]

Just as important, for emerging socialist countries wanting to replicate the growth of the Soviet Union, the adoption of the Soviet management system also meant the adoption of the key practices of High Stalinism: (1) party control over management; (2) use of mass-mobilization campaigns; (3) militarization of management rhetoric, in which the shop floor became the battlefront for production; (4) ideological education of workers; and (5) connection between production goals and patriotism.[26] These characteristics appeared in the management system of all state socialist countries, including North Korea.

The socialist factory was more than a production unit: it was also a site of political interaction. Factory management was hence a field of governance among state and nonstate agencies—a troika system comprising operation specialists, party delegates, and trade union representatives. The highest level consisted of the factory director (*chibaein*, appointed by ministries), the factory party chair, and the factory union chair. The troika structure was maintained at all levels, down to the lowest level of the work team (or brigade, *chagŏpban*), which was managed by the work team leader (*chagŏp panchang*), the party cell delegate, and the trade union chief.[27] Although one part of the triangular management system held more sway than the other two depending on the historical moment, all three of the parts were involved in the entire process of planning, bargaining, and producing.

In most instances, planning began with the directives issued by the State Planning Commission. The initial directives entailed preliminary targets of how much to increase or decrease total input, total output, and cost.[28] Once the factory received the directives, its planning department drafted the initial plan, which was the result of negotiations and bargaining between party, union, and production representatives at the factory. The State Planning Commission, then, used this initial plan to create a second set of factory directives, which was now a more detailed plan in reference to the national economic plan. The factory took the second set of directives, now with less room for change, and prepared the final plan through more bargaining and negotiations at the factory. The final plan was ultimately approved by the factory director. Based on this plan, another process of bargaining began, this time for financing and for acquiring materials necessary for production.

An important type of socialist management was the "one-person management system" (*yuil kwallije*). It is based on the principle of *edinonachalie,* which is usually translated as "one-person rule"—that person usually being the chief director of the factory. (At the other end was *kollegial'nost'*, "collective rule.") As the name implies, the final decision maker in one-person management was the factory director. Once a plan had been agreed to, the responsibility for the execution and completion of the plan lay with the director. To be sure, the everyday workings of a factory were too complex for any one person to oversee entirely, but, as Joseph Berliner says, the actual practice of *edinonachalie* conveyed a sense of "unified authority":

The notion behind *edinonachalie* is that a line official at any level assumes full responsibility for the entire unit over which he has charge, and he alone may issue orders to people under his jurisdiction.

For example, if the director or the chief of planning department wants something done in a shop, [he or she] may not issue orders to the foremen, but only to the shop chief. Similarly, the shop chief may not issue orders to a worker over the head of his foreman, but only to the foreman directly.[29]

One-person management was hence the management of production by specialists who fulfilled the plan and controlled its variations (anarchy) within the labor process, as constant bargaining and negotiations in attaining resources created shifting (anarchic) production settings.

Introduced in the Soviet Union in 1918, one-person management was the guiding method under both Lenin and Stalin. It became especially prominent from 1929 on, when it was officially adopted by the Communist Party in response to the Shakhty Incident of 1928, in which the alleged bourgeois engineers in the City of Shakhty conspired to sabotage the socialist economic system. In this respect, as Hiroaki Kuromiya notes, one-person management entailed the goals of minimizing reliance on bourgeois experts, training communist workers into specialists, and placing a true proletarian control over the complex process of production. At the same time, according to Kuromiya, a common perception of one-person management was that by reducing the roles of the party and trade unions in the factory, it allowed the despotism of directors.[30] The despotic quality was thus innate in *edinonachalie* because proletarian control was, in the language of revolution, dictatorial control over all other types of management. By the late 1930s, the one-person system fell out of favor in the Soviet Union when factory directors were perceived to be failing both to meet the demands of production and party goals and to train new capable directors. Massive removals of directors took place in 1937 and 1938, and one-person management gave way to a party-dominated system.[31] Many other socialist states adopted the one-person management system at some point in their history, and, like the Soviet Union, they experienced a similar transition toward a party-dominated system.

Transition to Party Management

The major changes to North Korea's factory-management system occurred in three stages: the brief period of autonomous management by workers and specialists from 1945 to 1946; the period of one-person management from 1946 to 1961; and the period of party-dominated management called the Taean Work System, which has been officially in place since 1961.[32] The autonomous characteristic of the first period came from the postcolonial context, in which Japanese colonial managers had left the factories but a state capable of nationalization had not formed. For a year, without a centralized union or government, production in North Korea was jointly managed by Korean, Soviet, and Japanese workers and engineers. The second period—the period of one-person management—took place in the setting of rapid nationalization, wartime production, and especially postwar reconstruction. As the state focused on rebuilding the country after a destructive war, the role of the factory director and other specialists became essential in sustaining production.

At the same time, the postwar decade was a transitional moment: the transition toward the third period of party-dominated management, leading to the implementation of the Taean Work System in 1961. Several events in the 1950s caused this shift: the rise of Kim Il Sung and his political faction as the unchallengeable authority within the Korean Workers' Party; centralized ownership of all forms of production by 1958; and the success of party-led mass campaigns for labor mobilization and productivity. The North Korean state's response to these events, from the late 1950s, much like Stalin's response in the 1930s, was a substantial expansion of party influence in all aspects of life, including working life. In December 1961, the party's involvement in factory management became official with the adoption of the Taean Work System—named after the Taean Electric Factory in the city of Namp'o, which Kim Il Sung had visited that winter and had been impressed by the authoritative role played by the factory party committee in overall production.

North Korea's one-person management system—*yuil kwallije*—relied on the director, who was supposed to understand the activities of operation, set clear goals, distribute the workload properly, and guide the execution of the plan.[33] Although it was the director's responsibility to fulfill the state plan, the troika system could not be easily ignored because the director had to depend on party and labor units at the factory to elicit the workers' morale.[34] Beyond the troika structure, the factory director had to answer to the authority of the government bureau, which was further managed by the ministry. And the authority over the ministry lay with the head of the cabinet, the premier, a position held by Kim Il Sung during the postwar years.[35]

The two decades after liberation were a remarkable and yet uneven period for North Korea. On the one hand, North Korea was successful in rapidly increasing production, which resulted in undeniable absolute growth. Between 1946 and 1969, the total industrial output is said to have increased twenty-one times, or at an incredible rate of 42 percent annually.[36] On the other hand, economic success was accompanied by certain problems. Even during the best years of growth, North Korea suffered from a labor shortage, frequent job relocation of workers, and sluggish productivity in some sectors. Job relocation was especially a serious problem: throughout the 1950s, Kim Il Sung spoke about the ubiquity of this problem in construction,[37] transportation,[38] machinery manufacturing,[39] and forestry.[40] One perceived cause of incongruity in production was lack of responsibility in management, which was manifested as redundancy, disorder, and inefficiency among state agencies and factory directors.[41] A way of resolving such irregularity was through the practice of "production culture" (*saengsan munhwa*), which "demands the cleanup of outdated, antiscientific ways" to ensure "all workers may possess high levels of technological, economical, and cultural minds."[42] A reinvigorated culture of production would take what had been "mere procedure" under one-person management and transform it into genuine interest and responsibility among the productive masses.[43] The party's decision in the late 1950s to expand its authority in production management was the first step in creating this new culture of production.

The changes in management taking place in the late 1950s showed a shift within the troika relationship in which the factory party chair became the most powerful voice over the union representative and the factory director. The era of *edinonachalie* came to a close in this setting, although the factory director continued to function as the chief operation specialist. The expansion of party authority was also part of a nationwide movement to reorganize the Korean Workers' Party in the aftermath of the August Factional Incident of 1956. The momentary crisis of Kim Il Sung's power propelled him and his supporters to remove political challengers and to further integrate the party in all domains of life. The increase of party control in production thus occurred simultaneously with the increase of party control in general. The best-known case of party penetration into daily life is the Ch'ŏllima Work Team Movement of 1959, which sought to translate party interests of high productivity and ideological unity into everyday language, competition among workers, and motifs for art and education.

The Taean Work System, publicized in mid-December 1961, was the culmination of this change. On December 7, party leaders, including Kim Il Sung, visited the Taean Electric Factory located at Namp'o, 50 kilometers (31 miles) southwest of Pyongyang. The visit, which lasted for ten days, was part of the party's Central Committee plan, approved just days before the visit, to overhaul North Korea's management system.[44] At the end of the visit, Kim Il Sung declared one-person management a system with "many remaining capitalist wastes," such as bureaucratism and individualism.[45] In contrast, Kim claimed, the Taean System was a collective system with "many communist elements," in which the "factory party committee manages the factory as the highest leadership organ" and where the "responsibility goes to no one person but to all party members, workers, directors, and engineers."[46] More specifically, the Taean System was to be rooted in four principles: (1) the adherence to the so-called mass line in the planning process, in which the workers were actively involved in the creation of production goals; (2) the merger between production and technology enabling the workers to constantly work with engineers and learn about technology; (3) the guaranteed supply of materials from one area to the next to make production consistent; and (4) the elevation of the party Central Committee to the top of the management chain so that the party's political mission and economic policy could be followed simultaneously.[47]

China went through a comparable trajectory during this period. Having witnessed the Soviet Union's remarkable overall economic growth, China adopted the one-person management system in the early 1950s. As Franz Schurmann writes in his classic study *Ideology and Organization in Communist China* (1966), one-person management was implemented in China to tackle the problems of irresponsibility and bureaucratism and to introduce labor heroism at the production level. The system gave factory managers the authority to make the final decision on labor, materials, and money; to impose punitive actions on workers who tampered with state property; and to take independent action to fulfill the plan.[48] These features were also observable in North Korea. A key difference, however, was variation according to sector and region in China, which ultimately led to China's rejection of one-person management. At the root of the variation was the concentration of heavy industries in Manchuria (with emblematic factories such as Anshan Iron and Steel Works), which contributed to the growth of independent power in factory managers, industrial ministries, and, in particular, the chair of the State Planning Commission, Kao Kang.[49] The Chinese Communist Party saw this development as a corruption of individualism and purged key officials and industrial technocrats, including Kao Kang, who committed suicide in 1955. With the party's increasing involvement in daily life in the second half of 1950s, the Eighth Party Congress announced a new direction, wherein one-person management would be abandoned in favor of management by the factory party committee.[50]

The Taean Work System is still the official method of factory management in North Korea, although in practice the large military economy and the growing private sector make the picture more complex. From the position of market-based countries, it may seem odd at first to have a party representative at a worksite, let alone a powerful one dominating the production decisions. But the substance of what the party does at factories is not odd: raising morale, creating a sense of belonging, emphasizing responsibility and efficiency, and equating work with abstract ideologies such as

Figure 2.1 A party worker conducting political education, Hŭngnam Fertilizer Factory, 1960s.
Source: Photograph courtesy of the Hŭngnam Fertilizer Factory Museum.

patriotism. These activities are also carried out by human-resource offices across the United States, South Korea, Japan, and other market-based countries. The efforts to increase productivity in North Korea thus has a human component: to cultivate the mind and the will—not through coercion but through collective vision. Here, the paradoxical relationship between form and content becomes particularly important: two different forms—socialism and capitalism—are connected to the same content—the ideologies of morale, belonging, and responsibility. The appearance of different forms is related to the type of misrecognition prevalent in the current capitalist stage of world history: the misrecognition of the exterior as a direct reflection of the interior. The mechanism behind the appearance of commodity as value determined by the market (and not by collective labor) is also behind the perception of the ideology of state socialism as different from the ideology of capitalist industrialism.

Calibrating and Monetizing Work

The qualitative ways of raising productivity—the party's emphasis on unity and responsibility—occurred alongside the quantitative ways of raising productivity. Two main categories were used in the practice of labor calculation: calibrating efficiency in the labor process and monetizing work through various types of wage. Calibrating efficiency involved changes to the labor process on the shop floor. Specifically, this meant rationally managing resources by maximizing the workload, work time, and work space. Increasing efficiency was therefore about increasing industrial efficiency, a noncoercive method not requiring changes to the worker's own physical effort. In this sense, there was no such a thing as socialist efficiency, only the efficiency related to industrialism. The practice of monetizing work, however, was more problematic. North Korea had to claim that the wage in socialism was absolutely different from the wage in capitalism. Wage was a measurement of exploitation, after all: it was only a fraction of the total surplus value produced by the worker and was determined by the market, whose aim of maximum profit kept the wage as low as possible. In contrast, wage in socialism could not be a market expression of the value of labor because labor power was no longer a commodity sold and bought on the labor market. Now, at least in principle, wage was a transparent and just redistribution of the total surplus after a certain amount was kept by the state to satisfy collective need. Throughout the postwar period, the journal *Rodong*, published by the GFTUK, constantly featured articles on efficiency and wage. These articles championed various practices in efficiency and wage, which could potentially increase productivity without increasing the number of workers.

Industrial Efficiency

The practice of efficiency in work was based foremost on the standardization of workload. This entailed the adoption of "advanced and scientific technology and work methods" reflecting the new standards claimed to be created by the "patriotic devotion" of workers themselves.[51] The nation-wide campaign to standardize the workload began soon after the Korean War with Cabinet Directive No. 108 (September 18, 1953), which established the Standard Workload Audit and Inspection Committee. This committee collected data from 564 firms and 4,194 job types, showing an average 45.5 percent increase in workload across the board.[52] Production figures from the period of the Korean War formed the base against which the increase was determined.[53] All work was thus measured against the productivity level of war communism. Kim Il Sung was aware of what some workers were capable of during war. "Last winter we mobilized a People's Army regiment for forestry work," Kim said, referring to the winter of 1952. "The solders achieved a productivity level of 1,000 percent over the standard workload applied currently. What does this situation show us? There is no secret or mystery. The previous workload standards are already outdated today."[54] The dire experience of working during war—which demanded a great amount of sacrifice and legitimated the condition of difficult work—became the new measure of labor in the postwar period.

The first industrial sector to receive a new workload standard was mining.[55] Important production sites such as Kŏmdŏk Mine, the largest producer of zinc, in the city of Tanch'ŏn in South Hamgyŏng Province, saw a workload increase of 51.8 percent by the end of 1958.[56] The next sector was chemical and other heavy industries: at the Hŭngnam Fertilizer Factory, the largest producer of nitrogenous fertilizer, the workers saw their workload standard raised by 53 percent.[57] The general guideline for all industrial sites was to establish a high standard based on the production level of superior individual workers and then establish "progressive work-load standards" (*rujinjŏk rodong kijunnyang*) below that high standard.[58] Although the new labor standards certainly contributed to the overall growth of postwar industrial economy, the practice of increasing work-loads faced problems of inconsistent timing of implementation, shortage of materials needed for higher output, and inadequate management of operations.[59]

The second type of efficiency practice involved the modification of work time. The accepted view here was that even with a low amount of labor power, a rational and efficacious use of labor time was sufficient to increase productivity.[60] The time a worker spent at a job was uneven, even for the best among them. Not all work time was equally efficient, which became apparent with the creation of a temporal map of productive time. In such a map, time at the work station was divided into different parts. Typically, time was first divided into when the machine was running and when it was not. The time when the machine was running was further divided into when the running machine was actually productive and when it was running idle. The time when the machine was not running was then divided into when the stoppage was necessary (for oiling, maintenance, cleaning) and when the stoppage was unnecessary and hence avoidable (electrical problems, shortage of raw materials). Each division was a separate target of improvement.

Table 2.1 is a sample of work-time management created by specialist Kong Chint'ae for forty-six cutting machines. In his analysis, Kong noticed that the many causes of machines not running were unrelated to produc-tion needs. "By eliminating the unnecessary stoppage of machines," Kong said, "the time when the machine is cutting can be increased. . . . As such, the causes for machine stoppage and irrational usage were exposed in detail."[61] The details of unevenness of labor became apparent once labor was translated into time: time revealed the incongruous terrain of labor. Simultaneously, the dissected representation of labor time enabled further domination by labor: nonproductive activities such as talking to cowork-ers and leaving the workstation—activities "exposed" by work-time analysis—were treated as wasteful time, although such activities could help the workers deal with the monotonous and strenuous production environment.

TABLE 2.1

Machine-Time Use Analysis, North Korea, 1958

Time Group	Work Type	Time (minutes)	% of Total Machine-Time Use
Machine running	Cutting	13,591	61.7
Machine not running due to production needs	Oiling, cleaning, exchanging parts, changing shifts, etc.	3,478	15.7
Machine not running due to management or workers' unnecessary stoppage	Repairing machines; waiting for raw materials, parts, inspection, directives, etc.	2,611	11.8
Machine not running due to workers' behavior	Talking, deserting work station	1,328	6.0
Machine not running due to workers' physiological needs	Going to the bathroom, eating, taking breaks	1,072	4.8
	Total	**22,080**	**100.0**

Source: Figures compiled from Kong Chint'ae, "Kongjak kigyedŭl ŭi riyongryul chego rŭl wihan rodong sigan ŭi ch'ŭkjŏng" (Work-time measurement to improve the use rate of manufacturing machines), Rodong, no. 8 (1958): 40–43.

In another labor-time analysis, specialist Yang Inhyŏk discovered that a group of supply workers spent 33.5 percent of their shift time writing reports on how much they manufactured. He also noticed that 19.5 percent of their time was "lost" on various stoppages, such as production interruptions, work breaks, and pauses related to "bodily functions." "There is too much misused time!" Yang exclaimed. "This kind of labor-time expenditure can be decisively reduced once organizational and technological conditions of this task are analyzed." His suggestion for reducing the reporting time and unnecessary stoppages was to calculate the quantity of supplies by "weight instead of pieces" and to use "cards" instead of "books" to make reporting faster. Furthermore, he suggested that machine workers, who used the materials provided by the supply workers, should participate in hauling the materials to their work stations. Yang concluded that if these changes did not raise the productivity, then the problem might not be the supply workers: it might be that there were too many machine workers relative to supply workers, so the factory management should consider reducing the overall number of machine workers.[62] In Yang's analysis, the productivity of supply workers was not a matter of individual exertion but a matter of efficacy with things around them. The counting by weight and the use of cards are examples of efficacy not requiring an increase in the workers' physical effort.

The third target of efficiency practice was work space. The appropriate spatial distribution of machines and workers was a key marker of industrial efficiency. Labor acquired an additional level of domination through spatial manipulation. At the Pyongyang Textile Factory, specialist Kim Insŏn reported that workers doubled their production of fabric without an increase in the number of workers by "making ordinary what is an advanced manufacturing technique." Along with mechanization of what used to be manual work and rebuilding the motors to run faster, the "manager-workers" at the factory paid great attention to maximizing the production space. In textile work, Kim went on to say, "more so than in other types of work, an arrangement of workers without the consideration of their skill levels will result in machine stoppages and a decline in labor productivity." At weaving machines, the management placed higher-level workers (those responsible for the quality of the weave, cutting the yarn, and communicating with the team leader) at the machine-front area and lower-level workers (those responsible for preventing the knotting of the weave and the severing of the yarn) at the machine-rear area. The workers were then directed to move in a pattern to handle only the front or the back, never both (figure 2.2). The spatial improvement at this textile factory supposedly cut down the time spent at each machine per rotation by 3.5 seconds and stabilized the workers' movement at 126 steps a minute among the machines.[63]

For specialist Kim Ch'unsang, a fundamental issue in the spatial arrangement of workers was the sequence of movement. If one job entailed stopping the machine and another job did not, then Kim recommended the job requiring machine stoppage be carried out first. For instance, when a worker was faced with task of changing the bobbin, which required stopping the motor, or mending a flaw in the fabric, the worker needed to change the bobbin first. When a task involved the stopping of multiple machines, Kim advised that the first step should be handling the machine needing the shortest amount of time. In a situation where "one machine needs mending a single broken thread (taking fifteen to eighteen seconds) and another machine needs mending three broken threads (taking thirty to forty seconds)," the machine with a single broken thread should be handled first.[64] Kim did not mention exactly why such a method would improve productivity, but he assured the readers that following his advice would improve the speed of spatial movement and efficiency of production. Again, what is salient here is the effort to control productivity not through individual workers' physical exertion but through the recalibration of the work setting.

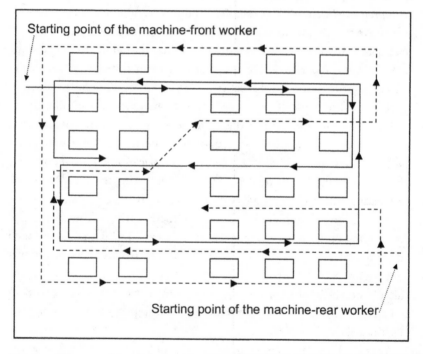

Figure 2.2 Diagram of the direction of textile workers' movement on the shop floor, 1958.

Source: Kim Insŏn, "Sŏnjin kisul chagŏp pangbŏp ŭl toip hayŏ sae kijunnyang ŭl ch'angjo" (The creation of new standards by adopting advanced technologies and manufacturing methods), Rodong, no. 12 (1958): 52.

Figure 2.3 A textile factory at Sariwŏn, North Hwanghae Province, 1990s.
Source: Chosŏn Hwabosa (Korean Pictorial Agency), *Kim Ilsŏng chusŏk kwa onŭl ŭi Chosŏn* (Premier Kim Il Sung and North Korea today) (Pyongyang: Oegukmun Chonghap Ch'ulp'ansa, 1993).

Socialist Wage

Industrial management found another rational expression in the monetization of labor through wage. In 1955, two labor researchers, Yun Ŭisŏp and Ch'a Sunhŏn, wrote a definitive book on wage in which they defined *socialist wage* as a "remuneration for labor and not the price of labor power," unlike in a capitalist economy.[65] This distinction was a formal one, however, because, strictly speaking, there was no true way of determining wage except as a socially accepted amount (as it is also done in capitalism, albeit based on the market) and because the socialist wage system also depended on surplus, which was appropriated by the state before it could be turned into wage.

Three types of wage were important during North Korea's early industrial period: the fixed wage (*chŏngaek imgŭm*), calculated according to the length of labor time expended; the piecework wage (*togŭp imgŭm*), calculated according to the quantity of goods produced at a certain level of quality; and the incentive wage (*sanggŭm imgŭm*), given as a reward once a certain level of production was achieved. Usually, a worker's actual wage was a combination of fixed wage or piecework wage *and* incentive wage. The fixed wage was the form of wage reserved for office workers, artists, health workers, engineers, and education workers, whose "product" was not concretely assessable, and the piecework wage was paid to those who labored outside the office, whose work created quantifiable products. The postwar period saw the beginning of the overhaul of labor compensation, with the goal of eventually eliminating all payments-in-kind. This motion was started at the Third Party Congress in 1956, where a decision was made to "consider abolishing the distribution system of manufactured goods and food provisions."[66] In the effort to transform from payment-in-kind to payment-in-money, the wage of all workers was raised throughout the 1950s: in April 1954, by 25 percent; in November 1956, by 35 percent; in January 1958, by 10 percent; and in January 1959, by 40 percent.[67] However, even at the end of the 1950s payment-in-kind seems to have been common.[68]

In North Korea, as in other state socialist countries, the type of wage considered superior to others was piecework wage, for several reasons. First, it determined wage according to concretely expressed results and hence eliminated the "tendency to remain average" (*p'yŏnggyunjuŭi*). Second, it increased the workers' cultural and technological levels in that culture and technology were directly related to the workers' personal profit. Third, it strengthened the workers' consciousness and promoted self-regulation. And fourth, it advanced the workers' awareness of "social property by merging social profit with personal profit."[69] Because the workers received according to what they put in, the piecework wage was accepted as the most just and most socialist type of wage. The great irony was that the piecework wage was also the preferred method of compensation in capitalist production and thus a setting for exploitation, as Marx had noticed many years earlier. The piecework system was a setting for exploitation because a worker could be persuaded by the earning potential to produce without concern for the intensity of exploitation. This latent problem (which surfaced in the everyday space of the shop floor) was resolved with the claim that in North Korea piecework occurred under the conditions that protective measures and shortened labor-time had been adopted and that the workers were aware of the unity between personal profit and state profit.[70]

First introduced to the transportation sector in May 1947, the piecework wage was accepted by the government as an effective way to deal with the problem of underproductivity—"working for average."[71] According to Yun and Ch'a, "an extensive and accurate operation of piecework wage is necessary to liquidate the tendency to work for average wage."[72] The goal in the postwar era was to bring more than 60 percent of workers under the piecework-wage system.[73] In principle, the piecework wage was best suited to dangerous work (*yuhae nodong*), such as mining, because work time could be flexible as long as production goals were met. The minimum piecework wage therefore became higher as the physical danger attached to a job became greater. Work in heavy industries received a higher minimum wage than work in light industries such as textile, paper, and rubber manufacturing. But the piecework wage within heavy industries also had a wide range: automobile transportation was at the lower end (106.5 percent of light labor), and railroad transportation was at the higher end (123.6 percent of light labor).[74] The highest wage was given to mining workers (149.6 percent of light labor).[75] The notion of *equal amount of labor for equal quantity of products*—as endorsed by Lenin in *The State and Revolution*[76]—found practical expression in the piecework wage, even though this method of compensation was also widely and egregiously practiced in capitalist countries.

How such calibration and monetization of labor and the subsequent increase in total productivity actually made the workers' livelihood better is not too clear. Behind the claims of a 2,000 percent increase in industrial output, a 683 percent increase in national income, and a 539 percent increase in labor productivity between 1946 and 1960,[77] the situation of North Koreans' everyday life was marked by stressful work and uneven material returns, including in 1955 what amounted to a famine, which was especially devastating to the people in the northern regions.[78] This situation was further exacerbated by the general milieu of obligatory political education. Between 1950 and 1979 at the international level, whereas the average annual growth rate of gross domestic product was similar between state socialist countries and so-called capitalist countries (3–6 percent for both sides), the average annual rate of investment in fixed assets was twice as high in state socialist countries (6–11 percent compared to 4–7 percent in capitalist countries), indicating low returns on investment (thus low productivity) and low consumption for the sake of state investment.[79] The industrial initiative of countries such as North Korea in the 1950s was a complex endeavor. Ideological and discursive programs (mass campaigns, patriotic motivation, hero workers) took place along with modern industrial management (time–space calculations, wage standards). It is often the case that the former covers up the latter in the historical imagination of places such as North Korea, but beyond the imagination is the historical reality of modern industrialism.

My contextualization of North Korea's postwar industrial practices within the universal framework of capitalism is similar to Jake Werner's analysis of China within the framework of Fordism, the global process of capitalist subsumption critically put into words first by Antonio Gramsci. Werner observes in urban China of the 1950s an industrial work culture signaling Fordism in practice. In particular, he identifies in urban China four Fordist characteristics: a restructuring of production based on industrial rationality; a new culture of work integrating the diverse population; a reconstitution of the nation as a productive whole; and a public rhetoric of equality masking the contradictions and hierarchy within the labor process.[80] Comparable features are found in postwar North Korea. Especially notable is Werner's assertion that global Fordism was a "determinant response following from a shared global experience of the crisis of war and depression, incorporating and further elaborating existing social forms of organization like the bureaucratic corporation and forms of consciousness like the modern nation in an attempt to overcome the crisis."[81] The mid–twentieth century, after a series of devastating wars across regions, was a period of both crisis and reconstruction throughout the world. Capitalism found multiple historical formations in this setting—Keynesianism, Third-Worldism, developmentalism, the welfare state, and so on. And despite inspiring revolutionaries such as Lenin and their remarkable achievements, state socialism can be added to this list. Whether in the United States or in North Korea, a prominent feature was the culture of work reconfigured according to the rationality and calculation of industrialism. Nevertheless, how much the state became involved in the formation gave rise to distinct historical experiences. That is to say, in postwar North Korea the workers indeed experienced their everyday life as some kind of new socialist reality.

CHAPTER 3

Producing the Everyday Life of Work

The proletarian state is the structural timber, not the structure itself.
—LEON TROTSKY, *PROBLEMS OF EVERYDAY LIFE*

E veryday life is a product. This description refers not only to the ideal and moral image of everydayness created by the state, religion, or other hegemonic forms but also to the mundane and repetitive side of daily life. Both are made, and both have the same ideological structure revealing the workings of power. In this chapter, everyday life is considered specifically as modes of production and administration. Work became an indispensable area of state control in postwar North Korea. The ultimate space of this control was everyday life. To organize work and set production in motion, the everyday had to be seized by the state. In the process of seizure, everyday life was remade and infused with the ideology of work and the insistence of totality between living and producing.

Because everyday life is constantly organized by the state, it would be incorrect to suggest that everyday life is a modern condition. Was not the Neo-Confucian transformation of Chosŏn Korea starting in the fifteenth century precisely the gradual merger of everyday life with ritual practice based on the male primogenitary lineage? There is, however, a modern aspect of everyday life described in these pages. It is only in the modern era—that is, with the rise of industrialism and the dominance of the wage-labor market—that everyday life emerged as an explicit category of its own. In considering everyday life of the modern type, this study principally refers to the thought of Henri Lefebvre (1901–1991). For Lefebvre, the modern world reduced the everyday into "organized passivity" both in work and in private life.[1] More specifically, everyday life became a mode of production and a mode of administration, where the state and industries collaborated to achieve their aim not through coercion but through self-determination.

North Korea's dire postwar situation was conducive to the production of everyday life centered on work. The casualties, population displacement, and economic damage brought on by the war were great, but these factors also provided a space for political reorganization benefitting Kim Il Sung and his faction of former partisans of Manchuria. The war's impact on the industrial economy, too, was large, but it was uneven (not everything was destroyed), allowing the state to reinitiate industrialization across the country. The postwar period therefore saw a double movement of consolidating power and consolidating production: on the one hand, the emergence of Kim Il Sung and the partisan faction as the unchallengeable authority in the party, legislature, and military, eliminating in the process those who challenged him and the legacy of the partisans and, on the other hand, the appropriation of all surplus by the state through the control of unions, the nationalization of private enterprises, the cooperativization of agriculture, and the transformation of farmers into agricultural wage-workers. This double movement was a necessary foundation for the emergence of a new everyday experience.

In this chapter, I approach North Korea's postwar everyday life in three parts. The first part is ideological, explained with a particular emphasis on the notion of repetition. Through repetition in everyday space, the extraordinary work performance of labor heroes found its historical meaning among ordinary workers. The second part is practical, exemplified by production campaigns taking place in all sectors of industry. Commonly known as mass movements, these production campaigns emphasized competition, the work ethic, and the patriotic significance of hard work. The central feature of mass movements was their spontaneous origin from *and* voluntary practice among the workers in the everyday space of the workplace. The best-known mass movement is the Ch'ŏllima Work Team Movement, which began in 1959 and became an iconic cultural fixture that has lasted to this day. And the third part is the sense of totality, where communal needs and state needs are simultaneously—and at least formally—satisfied in everyday space. The ideology of repetitive work, the mass movements to increase production, and the infrastructure of housing, education, and leisure merged in the space of everyday life to create a discursive and practical coherence, a totality between living and work-ing. The moment of totality, however, was also the moment of disinte-gration because no totality is complete in practice and because totality always holds certain layers of antagonistic relations that prevent any true totalization. Nevertheless, the attempt at ideological and practical con-trol over everyday life was necessary to fulfill the state's goals of industrial-ization and socialist construction. Despite the contradictions and failures, North Korea of this period seemed—certainly to its own people but also to many outside—like a single machine moving in the direction of human progress.

When the War Was Over

Industrial Economy in the Aftermath

Toward the end of the colonial period, the northern part of Korea was undergoing an economic change that can only be called industrialization, albeit to support the costly (and losing) war waged by imperial Japan in the Pacific and Northeast China. There was industrial development in the southern part as well, and until around 1940 the level of production was similar between the two parts, if not higher in the South. However, with the demands of war in the Pacific and China, industries in the North grew rapidly, especially the mining, electric power, and railroad sectors. At the end of 1944, colonial Korea was producing 50.7 percent of the fluorite, 85.7 percent of the tungsten, and 100 percent of the cobalt and nickel used in the Japanese Empire.[2] Almost all mining facilities were in the North, and 80 percent of the electric power generating facilities were built in the North. Japan built ten hydroelectric dams along the two rivers on the northern border with China, the largest of which was the Sup'ung Hydro-electric Dam on the Amnok River, capable of producing a quarter of all electricity in the North. In 1945, the North was able to produce 1.5 mil-lion kilowatts of electricity that year, whereas the South's annual capacity was only 237,000 kilowatts.[3] Japan's capacity was seven times that of north-ern Korea, but when populations are taken into account, northern Korea actually produced more electricity per capita than mainland Japan (162 kilo-watts per capita in northern Korea versus 144 kilowatts per capita in Japan).[4] The railroad network, too, was concentrated in the North, with

4,009 kilometers (2,485 miles) of track compared to 2,488 kilometers (1,543 miles) in the South; and when the length of railroad per capita is calculated, the rate was higher in the North than in Japan (430 meters [470 yards] per capita in North Korea and 350 meters [383 yards] per capital in Japan).[5]

North Korea was indeed an industrializing place. Right before the Korean War, there were a thousand production facilities in operation, employing more than 200,000 workers (see chapter 1). What were they producing? What made up North Korea's industrial economy in the mid–twentieth century? According to a Soviet report from 1950, North Korean products exported to the Soviet Union—and directly managed by the Ministry of Industry—included pig iron, electrolytic copper, zinc, cadmium, lead, ferrosilicon, carbide, caustic soda, ammonium sulfate, gold, silver, laundry soap, starch, and cement.[6] In fact, almost all the gold, silver, and cadmium produced by North Korea during this period was sent to the Soviet Union.[7] Where was production taking place? What were some important production sites of this period? Some clues are found in a document titled "Ch'on'gubaek sasipgunyŏndo taesso such'ulp'um ch'ulha silchŏkp'yo" (The record of export items to the Soviet Union in 1949) sent by Deputy Minister of Industry Ko Himan to Vice Premier Kim Ch'aek on January 10, 1950. In that year, the Ministry of Industry was operating sixteen large factories and twelve mines for trade (see table 3.1).[8] All had been built by Japanese companies during the colonial period. This group of mines and factories would continue to be the most important production sites after the war. Hwanghae Iron and Steel Works in South Hwanghae Province, which produced all the exported pig iron, had the only functioning blast furnace after the war, and Hŭngnam Fertilizer Factory in South Hamgyŏng Province was one of the largest chemical factories in Asia. The Pon'gung Chemical Fertilizer Factory, also in South Hamgyŏng, which would become in 1961 the emblematic Vinalon Factory, produced most of North Korea's carbide, an important item in making iron and, of course, vinalon. The total value of export to the Soviet Union in 1949 was 258,730,000 rubles (US$64 million).[9] All the export to the Soviet Union between 1949 and 1950 was payment-in-kind. In a secret military agreement between North Korea and the Soviet Union in March 1949, the Soviet Union had agreed to supply North Korea with weapons, and North Korea had agreed to pay with metals, chemicals, and foodstuffs. North Korea was a state short on cash but long on ambition to build a military strong enough for an invasion of the South. What is particularly notable (and disturbing

TABLE 3.1

Sites and Products Controlled by the Ministry of Industry,
North Korea, 1949

Industry	Production Site	Products for Export
Mining	Tallok Mine, Ŭngok Mine, Kimhwa Mine, Ch'ŏlsan Mine, Kŏmdŏk Mine, Musan Mine, Nam'gye Mine, Sŏnch'ŏn Mine, Hasŏng Mine, Iwŏn Mine, Ch'ŏnghak Mine, Kaech'ŏn Mine	tantalum, beryllium, monazite, zinc ore, iron ore, magnesite, talc, silicon dioxide, flake graphite, earthy graphite
Smelting	Hŭngnam Smeltery, Munp'yŏng Smeltery, Namp'o Smeltery	electrolytic copper, electrolytic lead, cadmium, bismuth, monazite, arsenious acid, lead oxide, zinc oxide
Steelworks	Sŏngjin Steelworks, Kangsŏn Steelworks	ferrotungsten, ferrosilicon, high-speed steel, special-purpose tool steel, carbon tool steel, round steel, angle steel
Steelmaking	Hwanghae Iron and Steel Works	steel sheet, pig iron, angle steel
Fertilizer	Hŭngnam Fertilizer	monazite, fertilizer, laundry soap
Chemical	Ch'ŏngsu Chemical, Pon'gung Chemical	carbide, acetylene black, abrasives, caustic soda
Explosives	Hŭngnam Explosives	ammonium nitrate, blasting fuse, detonator, ammonium nitrate explosive, barium chlorate
Cement	Ch'ŏnnaeri Cement	cement
Silk	Ch'ŏlwŏn Silkmill, Hamhŭng Silkmill	raw silk

TABLE 3.1 (continued)

Industry	Production Site	Products for Export
Cereal	Pyongyang Cereal	starch
Shipbuilding	Ch'ŏngjin Shipbuilding, Wŏnsan Shipbuilding	barges

Source: Ministry of Industry, DPRK, "Such'ulp'um ch'ulha silchŏkp'yo," in Pukhan kyŏngje kwan'gye munsŏjip, vol. 2 (Chunch'ŏn: Hallimtaehakkyo Aseamunhwayŏn'guso, 1997), 538–543, cited in Kimura Mitsuhiko and Abe Keiji, Chŏnjaengi mandŭn nara: Pukhanŭi kunsa kongŏphwa (The country made by war: The military industrialization of North Korea), trans. Ch'a Munsŏk and Pak Chŏngjin (Seoul: Mizi, 2009), 296–297.

perhaps) about this agreement was the large amounts of starch, grains, and rice included in "foodstuffs."[10] Even during the war, when millions of North Korean people were lacking adequate food, shipments of rice were heading for Moscow.

The Korean War's damage on North Korea's industrial economy was large but not as complete as one is led to believe by the story of a single building being left standing in Pyongyang or of a B-29 bomber chasing a single motorcycle because targets had become so scarce.[11] First of all, there was a kind of wartime industry in that many factories were converted to weapons-making facilities and relocated to safer areas (some underground) to resume production (see chapter 1). The heavy industry's production of supplies for the battlefront was the most important goal of wartime industry. At the same time, the reconstruction of light industry, which manufactured consumer goods, also began during the war when in July 1951 the Ministry of Industry was split into the Ministry of Heavy Industry, the Ministry of Light Industry, and the Ministry of Chemical and Construction Industries. The core of the labor force during the war were women, who worked long hours mostly in light manufacturing, making clothes and processed foods.

The accounts of war damage to North Korea's industrial economy provide an uneven picture. At one extreme, the war resulted in the destruction of 8,500 industrial sites, 600,000 housing units, 5,000 schools, and 370,000 hectares of rice fields, which translated into a monetary value of 420 billion won (approximately US$400 million), about four times North Korea's gross national product in 1953.[12] These numbers are high, and the exact places of these 8,500 industrial sites are unknown, but the picture is sufficiently grim. The air-bombing campaigns of the Far East Air Forces also tell a similar story. In June 1950, 90 percent of North Korea's electric power potential was wiped out; and by the end of 1950, 60 percent of Sinŭiju City was burned down, 90 percent of Hweryŏng City was destroyed, and 65 percent of Kanggye City was set ablaze.[13] But as far as industrial damage is concerned, only a small percentage of the bombs were used for industrial targets. An assessment made by Far East Air Forces at the armistice shows that out of more than 17,000 tons of bombs delivered during the war, about 2,000 tons (12 percent) were delivered to industrial targets, with the rest going to supply areas, airfields, and cities.[14] Among the damaged industrial sites, fifty-two factories stopped most of their production by the end of 1950.[15] They include the most critical facilities for export-oriented products—large facilities such as the Hŭngnam Fertilizer Factory, the Pon'gung Chemical Fertilizer Factory, and the Ch'ŏngjin Chemical Textile Company.[16] But other facilities actually increased production: at a machine factory in Sun'an (northwest of Pyongyang), the workers increased the production of aluminum plates by 300 to 400 percent.[17]

Overall, the total industrial output in North Korea immediately after the war was 64.1 percent of the output in 1949 (or more than twice the output in 1946).[18] On the ground, however, the output was different for different industries. In 1953, the industrial sectors suffering the most from the war, compared to their output in 1949, were power (26.5 percent of output in 1949), fuel (11.3 percent), metallurgical (10.6 percent), chemical (21.6 percent), textile (1.5 percent), paper (26.3 percent), and fishing (24.0 percent). Some sectors actually saw an increase in output: metalworking (123.9 percent), pharmaceutical (136.4 percent), glass and ceramics (153.6 percent), leather and shoemaking (145.0 percent), and oil and fat (129.3 percent).[19]

There were regional differences as well. Compared to the output in 1949, most provinces experienced a decrease: South P'yŏngan, 59 percent; North Hwanghae, 26 percent; South Hamgyŏng, 36 percent; North Hamgyŏng, 73 percent; Ryanggang, 62 percent; and Kangwŏn—the most damaged of all provinces—16 percent. Yet two provinces saw an increase in industrial output, and one province did not change: North P'yŏngan, 212 percent; Chagang, 345 percent; and South Hwanghae, 100 percent.[20] The capital Pyongyang, where only one building is said to have stood at the end of the war, had an industrial output in 1953 that was 43 percent of the output in

1949.[21] Damage was thus spatially uneven. Kangwŏn and South Hamgyŏng, two provinces on the east coast, and North Hwanghae, which borders South Korea, suffered the most: the first two because they were centers of cement, chemical, and machine production, and North Hwanghae because it was a crucial supply route and the location of a large steel factory, Hwanghae Iron and Steel. But the provinces in the North, especially the four provinces sharing a border with China, had industries that remained intact enough to continue production during and after the war.

When the damage is assessed on the basis of key products, the pattern is once again uneven. The items whose production were most affected by the war were mining and heavy industrial products (coal, graphite, steel, coke, cement). The most important items for the Ministry of Industry—the items for export—saw a large decrease in their production: in 1953, North Korea did not produce any meaningful amount of pig iron, ferrosilicon, caustic soda, or ammonium sulfate, and cement production was just 5 percent that of 1949.[22] However, the production of certain items of light industry—essential for day-to-day survival—continued (even expanded) during the war. Compared to the output of 1949, the production of fabric was 168 percent (21,623 kilometers [13,406 miles]); footwear, 123 percent (7 million pairs); soy sauce, 99 percent (17,730 kiloliters [4,684 gallons]); vegetable oil, 85 percent (6,994 tons); and tobacco, 70 percent (4,241 tons).[23] Grain production in 1953 (at 2,327,000 tons) was 88 percent of the 1949 level, and rice production actually increased from 1,158,000 tons in 1949 to 1,229,000 tons in 1953, albeit still insufficient to feed the population.[24] There is little doubt that the Korean War brought much destruction to North Korea, but the pattern of this destruction was uneven. Heavy industry and the mining industry, considered the most important industries for North Korea due to their role in export, were decimated, but much of light industry remained intact. Bombs and bullets over North Korea razed the cities and killed millions, but they did not destroy all industries, which was a fortuitous circumstance for a state in pursuit of industrialization.

Plan for Reconstruction

The first party document outlining postwar reconstruction was a comprehensive plan on mass education, export economy, labor mobilization, and agricultural collectivization. A close look at this document is important for understanding North Korea's process toward state socialism. Titled "Chŏngjŏn hyŏpchŏng chegyŏl kwa kwalyŏnhan chŏnhu inminkyŏngje pok'kupalchŏn ŭl wihan tujaeng kwa tang ŭi kŭmhu immu e taehayŏ" (On the struggle and party tasks for the recovery and development of postwar people's economy in relation to the Armistice Agreement), the plan was passed at the Sixth Plenum of the Korean Workers' Party Central Committee, held August 5–9, 1953.[25] It has six sections: "Results of the Victorious War," "Causes of the Victorious War," "Tasks in Mass Politics and Propaganda," "Basic Economic Projects," "Shortcomings of Production Sites," and "Ideological Struggle of the Party." Among them, the third and fourth sections are the most revealing.

The third section on mass politics and propaganda has five parts: "Political and Ideological Attentiveness," "Patriotism and Heroism," "Relations with Other Socialist Countries," "Political Projects on South Korea," and "Antiespionage Struggle." A key feature in this section is patriotism, which was seen as necessary in all areas, whether in the mobilization of workers for national reconstruction or the call for the expulsion of the US military from South Korea. Patriotism is not an innate quality of human beings; it is constructed under certain conditions—for example, the condition of imperialism or the condition of industrialization. The violence, displacement, and poverty caused by the war, along with the drive toward industrialization, provided an ideal setting to instigate the patriotic spirit. The 1953 plan states, "The patriotic sacrifice and mass heroism shown by the Korean people shall be continuously exalted, and by revealing the beastly atrocities of the enemy, hatred and enmity shall be continuously promoted within the masses."[26] The postwar situation was, in a way, a situation of possibilities, and although patriotism and hatred are not innate emotions, they were made by the state to become the collective emotion necessary for the production of surplus.

The fourth section of the plan, "Basic Economic Projects," begins with the announcement that 1953 would be the year of preparation for recovery, followed by three years of raising the economy back to the prewar level (the Three-Year Plan) and then by five years of constructing a fully state-controlled economy (the Five-Year Plan).[27] Laid out here was the initial blueprint for state socialism: the eventual ownership by the state of the means of production and its entire surplus. Under the heading "Important Industries Requiring Immediate Reconstruction," nine industrial sectors are listed (see table 3.2).[28] These were industries whose products were not for immediate consumption but were manufactured in order to produce other things. The primary industries were steel, machinery, chemical, and mining because they were the industries where the final products were the means to make other products—namely, consumer and agricultural products for daily use. Under the logic of state socialism of the twentieth century, the development of heavy industries was essential to changing the means of production from exploitative capitalist means to egalitarian socialist means. The production of things with which to make other things—thereby gradually making work easier and more efficient—was the revolutionary mission of heavy industries.

Besides the potential to advance workers' liberation, the heavy and mining industries were crucial in postwar North Korea for another reason: they generated monetary value. Raw materials were extremely valuable as export items to the Soviet Union before and during the war, and that same strategy was followed in the plan issued in 1953. In fact, in 1953 and 1956, metals and minerals made up 85.2 percent and 89.8 percent of total export, respectively.[29] Iron and steel factories at Hwanghae and Sŏngjin were the key sites for the production of pig iron and rolled steel, and all mines were ordered to be restored in two years with the aim of exporting minerals and metals worth 100 million to 300 million rubles (US$25–75 million) a year.[30] In the plan, there is an interesting section on private manufacturers. The Ministry of Construction Industry was given the task to organize private manufacturers of construction materials (brick and roof tile makers) and allow their operation.[31] The Ministry of Light Industry was given the tasks to purchase raw silk from private manufacturers and to organize these manufacturers into a nationwide network of silk producers.[32]

The plan's "Basic Economic Projects" included the initial transformation of small farmers and slash-and-burn farmers into workers of collective or state-owned farms. The state consolidation of private farms (cooperativization and collectivization) had begun during the Korean War: by the end of 1953, there were 800 cooperatives comprising 12,000 farming households.[33] However, because most farming was still done by private family farmers—the result of the sweeping land reform in March 1946—it became necessary to allow private land and private means of production while organizing cooperatives at a wide scale.[34] The gradual collectivization of agriculture was to begin with two initiatives: first, land improvement through mechanized irrigation and distribution of fertilizers and, second,

TABLE 3.2

North Korean Industries Requiring Immediate Reconstruction After the Korean War

Industry	Task
Steel	Restore Hwanghae Iron and Steel Works and Sŏngjin Steelworks, to begin producing pig iron and rolled steel by 1954; build zinc factory at Ch'ŏngjin by 1960, to begin producing steel pipes, rails, wheels, and other zinc products; build a quarry at Tŏkch'ŏn and transfer or build steel factories at Tŏkch'ŏn
Machinery	Import a large amount of machine tools; increase production of lathe tools and motors; produce machine parts for transportation, automobiles, mining, agriculture, and shipbuilding; build machine tools and auto parts factories at Hwech'ŏn, to begin producing 6,000 cars a year from 1957; commence construction of mining tools and machine tools factories at at Sinŭiju
Weapons	Increase productivity at Factory Number 65 and Factory Number 45; relocate Number 26; commence construction of Number 82 to begin production in 1954; become self-sufficient in producing mortars and ammunition
Shipbuilding	Immediately construct a shipyard at Namp'o capable of manufacturing patrol boats, fishing boats, and river shipping boats; provide boats for the fishing industry
Mining	Restore basic production of entire mining industry within two years; mechanize the mining industry; increase export amount to 100–200 million rubles (US$25–50 million) a year; immediately develop a copper mine at Kapsan and a lead mine at Kaech'ŏn; restore refineries at Munp'yŏng and Namp'o
Electric power	Fully restore current power plants; install new generators as part of the Three-Year Plan; increase production to 1.5 million kilowatts per year; domestically produce electrical materials such as motors and transformers

TABLE 3.2 (continued)

Industry	Task
Chemical	Build facilities to make gunpowder, detonators, and fuses for military and civilian purposes; restore ammonium sulfate factory at Hŭngnam; relocate Ch'oan Fertilizer Factory to Sakju; restore the Chosŏn-Soviet Oil Company and the Synthetic Fuel Factory at Aoji; build facilities to produce synthetic rubber; produce sulfur from the waste of refineries; restore fiber factories by 1955 to supply raw material for the weaving industry
Construction	Organize private manufacturers of construction materials and allow small-scale private operations; restore brick-and-tile factories at Pyongyang, Hamhŭng, Ch'ŏngjin, Kangyŏng, Ŭiju, Wŏnsan, Kusŏng, Kaech'ŏn, Haeju, and Sariwŏn; restore all cement factories to produce 300,000 tons a year; build facilities to make cement substitutes with slag from refineries; build factories that produce cement sewer pipes at a rate of 2,000 kilometers (1243 miles) a year
Light industry	Expand textile factories at Pyongyang and Kusŏng to produce 70 million meters (77 million yards) of fabric a year; restore pulp factories at Kilju and Sinŭiju; cultivate reeds on the banks of Chaeryŏng River, Taedong River, and Ch'ŏngch'ŏn River; restore rubber-shoe factories to produce 30 million pairs of rubber shoes a year; produce 1 million leather shoes a year; restore factories that produce soy sauce, bean paste, bean oil, milk, canned goods, wine, and tobacco; build a candy factory at Musan; process silk purchased from private manufacturers and organize them

Source: Adapted from Kuksa P'yŏnch'an Wiwŏnhoe (National Institute of Korean History), *Pukhan kwangye saryojip* (Historical material on North Korea), vol. 30 (Kwachŏn: Kuksa P'yŏnch'an Wiwŏnhoe Press, 1998), 362–367.

farmland expansion through land reclamation.[35] The damages caused by the war required intensive state assistance to private farms, and this assistance was the roadway to the state's appropriation of the private means of production owned by the farmers.

On the issue of trade and foreign aid, the plan stated, "Export must be carried out as a state-wide and people-wide movement"—a "powerful struggle for the acquisition of foreign currency."[36] The goal was to reach an export value of 350 million rubles (US$87.5 million) by 1955, an amount about 100 million rubles higher than the amount North Korea had paid the Soviet Union for the latter's material support during the Korean War. The most consequential and yet least mentioned topic in connection with international commerce was foreign aid. The only sentence on foreign aid says North Korea considered material aid from "brotherly" states of the utmost importance in postwar reconstruction.[37] Indeed, this was true: between 1954 and 1957, North Korea received 1.0 billion rubles (US$250 million) from the Soviet Union, 1.3 billion rubles (US$325 million) from China, 545 million rubles (US$136 million) from East Germany, 362 million rubles (US$90 million) from Poland, 113 million rubles (US$28 million) from Czechoslovakia, 25 million rubles (US$6 million) from Hungary, 65 million rubles (US$16 million) from Romania, and 20 million rubles (US$5 million) from Bulgaria.[38] Albania's aid during the period was in the form of crops; and Mongolia gave 6,054 horses, 39,760 sheep, 18,693 goats, and 446 dairy cows.[39] In all, between 1946 and 1961, North Korea received in foreign aid more than 5 billion rubles (US$1.3 billion), or about 500 rubles (US$125) per capita per year, a scale of aid matched in the world only by the aid given to South Korea.[40]

Related to foreign aid was the immense project of urban reconstruction taken up by eastern European countries. Hungary helped to rebuild Pyongyang; Czechoslovakia assisted in rebuilding Ch'ŏngjin; and East Germany was heavily involved in the reconstruction of Hamhŭng.[41] As a gesture of solidarity and as part of war reparation to the Soviet Union, these socialist countries (most of them fledgling themselves), who had little prior relationship with Korea, helped rebuild these major cities. Traces of reconstruction by these countries are still scattered throughout the urban landscapes of Pyongyang, Ch'ŏngjin, and Hamhŭng. The reconstruction of Hamhŭng, the second-largest city of North Korea and a major industrial center, was especially an urgent task, and when the East German prime minister, Otto Grotewohl, pledged to help rebuild a North Korean city,

Kim Il Sung responded in a letter to Grotewohl on July 6, 1954, that Hamhŭng was the city chosen to receive East Germany's reconstruction effort.[42] The reconstruction of Hamhŭng, which lasted from 1954 to 1962, is dealt in greater detail in chapter 5, so it is sufficient here to mention that rebuilding the city was a comprehensive project, including the construction of housing, office buildings, factories, the power grid, and underground facilities.[43] The project also entailed the rebuilding of chemical, machine, and fertilizer factories along the Sŏngch'ŏn River, an important river flowing from the Kŭmp'ae Mountain Pass in the northern part of the province through the western edge of Hamhŭng down to the East Sea. One of these factories was the Pon'gung Chemical Fertilizer Factory, which would be transformed into the Vinalon Factory in 1961.

Consolidating Politics for Production

Triumph of Partisans

North Korea's political world had to be shaken up twice for it to emerge as singular and cohesive. The first time was during the Korean War, and the second was during the August Factional Incident of 1956, when Kim Il Sung was openly criticized and the party fell into momentary disarray. The Soviet Union and China intervened, and Kim Il Sung was forced to make a humiliating apology, but this event launched the most significant political purging in North Korea's history. The two moments of crises— the war and the August Incident—were the stages from which Kim Il Sung and his faction of former partisans of Manchuria emerged by 1961 as the unchallengeable ruling faction of North Korea.[44]

The rift in North Korea's postwar political world first became visible along the issue of heavy industry. The debate on whether to give priority to heavy industry or light industry during reconstruction had been taking place since Kim Il Sung's speech "Modŭn kŏsŭl chŏnhu inminkyŏngje pok'ku palchŏn ŭl wihayŏ" (Everything toward postwar recovery and the development of the people's economy), given to the party's Central Committee on August 5, 1953, in which he said the impossibility of simultaneous reconstruction of all sectors of the economy due to the level of destruction demanded giving priority to heavy industries.[45] However, Kim Il Sung wavered on the issue after North Korea's state visits to the Soviet

Union and China (with Kim going only to China) in October 1953. One reason for this wavering was the observation of China's own difficulty with agricultural collectivization carried out for the purpose of industrial growth. Another reason was the idea of equal development between heavy and light industries spreading in the socialist world, an idea attributed to Georgy Malenkov, who had emerged as the leader of the Soviet Union, albeit only for a few years, after Stalin's death on March 5, 1953.

A strong support of Malenkov's policy came from Pak Ch'angok through a report on the Three-Year Plan given at the Seventh General Meeting of the Supreme People's Assembly on April 20, 1954. Pak Ch'angok, the new chair of the State Planning Commission and a leader of the Soviet Korean political faction, reported that with dual industrial pursuit the total production of consumer goods in 1956 was projected to be twice the output of 1949, and for heavy industry it would be 1.3 times the output of 1949, with the ultimate goal of abolishing the distribution system of foods and manufactured goods.[46] Pak called for economic planners to pay attention to both industrial development and people's everyday needs, although the latter would be satisfied through large amounts of imports rather than through local production.[47] The message of dual development, however, became lost as the criticism of Soviet Korean leaders gained traction. The main criticism of Soviet Koreans was that they indiscriminately followed the Soviet Union—a tendency denounced as dogmatism (*kyojojuŭi*) in the years to come. At the end of 1954, while Soviet Koreans were losing their positions and authority, the direction of industrial policy became set: economic priority would be given to heavy industries, while consumer goods would be made available through foreign aid and imports. On December 14, 1954, the newspaper *Rodong Sinmun* reported that the Supreme People's Assembly's cabinet had passed an economic plan based on Kim Il Sung's advice to the party Central Committee in August 1953 and focused primarily on expanding heavy industry, with the secondary aim of developing both light industry and agriculture.[48]

The public criticism of the Soviet Korean faction launched in 1954 was a continuation of the purge begun during the Korean War. The first leading official to fall was Hŏ Kai, vice chair of the party Central Committee and vice chair of the party Organizing Committee. Born in Khabarovsk and educated in Moscow, Hŏ Kai had joined the North Korean government in 1945 as a Communist Party of the Soviet Union cadre well trained in party operations. When the Korean War broke out, Hŏ saw the war as an

opportunity to reorganize the party membership and so promptly implemented disciplinary actions against 450,000 of the 600,000 party members.[49]
At a party Central Committee meeting in November 1951, Kim Il Sung
denounced the mass expulsion and criticized Hŏ for being excessively
bureaucratic and preoccupied with retribution. Hŏ was soon removed from
his positions and demoted to the honorary position of vice premier of the
Supreme People's Assembly, a decision with which Stalin may have agreed.[50]
Hŏ Kai is said to have committed suicide in July 1953. Pak Ch'angok fared
better at first and even joined the public criticism of Hŏ, but he was eventually reprimanded: in January 1956, he was expelled from the party
Politburo and relieved of his position as chair of the State Planning
Commission.

With the Three-Year Plan winding down, the North Korean state
solidified its policy on economic reconstruction, which, based on Kim Il
Sung's original plan of 1953, gave priority to the development of heavy
industries in machinery, chemicals, iron and steel, and mining. The debate
on the course of industry was over, but it exposed a lasting rift in North
Korea's political world. This rift became most severe in 1956 when the issue
of personality worship of Kim Il Sung and ongoing economic woes,
including a severe food crisis in 1955, divided the political world into Kim
loyalists—led by former Manchurian partisans and joined by Kapsan and
domestic communists—and those who wanted to rebuke him, an opposition formed by members of the Soviet Korean and Yan'an (Chinese Korean)
factions.

The year 1956 was a turning point in the history of state socialism. It was
the year of the "secret speech" by Nikita Khrushchev at the Twentieth
Congress of the Communist Party of the Soviet Union. In the speech,
delivered on February 24 in a closed session of party delegates, Khrushchev
denounced Stalin for his oppressive method of rule and for creating a mania
around himself to gain almost absolute authority:

> It is clear . . . that Stalin showed in a whole series of cases his intoler-
> ance, his brutality and his abuse of power. . . . [H]e often chose the
> path of repression and physical annihilation, not only against actual
> enemies, but also against individuals who had not committed any
> crimes against the party and the Soviet Government. . . . Stalin very
> energetically popularized himself as a great leader; in various ways
> he tried to inculcate in the people the version that all victories gained

by the Soviet nation during the Great Patriotic War were due to the courage, daring, and genius of Stalin and of no one else.[51]

This speech sent an unsettling wave across the socialist world. The message was that nobody would be safe from scrutiny (not even the "Man of Steel") and that reform was beginning at the center of the revolutionary world. Specifically, the message coming out of Moscow was that no single person should amass absolute power.

The leadership of North Korea took caution, but, as Sŏ Tongman points out, the problem of the personality cult had already been attributed to individuals such as Pak Hŏnyŏng, thus leaving Kim Il Sung momentarily shielded from an open attack.[52] The Third Congress of the Korean Workers' Party, held April 23–30, 1956—an international event attended by 914 party delegates as well as by representatives from the Soviet Union, China, Poland, Czechoslovakia, East Germany, Hungary, Romania, Bulgaria, Albania, Mongolia, Vietnam, Japan, and Indonesia—reflected this wary stance. The rhetoric toward Kim Il Sung had changed. Adulatory terms for Kim such as *suryŏng* (leader) were absent, and the discussion of personality worship, as mandated by Moscow, did not mention him. Rather, when the discussion took place (led by members from the Kapsan and domestic communist factions such as Han Sangdu, Han Sŏrya, and Pak Chŏngae), the targets of criticism were Pak Hŏnyŏng and other members of the South Korean Workers' Party faction. "Unsound elements within the leadership of the South Korean Workers' Party," Han Sangdu, the party chair of North Hamgyŏng Province, said, "worshipped Pak Hŏnyŏng like an idol, committing anti-party deeds as long as the order came from him."[53]

Although Kim Il Sung and his faction avoided open criticism at the Third Congress, the impact of Khrushchev's message and the presence of foreign officials such as Leonid Brezhnev and Nie Rongzhen at the congress created a difficult situation for Kim and his faction with respect to their wish to rearrange North Korea's bureaucracy in their favor. At the end of the congress, the delegates elected a Central Committee of seventy-one members, four members more than the committee chosen at the Second Congress in March 1948.[54] The Chinese Korean—Yan'an—faction remained the largest group in the Central Committee, with nineteen members, followed by the domestic communist faction, with thirteen members (see table 3.3).[55] Kim Il Sung's faction was powerful, but it was still a small minority in the committee, with eight members.[56] The Soviet Korean

TABLE 3.3

Composition of the Korean Workers' Party Central Committee, 1946–1961

Faction/Group	First Congress, August 28–30, 1946	Second Congress, March 27–30, 1948	Third Congress, April 23–29, 1956	Fourth Congress, September 11–18, 1961
Manchurian partisan	4	6	8	31
Kapsan	—	2	3	6
Yan'an	19	18	19	3
Soviet Korean	8	16	9	1
Domestic communist	10	13	13	11
South Korean Workers' Party	—	—	7	2
Others	2	12	12	31
Total	**43**	**67**	**71**	**85**

Source: Adapted from Sŏ Tongman, *Pukchosŏn sahoechuŭi ch'eje sŏngnipsa, 1945–1961* (The formation of state socialism in North Korea, 1945–1961) (Seoul: Sunin, 2005), 177–178, 217, 550–551, 795–796.

faction saw a significant loss, from sixteen members in 1948 to nine in 1956, reflecting the political purges it had been experiencing since the Korean War.[57] The South Korean Workers' Party faction, which had joined North Korea in 1948 and had made up one-third of the Central Committee in 1949, also saw a drastic decrease in membership. By mid-1956, the authorities of the Soviet Korean faction and the South Korean Workers' Party faction had greatly diminished. The Yan'an faction appeared to remain strong, but this would change in the coming months.

Those critical of Kim Il Sung were mostly from the Yan'an and the Soviet Korean factions. The shared criticism of Kim Il Sung on the issues of industrial policy (that he was unduly focused on heavy industry), agricultural collectivization (that he was premature and reckless), and personal power (that he sought public glorification) turned into an anti–Kim Il Sung movement when he was out of the country visiting the Soviet Union, eastern Europe, and Mongolia. With the Three-Year Plan almost complete and the Five-Year Plan (originally 1957–1961 but ended in 1960) in preparation, Kim Il Sung and nine others went on a five-week trip (his longest foreign trip) in the summer of 1956 (June 1–July 19) to secure aid, loans, and trade deals.[58] The anti-Kim movement was organized and led by Ch'oe Ch'angik (vice premier and member of the party Standing Committee), Yun Konghŭm (commerce minister and member of the party Central Committee), and Ri P'ilgyu (chief of the Machine Industry Bureau), who were joined by prominent supporters such as Sŏ Hwi (chair of the GFTUK), Kim Kang (deputy minister of culture and propaganda), Kim Sŭnghwa (construction minister), and Pak Ch'angok (another vice premier). The anti-Kim faction was small but consisted of individuals from various arenas of the state—the party, the cabinet, the union—and all belonged to the Yan'an faction, except for two from the Soviet Korean faction, Kim Sŭnghwa and Pak Ch'angok. As serious as this movement was, it did not garner wide support: no one from the Kapsan or domestic communist factions joined the movement, and, in fact, some prominent individuals from the Yan'an and Soviet Korean factions (such as Nam Il, Pang Hakse, and Kim Ch'angman) remained loyal to Kim Il Sung.[59] The movement's intention, then, seems to have been to influence policy, curb Kim's authority, and stop the political purging of certain groups rather than to remove to Kim Il Sung from power.[60] Nevertheless, its initiation and success required the support of Moscow and Beijing. According to Andrei Lankov, while Kim Il Sung was outside the country, the anti-Kim faction met with the Soviet embassy several times to discuss its intention. Furthermore, Lankov writes that Beijing not only knew about the movement but helped to organize it.[61]

The open denouncement of Kim Il Sung took place at a plenum of the party Central Committee on August 30–31, which is why the name "August Factional Incident" is given to this particular event. The meeting had two main items on the agenda: a report on the five-week trip by Kim Il Sung and a report on public-health projects by Pak Kŭmch'ŏl (of the Kapsan faction). In his report, Kim talked about the trip and future projects related to the Five-Year Plan and addressed the issue of personality worship, a topic he could not bypass after having met with Khrushchev in Moscow. "This plenum recognizes the existence of a slight degree of personality worship in our country," Kim Il Sung said.[62] Excluding himself from this problem, he went on to say that the people manipulated by Pak Hŏnyŏng and Ri Sŭngyŏp would be reeducated and that the education effort would be expanded to all party members and the masses. After the report by Pak

Kŭmchŏl on public health, Yun Konghŭm, a leader of the anti-Kim movement, took the podium. He had not been part of the agenda. Yun criticized Kim Il Sung for cultivating his own glorification and pointed out the problems of a falling standard of living, overinvestment in heavy industries, and corruption among officials. "A policelike system is dominating the party," Yun said, "and a personality cult of Kim Il Sung is spreading; unnecessary individuals have entered the leadership."[63] It was a remarkable speech, the first open attack on Kim Il Sung, and it was supposed to be followed by speeches by other individuals in the anti-Kim movement. However, when Ch'oe Ch'angik, Pak Ch'angok, Sŏ Hwi, and Ri P'ilgyu attempted to speak, they were blocked by pro-Kim members and even by other Yan'an faction colleagues. The first day of the plenum ended with much commotion, but the anti-Kim faction was not arrested or punished, providing some members a chance to escape. Yun Konghŭm, Sŏ Hwi, and Ri P'ilgyu decided to leave the country together, and, along with another individual, Kim Kang, they departed Pyongyang by car that night (August 30) and crossed the Amnok River into China early the next morning.

The reprimand of the anti-Kim movement came swiftly. The next day, August 31, the plenum agreed to charge Ch'oe Ch'angik, Yun Konghŭm, Sŏ Hwi, Ri P'ilgyu, Pak Ch'angok, and others with the crimes of (1) damaging the party stature by spreading false information to the public; (2) creating an anarchic mood within the party by exaggerating the problem of personality worship; (3) plotting to harm government and party officials by calling them incompetent without any real basis; (4) spreading anti-Marxist, factional ideas against the party's effort to bring unity; and (5) violating ethical principles regarding work and private life.[64] Ch'oe Ch'angik, Yun Konghŭm, Sŏ Hwi, Ri P'ilgyu, and Pak Ch'angok were promptly removed from their positions and stripped of their party membership.

When the meeting ended on August 31, a nationwide purging of individuals in the Yan'an faction and the remaining individuals in the Soviet Korean faction began at provincial and city branches of the party. The exact size of this initial purge is unknown, but it was temporarily stopped three weeks later when Moscow and Beijing intervened. While the Eighth Congress of the Chinese Communist Party was taking place (September 15–27), Chinese defense minister Peng Duhuai (the former chief commander of the Korea-China Joint Forces) and Soviet deputy vice premier Anastas

Mikoyan left the congress and arrived in Pyongyang on September 20, 1956. The original mission was to remove Kim Il Sung from the party leadership, but this mission was abandoned when it became clear that he and his faction dominated the Korean Workers' Party Central Committee. They instead convinced Kim Il Sung to open up a plenum of the Central Committee to reverse the decisions made at the previous plenum. Kim conceded, and a plenum was held on September 23. With Peng and Mikoyan in attendance, the plenum passed a decision reinstating Ch'oe Ch'angik, Pak Ch'angok, Yun Konghŭm, Sŏ Hwi, and Ri P'ilgyu to the party. The decision also stated that the Central Committee had "lacked the patient effort to reeducate" them and that the party would build on the criticism from the masses.[65]

The intervention by Beijing and Moscow was a humiliating experience for Kim Il Sung, but, as with the Korean War, it also provided an opportunity for him to eliminate his rivals and consolidate his power. The August Factional Incident was the second time North Korea's political world was thrown into disarray in this period, but when the international watch on North Korea subsided in the following months, Kim Il Sung and his faction relaunched the campaign to purge the Yan'an and other rival factions. This purge lasted from November 1956 to the end of 1959 and was a thorough campaign involving a nationwide party membership renewal drive; public trials of people in rival groups; teach-ins by the party at all administrative levels; crackdowns on intellectuals at Kim Il Sung University; repatriation of Soviet Koreans back to the Soviet Union; and banishment of Yan'an and Soviet Korean factions from the military.

The editorial board of *Rodong Sinmun* labeled the Fourth Congress of the Korean Workers' Party, held September 11–18, 1961, the "Congress of Victors." "There has never been a time when the party and the people have been united by a single ideological will as there is today," Kim Il Sung said in his speech at the congress.[66] An important change was in the party by-laws, which now stated that the "Korean Workers' Party is the direct successor to the glorious revolutionary tradition established by Korean communists in their armed struggle against Japan," referring to the guerilla activities of the Manchurian partisan faction.[67] Compared to the membership in 1956, the number of party members in 1961 (regular and candidate) increased by 146,618 to a total of 1,311,563.[68] Regarding personnel changes (see table 3.3), the eighty-five-member Central Committee now had only three members from the Yan'an faction (Kim Ch'angman,

Ha Angch'ŏn, and Kim Ch'angdŏk), down from nineteen in 1956; one member from the Soviet Korean faction (Nam Il), down from nine; and two members from the South Korean Workers' Party faction (Ch'oe Wŏnt'aek and Pak Mun'gyu), down from seven. Kim Il Sung's partisan faction held thirty-one seats (up from eight), with seventeen members from Kapsan and the domestic communist factions loyal to Kim Il Sung.[69] The domination of the partisan faction was also unmistakable within the legislature. The Third Supreme People's Assembly, which convened on October 22, 1962, had a total of 383 seats, with only three members from the Yan'an faction (down from fifteen), one member from the Soviet Korean faction (down from twelve), and three members from the South Korean Workers' Party faction (down from thirteen).[70]

By the end of 1950s, the political world of North Korea was consolidated by a single political group—the Manchurian partisan faction led by Kim Il Sung—after going through two critical periods, once during the war and another during the factional struggle in 1956. The result was an unchallengeable control of the cabinet, legislature, party, and military by Kim Il Sung and his loyalists. The once diverse world of North Korea's politics was reduced to a single chain of command, with the partisan faction as the representing body of the masses. One sign of Kim's faction becoming an unchallengeable authority was the publication, beginning in June 1959, of the faction members' memoirs, meant to be studied by the whole population as the legitimate foundation of North Korea.[71] Titled *Hangilppalch'isan ch'amgajadŭl ŭi hoesanggi* (Memoirs of Anti-Japanese partisans), these books were foremost about Kim Il Sung and the women and men who had fought in Manchuria against Japan.[72] Others, of course, had fought against imperial Japan (the Kapsan faction, the Yan'an faction), but they were either relegated to a position under the command of Kim or excluded from the historical lineage of North Korea. The final group to be purged was the Yan'an faction, whose members had fought for independence and against imperialism in their own way in China. The physical and symbolic exclusions of rival groups by Kim Il Sung and the partisan faction signaled a political victory for this once minor group.

The other side of eliminating the Soviet Koreans and Chinese Koreans was the garnering of loyalty from various groups and individuals, including the Kapsan faction and the domestic communists. Removing political rivals through crisis was necessary for Kim Il Sung and his faction's political power, but what mattered more was genuine support from those who believed in Kim as the sole transformative leader. This was the pivotal process substantiating Kim and his faction's political power. Bruce Cumings describes Kim's style of rule from early on as being open to all the masses, where "almost anyone could be a party member, regardless of class background," especially the poor peasants.[73] Between 1946 and 1948, while the number of workers in the party doubled, the number of poor peasants more than tripled: the "vanguard" in North Korea was not proletarian but an "inner core bound together by personal loyalty to Kim Il Sung."[74] Kim's organization policy relied on embracing the hitherto luckless people and training them to become party and military officials. This policy provided millions of people with status and position and formed a popular basis for Kim Il Sung's political power.[75] The inclusion of this popular base within his political influence allowed him to survive the August Factional Incident and gradually reorganize the bureaucracy in its aftermath. What made the late 1950s different, then, was that the popular base loyal to Kim now held elite bureaucratic authorities in the party, legislature, and military.

Collectivizing Agriculture

The consolidation of political power accompanied the consolidation of production. For political dominance to exist, dominance over production had to coexist. This was the double mission of North Korea's ruling class. This section deals with the completion of centralization of production, which had begun in 1946 with the land reform and the nationalization of major industries. The final project focused on agriculture: the full collectivization of farms into cooperatives and, at the same time, the transformation of farmers into wageworkers of the state. Centralized control of production was, in other words, bringing all types of producers and means of production under the state's management—the state appropriating the entire surplus produced by the total labor power and not letting any surplus remain in the private domain.

By 1955, the state was in charge of almost all nonagricultural sectors. State enterprises made up 90.6 percent of total nonagricultural production, cooperative enterprises 7.7 percent, and private production (handicraft and small-scale factories) only 1.7 percent.[76] Domestic trade, too, was carried out mostly through state networks, private trade falling to 12.7 percent by 1956.[77] Agriculture was different, however. The land reform of 1946, as tremendous as it had been, was not collectivist or socialist in nature. In redistributing land among small family farmers, the means of production remained in the private domain. The land reform was an egalitarian diffusion of private property, not the abolishment of it, as demanded by the principles of socialism. The cooperativization of all agricultural land began with the Three-Year Plan (1954–1956) and was completed during the Five-Year Plan (1957–1960, declared complete a year ahead of schedule). It would be helpful to note here that in North Korea the terms *collectivization* and *cooperativization* generally meant the same process: almost all collectivized farms were operated by cooperatives; the rest were state-operated farms whose function was no different from cooperatives. A good definition of *cooperativization* is given by Chong-Sik Lee: a cooperative farm is a system in which "land, draft animals, and major farm implements of farmers are turned over to cooperative ownership. All farm work is done collectively. . . . [Farmers] are paid solely on the basis of workdays."[78]

Eliminating private property was only the start. Another reason for cooperativization was output: the growth rate of agricultural output was far lower than the growth rate of industrial output. Between 1949 and 1956, whereas industrial output is said to have increased by 278 percent, grain and vegetable yields increased by only 11 percent and 40 percent, respectively.[79] Cooperativization was to increase output by increasing efficiency through mechanization and labor management. Why was increasing agricultural output important? Feeding a growing population with decent food was surely a concern; Kim Il Sung had made a habit of saying that his lifelong wish was to provide the people with rice and meat soup (*ssalbapkwa kogikuk*). But self-sufficiency in food production was not the decisive reason for increasing agricultural output. North Korea depended on imported foodstuff even at the height of its agricultural output.

Of higher importance in collectivization was the issue of class struggle. Small farmers were a class of petite bourgeoisie who, despite possessing the means of production, continued to live in backwardness and for immediate satisfaction. The transformation of such farming life—foremost providing relief from back-breaking work—would come from changing the means of production through mechanization. This task belonged to heavy industry: the tools and machinery manufactured by heavy industry would serve to improve the means of production in other industries. Whereas light industry produced items primarily for consumption, heavy industry produced items enabling further production. This is why in state socialism, in principle, heavy industry took priority over light industry and agriculture. Cooperativization was the process by which the farmers' surplus could be organized to stimulate heavy industry, which would in turn produce the tools to advance farming life.[80] Thus, in theory, cooperativization was part of a dialectical process in which the sacrifice of farmers for the sake of heavy industry would have the ultimate consequence of the farmers' own historical progress.

Furthermore, collectivization of farms was to bring changes to the value form of agricultural products, particularly as the divide between city and country would disappear. In a situation where nationalized industry coexisted with privatized agriculture, the alliance between workers and farmers was weak, bound by, as Kang Chiwŏn wrote in 1956, "connections created by the market . . . where farmers are forced to sell their own possessions . . . with the inevitable consequence of constraining the variety and amount produced, as farmers concern themselves with money profit earned from selling commodified products."[81] Likely to emerge from this situation was an unequal relationship between town and country, the former (as the market) dictating to the latter what and how much to produce. By collectivizing the means of production and distribution, where type, quantity, and price would be determined by the state based on collective need (not on profit), the farmers would be compensated according to their effort (in wage) and linked to the town not by market forces but by mutual interest. The product would cease to be a commodity: its exchange-value would disappear, and only use-value would remain for actual utility. Kang went on to say: "The alliance between workers and farmers is not a moral alliance. It is an alliance based on calculation and class interests: a class alliance with the aim of mutual benefit."[82]

The postwar collectivization campaign officially began in early November 1954, when the party's Central Committee passed a decision to "gradually shift the farmers from the practice of dispersed individual management to collective management, thereby guiding the countryside toward socialist development."[83] At the time, according to government data, 332,662 farming families (31.8 percent of total farming families) were working at 10,098 cooperatives (30.9 percent of total agricultural land).[84] The number of cooperatives increased to 14,651 by the time of the party's Third Congress in April 1956, providing work for 65.6 percent of total farming families.[85] During the next two years, all farming families came to be organized into cooperatives, with each cooperative becoming larger in size, thus reducing the total number of cooperatives. When the collectivization project was declared to be complete in August 1958, the number of cooperatives stood at 13,309.[86] At the end of the year, these cooperatives were further divided into 3,843 large cooperatives, providing work and livelihood for 1,055,015 farming families.[87] In addition, in October 1958 the government enacted the integration of villages with cooperatives, each administrative unit of a village (ri) now functioning as a single production unit of a cooperative, with authority given to village officials to supervise the farmers' economic domains.[88] Administrative control was concurrently the control of production. South P'yŏngan Province, the land north of the capital, had the most cooperatives, 647, followed by North P'yŏngan Province, 580, and South Hamgyŏng Province, 545.[89] These provinces not only held very fertile plains, including the Pyongyang Plains in South P'yŏngan and the Hamhŭng Plains in South Hamgyŏng, but also some of most emblematic industrial sites, including the Kangsŏn Steelworks in South P'yŏngan Province, the birthplace of the Ch'ŏllima Work Team Movement, and the Hŭngnam Fertilizer Factory in South Hamgyŏng.

According to government data, the portion of "individual peasants" in the total population, 66.4 percent in December 1953, had decreased to 16.6 percent in September 1956, and by the end of 1959, they were an insignificant group within the population.[90] In contrast, the category of "agricultural cooperative members" appeared in 1956, and by the end of the decade they made up 45.7 percent of the population.[91] The farmers, who numbered close to 7 million in 1949 in a country of 10 million people, were reorganized within a decade into a class of agricultural wage earners. They lost their identity as independent owners of means of production, and their products lost their value as commodities. All means of production came to be owned by the state, and the market no longer dictated what items were to be produced. Released from the capricious condition of the market, the farmers were integrated into a production regime in which agriculture served the purpose of fueling industrial growth by relinquishing their total surplus to the state. With the cooperativization of farms by the end of 1958, the state-controlled production system added agriculture under its domain. The farmers were the last but essential piece to this system.

As important as cooperativization was for state building and socialist theory, however, it was a miserable process for many ordinary people. The constant food shortage in the postwar period was most acutely experienced in 1955 as nothing less than a famine. The best description of this moment in the English language is in Balázs Szalontai's study *Kim Il Sung in the Khrushchev Era* (2005). The general low output of the postwar agricultural sector—due in part to the low technology family farmers possessed and in part to the war damage to the land—was compounded in 1954 by dry and cold weather patterns. In addition, grain reserve was depleted as rice and other grains were shipped to the Soviet Union as payment for the weapons Moscow had provided for North Korea during the Korean War. Hardest hit were northern regions: in North Hamgyŏng, 70 to 100 percent of the crops were damaged, and farmers could not recover seed grains for the next planting.[92] High agricultural tax was another crucial factor. In the mid-1950s, North Korean farmers were paying between 23 percent and 27 percent of their crop as tax, while in China, which experienced its own devastating famine in the late 1950s, the farmers were paying a lower rate, between 18.2 percent and 18.7 percent.[93] As hunger-related deaths appeared throughout the country, in May 1955 the Hungarian embassy documented people in the northern regions of North Korea heading south in search of food, even as people in the southern provinces, also without food, were gathering and eating wild grass and plants.[94]

North Korea's postwar agricultural policy was created and carried out for the benefit of heavy industries, a practice also observed in other state socialist countries, with effects both phenomenal and devastating. Agricultural cooperativization generally contributed to rapid increases in industrial output in these countries, as it did in North Korea, but actual returns to agriculture in better technology took time or arrived irregularly according to region. Imports of food items and consumer goods were also slow to come or distributed unequally. During the lag and imbalance in distribution, people experienced acute food shortages—famines that resulted in countless deaths. China's Great Leap famine of the late 1950s took the lives of tens of millions of people. In all cases, the main cause of famine was political. In China, as Frederick Teiwes has shown, the utopian aim of catching up to Western capitalist countries sustained Mao's choice to implement collectivization, which eventually made central-party leaders complicit and yet fueled provincial leaders to push the mobilization efforts to extremes. Mao's dominance in both elite and mass politics institutionally reduced the role of central-planning agencies and increased the influence of hitherto subordinate spending ministries and localities, which demanded more resources from planning agencies to carry out Mao's vision.[95] Similarly, in the case of North Korea, Kim Il Sung and his faction's immense authority, the existence of passive central politicians, and the local fervor to carry out party objectives seem to have been the key factors in the pursuit of collectivization despite highly uneven results, although there were less famine-caused deaths in North Korea than in China.

Socialism Led by the State

Socialism of the twentieth century is difficult to define. It is different according to region and period, to the point of emptying the term *socialist* of meaning.[96] What North Korea had become by the end of 1950s is difficult to comprehend in relation to the notion of emancipation found in the writings of Marx. This is because in North Korea at the end of 1950s nationalism was excessively practiced as an instrument of state and industrial control. One person's immense authority stymied diversity in political thought and prohibited democratic procedures. The party was too dominant for unions and the legislature to act independently on behalf of workers and citizens. The state management of industries and agriculture prevented communal distribution of surplus. And work had become too intense, competitive, and hierarchical to function as an emancipatory activity. Instead of work returning to back into life, as an activity no longer isolating and exploitative, as Marx had envisioned, the space of work and production in North Korea became a space of domination. Marx's sense of emancipation—as a "restoration of the human world and of human relationship to man himself . . . when as an individual man, in his everyday life, in his work, and in his relationships, he has become a species-being"[97]—was not clearly discernable in North Korea (or in any other state socialist country).

However, if socialism is approached from the perspective of production and property—that is, who controls the means of production and who owns property—while its emancipatory aspects are suspended, then twentieth-century socialism has more relevance. Production as a key area of socialist transformation is outlined as orthodoxy in the *Communist Manifesto*, in which the revolution of the working class initially requires the centralization of all instruments of production in the hands of the state. Specific measures include the abolition of property; the centralization of credit by a national bank; the centralization of communication and transport; the expansion of production sites owned by the state; and the integration of agriculture with manufacturing industries, thereby erasing the distinction between town and country.[98]

In terms of production and private property, North Korea at the end of the 1950s could be labeled socialist. More precisely, North Korea had a socialism centered on the state (state socialism), in which all means of production and the total surplus created from them were appropriated by the state, with the crucial feature of the party as the decisive apparatus on how the surplus would be utilized. The representative organizations of producers surely existed in the form of unions, but by the end of the 1950s their function was no more than to carry out the party's decisions. Industrial production was managed by the troika system of party, union, and enterprise management; agricultural production was managed by cooperative committees; and both were directed by the State Planning Commission. Distribution and consumption were also done through state-operated transportation and ration systems, although private plots were allowed in the countryside for raising vegetables and small domesticated animals, such as chickens, for local consumption. The force of the market (and market logic) was formally removed from all levels of production and distribution. These changes took place under two economic plans: the Three-Year Plan, which lasted from 1954 to 1956, and the Five-Year Plan, which lasted from 1957 to 1960, concluding a year early.

The state considered the Three-Year Plan a success, for during this period production levels were raised back to prewar levels.[99] And the Three-Year Plan claimed to have eliminated in the process the remnants of colonial industrial practices, initiated the cooperativization of the countryside, and built a material foundation to gradually increase the people's welfare.[100] The state also saw the Five-Year Plan as achieving what it set out to do: the completion of cooperativization of agriculture and the expansion of a centralized national economy.[101] As Kim Sanghak wrote in 1958, the plan was a blueprint to "strengthen the condition of planned development in all sectors of the people's economy." At the same time, Kim Sanghak was cautious about exaggerating the Five-Year Plan: "Even if the First Five-Year Plan is fulfilled . . . the overall level of industrial development in our country does not indicate the fulfillment of socialist industrialization. It would only indicate the establishment of the foundations for socialist industrialization."[102]

By the end of 1950s, the state's command over production signaled the establishment of the foundations for a state socialist economy. The control of production was possible only with the control of politics. But lest the 1950s be seen as a period in which Kim Il Sung and his faction achieved an impervious system of command, it should be said that "socialist corporatism" or the "guerilla dynasty" or the "suryŏng system"—which North Korea is understood to be from the 1970s on—was incomplete. This shift would require the creation of an ideological program for the masses: the canonization of chuch'e, the philosophy of subjectivity attributed to Kim Il Sung and ultimately exemplified by the adoption of a new constitution in 1972, which defined North Korea as the "socialist motherland of chuch'e." The beginnings of chuch'e, however, are to be found in the 1950s: Kim Il Sung is said to have first uttered the word as an ideological concept in the speech "Sasangsaŏp esŏ kyojojuǔi wa hyŏngsikjuǔi rǔl t'oech'i hago chuch'e rǔl hwangniphalte taehayŏ" (On eliminating dogmatism and formalism and establishing chuch'e in our ideological project), given to party propaganda workers on December 28, 1955, during a time of open criticism among competing political groups. Kim said in the speech: "We're carrying out a Korean revolution, not a revolution of another country. This Korean revolution is therefore the chuch'e of our party's ideological project."[103] Although meaningful to the particular situation in 1955, the concept was not yet used as an independent system of thought; rather, throughout the late 1950s and the 1960s, chuch'e was employed as a goal to be established, as an object of construction to be forged in politics, along with the arrival of state socialism.[104] Chuch'e as the philosophical and practical orientation formally guiding and integrating life, art, and government would be created at the end of 1960s.

Chuch'e is an overdetermining entity in North Korea, often masking the diverse causes of and contradictions to historical phenomena. How the state constructed hegemony in the postwar period is not about chuch'e. Rather, hegemony was built through the integration of work and everyday life. The everyday conceived and constructed by the state was neither passive nor segregated. It was a field of multiple organizing practices: everyday life as a "denominator common to existing systems including judicial, contractual, pedagogical, fiscal, and police systems," as Lefebvre described it.[105]

Everyday Life of Work

Ideology of Repetition

Kim Il Sung knew better than anyone else that *to control* really meant *to control everyday life*. The capacity to directly control the politics and economic development of North Korea, which he and his faction attained by the end of 1950s, was specifically the authority over officials and agencies of the party and the state. Power over 10 million citizens, however, required a hegemonic style of rule realized only in the everyday. For instance, in December 1957, just a little more than a year after the August Factional Incident, Kim was aware that what he did with the *nomenklatura* had to be different from what he did or how he portrayed himself to the general public. During this period of crisis and purging, which would fill the party and the legislature with loyalists to the partisan faction, Kim made an interesting speech to the workers of Hwanghae Iron and Steel Works:

> Without steel, we can construct neither cities nor the countryside, neither railroads nor ports. . . . In order to produce more steel, we must take care of workers' daily life. . . . Their daily life must be culturally cultivated. . . . Their household and village must be clean, and their life must be joyous. . . . Fruit trees should be planted so that landscape and livelihood become better. Streets and villages should be clean. . . . Party and social organizations need to strengthen the education of housewives so that households can be managed efficiently.[106]

This statement offers a glimpse into his way of ruling. Kim Il Sung as a politician and Kim Il Sung as a leader of the people were more than contradictory entities. On the one hand, as the ultimate authority of the state, Kim ruled *directly* and yet *abstractly*—directly because he had the authority to change personnel and to make policies and abstractly because all personnel changes and policies were carried out in the name of abstract ideas such as nationhood. Thus, in official history, Yun Konghŭm, Ch'oe

Ch'angik, Sŏ Hwi, and almost all other members of the Yan'an faction were removed from office not because they opposed Kim (in the August Factional Incident) but because they opposed the ideals of the nation and revolution. On the other hand, as the leader of the people, Kim ruled *indirectly* and yet *concretely*—indirectly because his style of command over the people was almost completely noncoercive, relying on the cultivation of loyalty and veneration through material and vocational support and concretely because the indirect style of rule depended on concrete means such as housing, jobs, clean streets, an orderly landscape, and a happy home life.

In other words, elite control was done directly but with abstract reasons, whereas popular control was done indirectly but with concrete reasons. They overlap at every moment, but the conceptual pairings of "direct rule/abstract reasons" and "indirect rule/concrete reasons" can nonetheless be distinguished. Why make this distinction? Because the simultaneous presence of seemingly contradictory elements—indirect and concrete manners of control, autonomous and dominated conditions of existence—is a definitive character of everyday life. Because the distinction begins to address everyday life as both a concrete reality and a concept wherein domination and social possibilities coexist. Because it helps us understand the everyday—rationalized and constructed by the ruling class—as a coherent world inhabited by people who are happy and willing to do what is asked of them.[107] Such people were written about in popular magazines such as *Ch'ŏllima*, often in letters sent in by the readers, as Han Kyŏnghwa did about her team leader Chŏn Ch'angok. According to the letter, Ch'ŏn started her day before anybody else, and, following the advice of Kim Il Sung to plant apple trees capable of providing flowers in the spring and apples in the fall, she spent her time before and after work cultivating the trees. "Whenever we look at the healthy apple trees," wrote Han Kyŏnghwa, "we can imagine our team leader Chŏn Ch'angok in front of us, carrying out the instruction of Comrade Premier . . . and we resolve to live like she does."[108]

Chŏn Ch'angok was not only a role model who inspired others to imitate her life but also an ideal worker of the state who did much more than what was asked of her. What is particularly important here is that through her willful daily action, as a subject who shaped her own future, she conformed to the words of Kim Il Sung and actualized them. In the everyday space of actualization, she produced and complied. Everyday life as both a mode of production and a mode of administration—this is the original thought of Henri Lefebvre. Ambiguous and contradictory, the everyday creates and satisfies its own needs, and at the same time it is a "base of exploitation and domination" where the "tragic" is dissimulated.[109] Chŏn Ch'angok's diligent work was legitimated when it heeded the call to produce. Her moment of self-determination was the very moment of domination. What was dissimulated in the everyday space was thus the (tragic) reality that her position of self-determination was possible only within her condition of subjugation. It is this aspect of everyday life—which disguises the condition of domination while revealing the experience of the subject—to which Lefebvre was referring when he said that "the everyday is a kind of screen . . . it both shows and hides."[110]

For hegemony to become genuine experience, it had to appear as the most ordinary setting of life. Where else but in the everyday could hegemony appear mundane? Where else but in everyday life could repetitive activities of work attain supraindividual meaning? "There is a young team leader at the Hŭich'ŏn Machinery Factory," Kim Il Sung said in 1954, "and despite losing an arm in the war, he performs 170 to 250 percent above his target each day. This comrade is a true patriot."[111] Where else but in everyday life could a monotonous, repetitive activity converge with the abstract notion of patriotism? Kim Il Sung praised the young worker because of his ability to be productive day in and day out: he was a patriot because he *repeated*. Repetition is exactly how the mundaneness of everyday life becomes extraordinary. As Khang Jeongseog points out, everyday life is history caught up in a vast repetitive cycle.[112] The initial claim here is that everyday life functions as modes of production and administration. This function is sustained by repetition: repetition is key to the ideological side of everyday life; repetition is the confirmation of human action in the symbolic world.

For a moment, it is useful to turn to the unique inquiries of Jacques Lacan and Slavoj Žižek. "Repetition is not reproduction," Lacan writes. Reproduction is a self-evident behavior that is in and of itself alienated from the original thing, like reproductions of paintings of masters (Lacan's example): the aim of reproduction is reproduction itself. Repetition, in contrast, "always has an element of structure." The etymological root of the German word for repetition, *Wiederholen*, is *haler*, "to haul," and it offers a clue to the meaning of repetition. Repetition, Lacan says, is "very close to a *hauling* of the subject, who always drags his things into a certain path that he cannot get out of."[113] Here is Lacan's clear and yet abstract description of the role of repetition: it leads the subject onto a "path that he cannot get out of." Through repetition, a subject is placed within the symbolic structures of history and language, from which he or she cannot escape.

The first moment of an act is unregistered in the symbolic structure: it is a moment of unbelievable, superhuman action, the moment when a hitherto ordinary worker does an extraordinary act. Repetition of the deed is the registration of that deed. Or, as Žižek puts it, "only through repetition is [an] event recognized in its symbolic necessity." Born as an anomaly, repetition allows an extraordinary event to become a historical possibility: an event "finds its place in the symbolic network; it is realized in the symbolic order."[114] This is the conceptual process of how a superhuman workload transforms into a realistic measurement by which a new workload standard is created. *Recognition-through-repetition* (as formulated by Žižek) thus always has a practical function of turning an uncommon act into an everyday force. But this process is not straightforward: it is not a simple reproduction the workers are forced to emulate.

In the process of recognition-through-repetition, as repetition takes on a historical function, there is oversight of the original act. This is another essential point Žižek makes: "Repetition rests upon the epistemologically naive presupposition of an objective historical necessity." The naive presupposition is nothing other than *misrecognition*. What is masked in the notion of repetition is how "historical necessity itself *is constituted through misrecognition*."[115] From this standpoint, the hegemonic force of the state acting upon the worker (at the moment of the worker's superhuman act) is misrecognized through repetition as a historically meaningful subjective act. *Recognition-through-repetition*, as Žižek makes it clear, is really *mis*recognition-through-repetition. The worker's original act is misrecognized as possessing a historical significance—as a heroic act for the nation and the people—while the objective reality of the worker as essentially a means of production for the state is momentarily masked.

In sum, everyday life always consists of mundane, repetitive aspects. Repetition, however, has an essential function. Unlike reproduction, repetition is foremost responsible for the insertion of an act within the structures of history and language, within the symbolic order. This symbolic recognition, however, is inscribed with an instance of misrecognition, the failure to recognize the initial act in its objective reality. With the addition of the notion of misrecognition to the understanding of repetition, the final, ideological side of repetition in everyday life becomes clear. Lefebvre says, "In everyday life, the deep, objective relation is disguised by direct, immediate relations, apparently real."[116] The disguise of objective relation is precisely the misrecognition appearing in historical reality. In this schema, repetition allows "immediate relations" (the initial act!) appear to be the reality of the everyday. Here lies the ideological moment (via Lefebvre): "Everyday life functions within certain appearances which are not so much the products of mystifying ideologies, as contributions to the conditions needed for any mystifying ideology to operate."[117] Appearances are more than what they seem: they are situations in the symbolic order arising from the misrecognizing process of repetition present in everyday life.

The misrecognizing process of repetition is what I call the *ideology of repetition*. Ideology ("any mystifying ideology") entails the misrecognition of the dialectical process of an act. The ideology of repetition, then, refers to the dialectical misrecognition of objective relations and at the same time the appearance of historical reality created by the repetitive condition of everyday life. In North Korea, the construction of everyday life as a system took place in the decade after the Korean War. A true citizen was one who returned to grueling and repetitive work day in and day out. Everyday life thus became a hegemonic system. It became simultaneously the site of struggle for revolution and the site of apparent harmony between antagonistic entities. As a system, everyday life fulfilled the population's needs while fulfilling the state's need for surplus accumulation. It expanded state power and yet made state power appear communal. The everyday became abstract and yet concrete.[118] In short, everyday life entailed ideology in its purest function—the ability to make antagonism appear as harmony. Before the era of *chuch'e*, there was the postwar era of everyday work and its ideology of repetition.

Masses Into Heroes

The ideology of repetition found expression in everyday life through mass movements. The essential aspect of repetition became a mechanism of state-led campaigns to increase production and productivity. Mass movements represented a noncoercive method of influencing production. They were not the only noncoercive method used, but they were the most comprehensive and publicized kind. Strictly speaking, they were state-led or party-led production campaigns, but because their origin was always attributed to ordinary people (from individual workers to teams), each campaign was called a "movement" (*undong*). The general aim of mass movements was clear: to increase production through competition. In the process, mass movements also sought to improve work ethics, bestow privilege upon highly productive individuals or teams, increase the overall standard of production, and connect labor to the abstract notions of nationalism and patriotism. The key mechanism was the repetition of competitive and intensive work unfolding in the space of everyday life. In this space, the antagonistic relation between the state (as the absolute owner of the means of production) and its citizens (as the source of labor power and the means of production) was concealed.

Mass movements to increase competition and production began prior to the founding of the DPRK. After liberation in 1945, workers were engaged in various campaigns at all levels (from the work team to the factory) to drive up production; some campaigns were started by unions, some by managers, and some by the workers themselves. These campaigns were soon adopted by the party and the state as the "mass line" (*taejung nosŏn* or *kunjung nosŏn*) of policy making and led to nationwide campaigns, which the workers in turn readopted to their specific situations. The mass line was a concept made famous by Mao Zedong, and within the Korean Workers' Party it was first initiated by the Chinese Koreans of the Yan'an faction. It is not clear what the first mass movement was, but the first time Kim Il Sung spoke about such a movement was in November 1946, when he mentioned that the Production Shock Movement was happening across all regions.[119] The first labor hero of North Korea is considered to be Kim Hoeil, a train engineer who started a coal-transport movement and who, hailed as North Korea's Alexey Stakhanov, later served as the minister of railroad transportation.[120]

The names of mass campaigns varied, and certain campaigns gave rise to other campaigns. Large campaigns between 1945 and 1961 included the Production Increase Shock Movement, the Production Increase and Competition Movement, the Collective Innovation Movement, the Ch'ŏllima Speed Battle Movement, the Ch'ŏllima Work Team Movement, and the Vinalon Speed Movement.[121] Smaller campaigns at the level of the factory and work teams were truly numerous and diverse in style. They included efforts to reuse scrap material, such as the Day Without Supplies Movement and the Pick-Up One More Piece of Cotton Movement. They included campaigns to save energy, such as the Burning Wood Movement and the

Figure 3.1 Shock workers of the Hŭngnam Fertilizer Factory, 1960s.
Source: Photograph courtesy of the Hŭngnam Fertilizer Factory Museum.

Grab the Flying Coal Powder Movement. And they included campaigns
to lower unproductive time, such as the Reduce One Second from Every
Motion Movement, the Rest After Five Hundred Shovel Scoops Movement, and the Rest After One Thousand Shovel Scoops Movement.[122]

All mass movements had the common feature of competition. In principle, competition was to influence both individual workers and the particular industrial sector as a whole. At the individual level, the competitive
zeal of workers was incited by openly comparing the person ahead and the
person falling behind.[123] At the enterprise level, the more advanced firm
assisted the underperforming firm, so the latter could follow the former,
eventually raising the overall output of the particular industrial sector.[124]
The impetus of competition was to increase the total industrial output
because it would bring changes at the everyday level. As Han Sangdu, party
chair of North Hamgyŏng Province (and belonging to the domestic communist faction), wrote, the Collective Innovation Movement had the aim
of raising the "brigade, the cell, and ultimately the entire firm to the high
level achieved by innovative workers." This, he said, required the "collective wisdom and patriotic and creative effort of the masses" which can be
accessed only when specialists "open their eyes to the daily advancing reality, enter the actual production space of workers, believe in the infinite
power of the masses, and solve the technical problems together with

them."[125] Mass movements were thus declared a systematization of the everyday process of work—born from the site of production (the "daily changing reality"), the place of sweat and toil, where extraordinary achievements in the everyday space became the very source of innovation and competition.

The actual situation of these movements at work sites was various. Competition created a labor process where management and production entailed inconsistencies. The standardization of competitive work was difficult to implement, and at the end of a month or quarter it was common to see work being carried out in a rushed manner, wearing down the machines and wasting materials.[126] At the level of the enterprise, better technologies and methods were often not properly transferred to underperforming firms. Even at those firms where labor heroes existed, the transmission of their work methods was not always successful. One such a case was the Aoji Mine, an important mine in North Hamgyŏng Province where during the Korean War a miner named Kim Chikhyŏn became a labor hero for developing an innovative blasting method. This method, which allowed continuous and multiple blasting, was not turned into a standard procedure passed down to other workers, however, and once he left the mine, no worker was able to apply his method.[127] The incongruities of the everyday work process are covered in depth in the next chapter, so it is sufficient here to mention that the principles of mass movements were different from their practice. To say the two aspects were contradictory is not enough. The everyday life of work created its own dialectical rhythm.

The system of mass movements was built in coordination with the system of labor heroes.[128] The role and meaning of labor heroes are examined in other chapters (especially in chapter 5). Here, labor heroes are approached as a state system, an institution of recognition, propaganda, public education, and monetary support related to workers whose labor performance was superior to others. The recognition of such workers had been happening in North Korea since the days of People's Committees in the postliberation period (Kim Hoeil is an example, but high-performing Japanese workers still remaining in North Korea were also recognized). They were honored, given material awards, and made into model workers for others to emulate. A system of recognition centrally administered by the state was established on July 17, 1951, during the Korean War, a year after the "hero of the republic" (konghwaguk yŏngung) designation was established (June 30, 1950) to honor courageous military personnel. Both labor heroes and republic heroes were chosen and awarded by the Standing Committee of the Supreme People's Assembly—usually on major holidays such as Kim Il Sung's birthday (April 15), the Founding Day of the DPRK (September 9), and the Founding Day of the Korean Workers' Party (October 10)—and announced through newspapers.

Labor heroes gained much privilege. In addition to receiving day-to-day respect from the community, the labor-hero system provided them with free public transportation, promotions in their jobs, and a high pension when they retired. They had access to health care reserved for high-ranking officials, and their children received preferential treatment in school admissions. To be sure, the system, which made them into privileged citizens, also made them into instruments of hegemony. Through images and stories of labor heroes, the state imprinted onto ordinary workers the ideals of sacrifice, loyalty, and honor. The ordinary workers were treated as passive beings who needed to emulate these heroes. The two processes—the recognition of extraordinary workers and their unilateral use by the state to increase productivity—cannot be separated. In the system of labor heroes, human possibilities and state hegemony occupied the same everyday space.

The most propagandized mass movement was the Ch'ŏllima Movement. The spirit and achievements of this movement had a wide effect on North Korea and have lasted to this day, reappearing once again as a national campaign in 2009.[129] The original Ch'ŏllima Movement is said to have started with the launch of the Five-Year Plan in January 1957, after the general meeting of the party Central Committee in December 1956, where a decision was passed to "expand mass campaigns among the masses . . . by penetrating down into the their everyday."[130] As expected, the moment of the movement's birth involves Kim Il Sung's contact with the people. After the Central Committee meeting, as the official story goes, Kim Il Sung and other leaders went down to a factory (whose name is unknown) to inform the workers of the party decision. As written in *Ch'ŏllima Kisu tokbon* (The Ch'ŏllima Riders handbook), "The party appealed to all workers to . . . break through the barriers and go forward in the spirit of *ch'ŏllima* [thousand-*ri* horse]. . . . We workers, who are loyal to the party and *suryŏng* [leader], . . . unanimously supported the party decision and . . . set out in the party's direction."[131]

Although the state recognizes the birth of the Ch'ŏllima Movement at the onset of the Five-Year Plan, the use of the term *ch'ŏllima* to refer to a mass movement cannot be found prior to 1958 (*The Ch'ŏllima Riders Handbook* was not published until 1963), although Kim Il Sung did utter the word as early as the 1930s in reference to the spirit of partisans. It is only in retrospect that the Ch'ŏllima Movement is said to have begun in 1957. An actual movement using the term began in 1959 as the Ch'ŏllima Work Team Movement. It was a planned campaign in conjunction with the party Central Committee's decision in September 1958 to complete the Five-Year Plan one year ahead of schedule. This moment was one of great consolidation of power: on the eve of the tenth anniversary of the DPRK's founding, the collectivization of agriculture was nearly complete; the last remaining private industries had been nationalized; and the party, state, union, and military were dominated by Kim Il Sung's faction, with strong loyalty from domestic communist groups. One effect of this power consolidation on the production regime was the mobilization of workers to quickly meet the objectives of the Five-Year Plan.

The Ch'ŏllima Work Team Movement is tied to the factory Kangsŏn Steelworks in South P'yŏngan Province. On March 9, 1959, after two visits to the factory by Kim Il Sung, a smelting team led by Chin Ŭngwŏn resolved to "complete the First Five-Year Plan within the year and inherit the noble revolutionary tradition of Kim Il Sung" and so started a production campaign within the factory.[132] Eight days later this team was the first to receive the title "Ch'ŏllima Work Team" from the Central Committee. Chin's team spawned a nationwide movement. At the end of 1960, 22,083 work teams and 387,412 workers were participating in the movement.[133] By 1963, more than 3 million workers were participating in the movement, with 13,626 teams receiving the title "Ch'ŏllima Work Team."[134] Chin Ŭngwŏn became a labor hero in 1960.

Totality of Everyday Work

Everyday life in the postwar period, defined by repetitive work and mass movements, had the effect of redrawing the relationship between working and living. The everyday was infused with the ideological aspect of repetition, which helped to forge a connection between mundane activities and historical meaning. The nationwide campaigns to increase productivity formally enveloped the entire population within the state-controlled regime of production. Such control was bureaucratic and ethical in nature: a

Figure 3.2 An early image promoting the Ch'ŏllima Movement. The caption reads, "Comrade, are you riding *ch'ŏllima*? Incinerate conservative passivity!"
Source: *Rodong Sinmun*, October 22, 1958.

Figure 3.3 Chŏng Yŏngman, *Kangsŏn ŭi chŏnyŏk noŭl* (Sunset at Kangsŏn), oil on canvas, 46 in. × 78 in., 1973.
Source: Image courtesy of the National Library of Korea.

Figure 3.4 Ch'ŏllima Riders calling for the speeding up of a repair project, 1960s.
Source: Photograph courtesy of the Hŭngnam Fertilizer Factory Museum.

mechanism of indirect control through mass mobilization and emotional connection. Real control was impossible, but in the impossible attempt to achieve it there arose a totality of life and work that aligned the needs of the community with the needs of the state. The production of everyday life was concurrently the production of its totality.

The coming together of the needs of the state and community involved the construction of coherence between ideology, bureaucracy, infrastructure, and human agency. Within three years of the armistice, the North Korean state had built and restored hundreds of schools, hospitals, clinics, nurseries, movie theaters, and clubhouses. By 1958, 22 colleges and 121 technical schools had been built (compared to one college and no technical school before liberation), along with numerous libraries and museums.[135] In print media, by 1957 there were 1,358 newspapers, magazines, and book publishers, with a total printing of 230 million copies.[136] The infrastructure of the built environment and print media also signaled an effort to strengthen the class consciousness of workers through education. Kim Tongch'ŏl, a Soviet Korean who served as the deputy chief of the Supreme Court before being dismissed in 1960, wrote about the necessity of this undertaking. He was concerned that the vestiges of old ideologies remained in the consciousness of workers: class education was thus necessary to "purge the bourgeois or petit bourgeois consciousness and arm them with advanced socialist ideology."[137] Such an ideological education was always practical— practice as the externalization of ideology. This is why from 1958 on all technical schools implemented the curriculum of 50 percent classroom learning and 50 percent productive labor, which included participating every year in a month-and-a-half-long, mass-mobilized labor project.[138] It is useful here to think further about the concept of totality.

Once again, my central thinker on this notion is Lefebvre, who saw everyday life as a total system of practice: as a product, as modes of administration and production, and as an ideological field. All state activities tended toward totality; totality is the guide of all knowledge and action: "It directs knowledge; it orientates investigations and plans them. It tends toward immanent structure. It desires power."[139] The state strives for totality through its apparatuses of law, education, housing, campaigns, and public projects. Despite the grand scale, however, the state's insistence on totality is based on a more fundamental aspect of the human act. This is the *will for totality*, which attempts to recapture a fragmented life: "to develop knowledge as an element of praxis, and to refuse to accept separations with that praxis." At the same time, Lefebvre suggests that this process, which describes the total human phenomenon, does not have any ontological essence. While rejecting the existence of ontological essence, Lefebvre, ever consistent as a philosopher of the quotidian, offers three dimensions of human totality: need, labor, and pleasure. Their interactions in practice constitute the process of "becoming" and "historicity."[140]

Need, labor, and pleasure are what Lefebvre calls a "coherent triplicity."[141] Human need is distinct because it is mediated by labor: human need transforms into capacity and power through social labor. However, need and labor cannot stand alone. Without pleasure, need is privation and frustration, and labor becomes a fetish where productivity and work ethic reign supreme. Need and labor explicitly demand pleasure. "Labor is indispensable if man is to appropriate nature," Lefebvre writes, "but pleasure alone makes this appropriation effective." The three dimensions determine human totality, but this totality is only a phenomenon, an observable linkage between knowledge and practice. Totality is not exhaustive or definitive: totality is always unfulfilling and incomplete. For Lefebvre, totality is not a circle satisfying itself but a "spiral which crosses history and establishes man's historicity."[142] This is a crucial point. At the level of practice, the struggle for totality leads to confrontation with other activities and demands their subordination. As such, totality is the predominance of a particular activity and a particular representation.[143] In sum, totality is essentially partial:

The moment [an activity] becomes totalized is also the moment when its immanent failure is revealed. The structure contains within itself the seeds of its own negation: the beginning of destructuring. Achievement is the harbinger of its withering away. . . . Totalization imposes doubt, collapse and disintegration. . . . [E]very attempt at totalization must be put to the test before the irreducible residual deposit—the everyday—can claim its demands, its status and its dignity, before we can consider raising it to the level of totality.[144]

Totality is by no means imagined, nor is it sheer repression. Rather, it is an indispensable quality of knowledge and practice arising from the interactions of need, labor, and pleasure. Totality is an effort to carry out a particular activity through struggle and thus contains struggle as its own seed. It is an incomplete phenomenon: the seed of struggle prevents any kind of fulfillment. As a state project, totality is the appearance of a particular predominant activity. Yet even for the state the appearance of totality confirms itself only in the everyday, the "irreducible residual deposit" in which every human struggle is carried out and every social project is tested. Hence, everyday life is simultaneously a practical field of production and administration and an ideological field of symbolic construction, with the two fields in turn giving rise to a totalizing reality in which social needs and state needs confront each other. Totality is a phenomenon of everyday life exhibiting both the confirmation and the negation of human activities. This dual characteristic comes from the fundamentally incomplete core of any totality, a core of struggle and confrontation—that is, antagonism. Such an understanding helps to distinguish in the everyday the moment of totality and its disintegration.

The quintessential state project of everyday totality was the construction of housing. Strictly speaking, housing was distinguished from work as a space of leisure, culture, and family. It was an environment that the worker entered after leaving the shop floor: housing was a place where surplus production did not take place. It was formally a domain of consumption (just as important as production) and hence a continuation of everyday life as part of the repetitive spiral of production and consumption. As repetition attained an ideological force on the shop floor, its function continued in the household through the act of consumption. In other words, as part of everyday totality, the nonproductive aspect of housing did *not* denote some kind of autonomy from the regime of production. Rather, housing simply represented a *noneconomic* aspect of the production regime (along with education and the arts) and played an indispensable role in the fundamental process of reproducing the means of production.

Despite losing more than 600,000 houses during the Korean War, out of a total of one million houses, the process of housing construction after the Korean War was a gradual process due to the priority given to industrialization.[145] The period of the Five-Year Plan (1957–1960) saw the planning and construction of 600,000 housing units, carried out with 13.4 percent of the entire construction budget.[146] The next period of nationwide housing construction was in the 1970s during the Six-Year Plan (1971–1976), when more than 800,000 units were built; the period of the Third Seven-Year Plan (1987–1993) also saw the construction of tens of thousands of housing units.[147] Yet, despite these efforts, North Korea has continually had a housing shortage. In the mid-1990s, there were around 3 million housing units in North Korea, but the housing supply rate hovered only around 60 percent (compared to 86 percent in South Korea in the same period).[148]

In theory, housing in North Korea was to be planned in agreement with socialist content, economic uniformity, and aesthetic orderliness, wherein the people's interests were to find harmony with industrial demands and spatial efficiency.[149] There are two types of housing in North Korea. *Permanent* houses (apartments in the cities and townhouses in the countryside) are centrally planned and built by the state, whereas *temporary* houses (prewar houses and rowhouses) were and are built outside the state budget, usually by the local government and cooperatives.[150] Except for prewar houses, all housing, whether permanent or temporary, is prefabricated. In Pyongyang, 80 percent of housing are permanent, but in other large cities only 20 to 40 percent are permanent; in smaller cities and industrial complexes, 90 percent of housing are temporary.[151] Because no structure can be privately owned, as written in the Constitution, all houses are owned by the state or cooperatives. There can be no buying and selling of real estate, and all residents pay a rent. Housing is distributed according to status, occupation, and rank—the best housing units in Pyongyang going to high-ranking party, government, and military officials.

The lowest level in the housing system is the *kun* (group), made up of several buildings providing housing for a total population of 1,000 to 2,500.[152] The next level up is the *soguyŏk* (subquarter), made up of four or five *kun*, followed by the *kuyŏk* (quarter), with a population of 40,000 to 50,000.[153] The largest level in the housing system is the *chiyŏk* (district), consisting of several *kuyŏk*, with a population of up to 150,000.[154] The most basic and inclusive housing unit is the subquarter, which, along with apartments for 4,000 to 5,000 people, ideally contains schools, kindergartens, daycare centers, food stores, home-goods stores, restaurants, grain-distribution centers, government offices, propaganda offices, maintenance offices, power-distribution centers, banks, clinics, bathhouses, laundry cleaners, beauty shops and barbers, warehouses, garages, gardens, sports facilities, playgrounds, and waste-treatment centers.[155] The size of a subquarter is about 4 hectares (10 acres), which translates into around 7 square meters (75 square feet) per person.[156]

Housing in the postwar period was planned and built as a comprehensive system, where workers found leisure, babies were cared for, and children received education, but at the same time it was a space where the workers recovered their strength to return to their jobs daily and where mothers had free children's daycare and thus no excuse to stay home. The free daycare centers were a step toward women's relief from domestic labor as well as the means to maximize their labor power. In fact, North Korea's notion of housing was particularly mindful of women. The expansion of household provisions, family restaurants, processed foods, kindergartens, and daycare centers was advocated with the goals of "alleviating the domestic burden of women" and "improving the convenience of mothers."[157] Kim Yŏngsu, once the chair of the People's Committee of North Hamgyŏng Province and deputy labor minister (as well as a Soviet Korean who was eventually demoted), wrote about women's emancipation in terms of housing and infrastructure. He said in 1958 that women's emancipation from household affairs would arrive when the technological revolution is fulfilled and the construction of socialism complete. "Then do we need to wait until the day when all conditions are met for our women to enter the workplace?" he asked. "No, women need to enter the workplace as soon as possible. . . . More daycare centers, kindergartens, restaurants, and laundromats will be built as women start going to work."[158]

The housing system was a practice of everyday life exhibiting a totalizing character. The individual's need for rest, leisure, and childcare *and* the state's need for increasing productivity and work morale were satisfied simultaneously within public housing (another relationship observed throughout the world). But as such the system's totalizing character also exhibited its impossibility. The moment of totality was also the moment of disintegration. In the case of the housing system, disintegration can be

Figure 3.5 Apartment complex in southwest Pyongyang, with stores in front, May 2014. *Source:* Photograph by the author.

seen on two levels. First, as a tangible state practice, the housing system never included enough infrastructure—not enough houses and not enough daycare centers; North Korea's housing supply rate was low and uneven. For those living in smaller cities and the countryside, the housing problem was left mostly in the hands of the people themselves. According to North Korean migrants in China, housing assignment was a slow process, and a person without a job was not assigned housing.[159] It was common for two or three households to share a single housing unit of only two rooms.[160] Second, as an ideological field, the claim of furthering women's emancipation by relieving women from household work was a misrecognition of the source of women's oppression. Relief from household work was a step in the right direction, but it provided no relief from the oppressive structure of patriarchy itself, which existed at home regardless of household work. Furthermore, the entrance into the workplace meant entrance into another arena of domination, now set up by the production regime. The state's fervor for industrialism entailed full appropriation of surplus and command over labor power. The failure of totality occurred at the levels of both practice and ideology. Housing was certainly a quintessential project of everyday totality, a meeting point of community needs and state needs, but at the center were the antagonistic relations of domination—patriarchy and surplus appropriation—prefiguring the disintegration of totality.

Ordinariness and repetitiveness were the very mechanisms establishing the everyday as the ultimate space of control. Certain historical conditions contributed toward this formation: the dominance of the political world by Kim Il Sung and his faction and the control of production by the state, resulting in centralized appropriation of surplus. Conceptually speaking, the everyday life of North Koreans entailed a totality that brought together communal needs and state needs through mass movements and repetitive labor. This description is not meant to paint a seamless image of everyday life. Lefebvre calls the everyday the "irreducible residual deposit." The everyday totality has an irreducible core of struggle, of antagonism. Thus, all forms of everyday totality—the housing system included—also anticipate their own disintegration, both in discourse and in practice.

CHAPTER 4

The Rhythm of Everyday Work, in Six Parts

Men do not fight and die for tons of steel, or for tanks and atomic bombs.
They aspire to be happy, not to produce.

—HENRI LEFEBVRE, *CRITIQUE OF EVERYDAY LIFE*

In a documentary film about the importance of women in North Korea's economy, produced in 2002, a group of women workers evoke the spirit of the 1950s.[1] The film refers back to postwar scenes of women workers participating in the construction of a dam and grinding away at machine-tool stations. Other footage shows young women students carrying bricks on their backs to rebuild their war-damaged school. The legendary labor hero Kil Hwaksil makes an appearance. The women workers of the contemporary period are inspired by the history, and they adopt the slogan "Let us live and work with the spirit of the struggle of the 1950s!" The film suggests that women workers of the new era should toil as their comrades did in the past, which is to say that they should work more than just *hard*. To live and work as people did in the 1950s is to make intense labor an everyday activity, to collapse the division between life and labor, to find happiness and fulfillment in the everyday space of work. The 1950s are a heady period in the memory of the North Korean people, a period of undeniable transformation.

How should everydayness be approached? What is the relationship between reality and the everyday? How can the seemingly chaotic and yet mundane activities of everyday work be understood in relation to power? What about agency? Can agency be located within everyday space, which is also the space of hegemonic power? What about ideology? How is the mechanism of ideological misrecognition deployed in the space of everyday work? This chapter, in six parts, is a study of North Korea's everyday work in the decade following the Korean War. It is an attempt to reconstruct a slice of everyday work at a particular historical moment. The main concepts of this chapter—choice, representation, resistance, contention, appropriation, and ideology—are relevant both to the historical reality of postwar North Korea and to the general questions of the everyday, socialism, and modernity. These concepts are analyzed in the context of everyday work depicted in the postwar cultural materials of fiction, poetry, paintings, documentary and narrative films, and popular memoir. One fictional work analyzed is Yun Sejung's novel *Yonggwangno nǔn sumshinda* (The furnace is breathing, 1960). The novel takes the reader into the contentious everyday space of a factory, its stories defying common assumptions about a place ruled by an authoritarian regime and guided by planned economy. It is a seminal text of this study.

As addressed in previous chapters, the everyday is in the first instance *not* autonomous from the state. On the contrary, it is a product of the state's attempt at constructing a totalizing discourse and practice: for state hegemony to be realized, it has to be consequential in everyday life. Various practices of North Korea's regime of production were carried out in everyday space, including calculations for industrial efficiency, mass movements for productivity, and housing that reproduced the conditions of labor. Everyday life and working life occupy the same conceptual and practical space. This chapter also proceeds from this initial notion of the everyday and makes observations about the incomplete nature of state hegemony: the core of antagonism sustains the incomplete nature of state totality. Everyday life is at the heart of the matter: hegemony and totality become ambiguous in the everyday, indistinguishable from choice and freedom in experience. Individual and collective choices and their consequence are genuine experiences often arising from the context of hegemony. Subjectivity is found to be a historically shaped experience contiguous with practices of domination. Ambiguity between domination and agency, however, is not the end point. The observation of domination and agency as experientially intertwined highlights the everyday also as a realm of possibilities.

Access to Everyday Life and the Problem of Choice

The short story "Kiltongmuduͦl" (Fellow travelers), written by Kim Pyoͦnghun and first published in the magazine *Chosoͦn Munhak* (Korean literature) in October 1960, is a representative work of fiction of the Ch'oͦllima Movement period.[2] It follows the theme of ordinary people heeding the call of the party and the state to increase production through hard work and innovations, which are to be discovered by the people themselves. The community possesses, the story claims, both limitations and possibilities activated by the people living in it in their ordinary circumstances. The everyday is dialectical, in the process of change. The two main characters of this elegant story are from two different generations and social positions. One is a man in his late forties whose name is not known. He is the party chair of P'ungsan County in Ryanggang Province.[3] The other is O Myoͦngsuk, a young woman worker at the Ch'oͦn'gae Cooperative of the same county.

One June afternoon the man is aboard a train returning from a provincial party meeting. His heart is heavy with all the tasks given to his district. When the train stops at a station, he encounters Myoͦngsuk arguing with a ticket agent, who is not allowing her to board the train because she is carrying live animals in a large pail. But when the whistle signals the train's departure, she quickly passes the ticket agent and jumps on board with her pail. The man helps her by taking her arm and the pail, which contains 50,000 carp hatchlings. Myoͦngsuk is on her way home, too. She plans to start a carp farm at her cooperative. The man is immediately intrigued by this young woman. She has been traveling since the previous afternoon, and she has not slept, for she must regularly change the water, pump the water with air, and feed the hatchlings. At a stopover station, she detrains to get some freshwater, but she does not return in time, leaving the pail on board. The man decides to take care of the pail and waits for her at the next stop, despite the urgency to hold a county party meeting the following morning. This mishap, which risks the two protagonists' immediate aims, brings them together.

Myoͦngsuk could have entered the university or a large factory after graduating high school, but she chose to stay at the cooperative. She was at first like most of her peers and did not want to "rot away in a mountain village," but after learning from village elders about the history of her hometown, a history of poor people who had gone hungry for too long, she resolved to stay and help: "I shall greet the dawn of communism from my hometown." Her plan is to study fish farming and eventually to provide fresh fish to her townspeople, but she receives no support from the cooperative manager, who considers her plan too ambitious. She thus ventures alone, initiating the plan with her own means. The pail with 50,000 carp hatchlings, to be raised in the village reservoir, is the beginning. The man—the county party chair—is inspired by her dedication and decides on the spot to make carp farming a countywide project, with Myŏngsuk in charge. She is unaware of his identity to the end. They part ways at her village station. She tells him to not say anything scornful about the manager of her cooperative. "The manager comrade is a good person," she says, "but he doesn't know anything about fish farming. . . . I will convince him myself." He promises and watches her walk away, a "painting whose beauty one cannot fully understand." "We emphasize it in meetings, and we read it in books," he thinks to himself, "but how difficult it is to melt into the real lives of each person, each worker, as the truth!" What this "it" is the story does not explicitly say, but "it" is surely to be discovered in the person of Myŏngsuk.

"Fellow Travelers" is a story about what *works*, what ought to happen, and what it means to properly follow the party. Myŏngsuk is the best of a new generation of people living and working under the revolutionary government. She represents a coherent being, a transparent medium between ideals and their realization. But she should not be mistaken for an automaton, blindly following orders from higher powers. There is humanness in her actions, which is to say there is conflict—the conflict between personal ambition and communal good, between consensus and individual will, between the plan and spontaneity. Her humanness presents the aspects of everyday work expanding against the flow of state power. The everyday is the practical space of planned campaigns such as the Ch'ŏllima Movement, but for such campaigns to actually work they require a type of action outside the plan: improvisation. Myŏngsuk is hence thrown into the paradoxical world of state socialism: she resolves to follow the great collective demand of revolution, but in doing so she must also depend on herself, ignore the pessimistic views of others, and act outside the boundaries of collective work. The anarchy of the plan is balanced, in the end, by individual intervention. Although the state tells the people *what* to do, it does not tell them *how* to do it—this *how* comes from the people. This separation between what (prescribed by the state) and how (improvised by the people) is precisely how the hegemonic order is maintained. The everyday has a cleavage dividing the ruling class from the masses, and this separation supports the appearance of "society," with members such as Myŏngsuk, as autonomous. Such a separation is represented in the story by Myŏngsuk never knowing that the man she meets on the train is the party provincial chair. She is instead led to believe her accomplishments are her own: the genuineness of her life is sustained, and the hand of the higher power in setting up the fish farm is temporarily made invisible.

This story provides a glimpse of life during the decade after the Korean War. There must have been people like Myŏngsuk who believed in the dream—the "dawn of communism"—and who appropriated this dream and turned it into actual practice, using improvisation, overcoming conflicts and disagreements, and fulfilling individual desires. Conceptually, such life can be located between the hegemonic projects of the state and the counterhegemonic practices of the community. Here in this space, life is neither passive nor resistive but a combination reconfiguring power and creating elements such as individual choice. Myŏngsuk could have chosen to compromise with what she already had at the cooperative, but she breaks with the normal order and goes out on her own. Some kind of "choice" is involved in this process. The North Korean state in the late 1950s was continuously launching ideological programs (mass movements) to increase production. These programs were carried out in everyday space and had an appearance of totality in which the fulfillment of state aims came to be identified with the satisfaction of communal needs. In the process, the state appropriated the everyday. This appropriation was partial: totality is inherently fragmentary because antagonism between the state and the community prevents any authentic domination. In the face of a powerful state, the people of North Korea made the most of their situation—not only materially (Myŏngsuk obtaining the hatchlings) but also subjectively (Myŏngsuk's will to bring about change). It can be said that the state plan and communal practice depended on each other for resources, ideas, and practical solutions. This relationship is similar to what James Scott calls *mētis*, "practical knowledge" necessary for a state's grand plan to work, especially that of a state with a centrally planned economy.[4]

The historian Alf Lüdtke investigates the everyday condition of people living in oppressive circumstances. Lüdtke looks specifically at the workers of fascist Germany, who passively or willingly participated in

Germany's fascist projects, including systematic genocide. He questions the view of the masses as victims of a larger scheme conceptualized by the few. He does not see them as perpetrators, either, but instead attempts to overcome such a binary view of them and to examine how they actually lived and experienced their historical reality. For Lüdtke, the everyday is a matrix in which the "people appropriate the conditions of their life and survival, making those conditions their own." For example, in his reading of a memoir of a former head of a labor camp in occupied Poland, he notices that she was at times confused and doubtful about her role at the labor camp, but she always came to enjoy the job of organizing, commanding, and having an impact, thereby creating or reinforcing a semblance of order and regularity.[5] In her daily activities, Lüdtke finds instances of both the willingness to participate in the fascist project and the tendency to distance herself from it:

> People participate in relationships of domination and follow their (occasional?) desire to be a part of things; but this very participation is undercut, time and again, by silent or self-willed distance. . . . For individuals, that constituted a mixture of responses, including assent, passive acceptance, going along with and participating in events—as well as "lying low," distancing oneself, or, here and there, resisting. These stances were not contradictory, they mingled. . . . Complicity could spring both from hesitant compliant acceptance or "enthusiastic" assent. Yet it was on this blend that German fascism's system of domination and exploitation relied, right down to its final moment.[6]

The people living under the influence of a despotic regime, even one as harsh as Hitler's fascist state, cannot be seen as passive, complicit victims. Their lives constitute a mixture of "stances" of assent and distancing, while always appropriating the conditions for survival, meaning, and fulfillment.

In the case of North Korea, advanced research on everyday life is being carried out by the Research Center on Everyday Life of North Korea at Dongguk University in Seoul. For these scholars, studying everyday life allows the understanding of specific structures of power reproduction and their relationship to macro social dynamics.[7] What happens "from below" is considered to be at times more important than the central bureaucracy in determining the social form: the other side of oppression, isolation, and alienation is North Korea's world "suggestive of tensions of diverse social relations."[8] In a study of North Korea's bureaucrats, center researcher Kim Chonguk describes the everyday of officialdom as one of dualism in which bureaucrats both submit to state hegemony and strategize resistance. The bureaucrats function within state apparatuses, and yet they are members of everyday community; they are both practitioners of dominant ideology and makers of everyday discourse; they are messengers of ruling culture while transmitting and developing everyday culture; they are followers within the state's symbolic world, and yet they comply with the demands of the people. In the workspace, the dualistic world of bureaucrats exhibits two types of stances, one of distancing (*kŏridugi*) and one of involvement (*kaeip*). As Kim Chonguk's study shows us, both stances are about survival and benefit, whether the bureaucrats are distancing themselves from smuggled goods, which provide a kickback, or involving themselves in the extralegal activity of receiving cash for allowing workers to do business at the market.[9]

Kim Chonguk's observation is similar to Lüdtke's. Both offer evidence of a reality not captured by party speeches, state policies, and propaganda—a reality in which actors appropriate various aspects of the hegemony and shape them to suit their livelihood. The everyday thus revealed is a space of multiple and composite experiences and practices existing contiguously but separately from ruling systems and their ideologies. Based on this understanding, it is now useful to *un*differentiate the everyday conceptually. In the first step, the everyday functions as modes of production and administration, a concrete space for a totalizing ideological practice. In the second step, the everyday can also be distinguished from official systems of control in that ordinary people appropriate the hegemonic aspects of everyday life (productive and administrative modes) and find meaning and practical benefits in those aspects, in the process occasionally resisting the hegemonic order. These two facets of the everyday are conceptual opposites, and yet they coexist in a single space as an undifferentiated field. For human beings, the oppositional and dialectical nature of the everyday is experienced as a whole: to distinguish hegemonic space from nonhegemonic space is impossible. And the same is true for the space of freedom: the simultaneous presence of freedom and domination in everyday space is experienced and misrecognized as reality itself (Lefebvre's irreducible residue). The dependence on the everyday is not limited to individual actions but is extended to state power as well; the state must rely on the everyday to enact its programs. *All* converge in and as everydayness.

In the third step, the everyday is about both the practical and substantive stuff of reality *and* their opposites. Reality is where coherence, experience, and resistance coexist with and are often inseparable from misrecognition, ideology, and domination. Human actions labeled as *distancing* and *resistance* are no more authentic than the state program of mass campaigns. Personal experience and ideological workings are thus indistinguishable from each other in their manifestations in the everyday. Such a paradoxical mode of existence, Lefebvre tells us, rests on the foundation of everyday life, where reality is "fictitious but terribly real; abstract but ever so concrete."[10]

This conceptual orientation is useful in reading a letter printed in *Kŭlloja*, a political theory magazine issued by the Korean Workers' Party Central Committee. The letter writer, Ri Kyedŭk, was chief of a tool shop at the Ragwŏn Machine Factory, an important production site manufacturing various machines used at mines and construction sites, such as cutting tools, tower cranes, and concrete mixers.[11] Ri Kyedŭk wrote about the problem of low efficiency in equipment use, which he thought was caused by unexpected changes to the production plan. Such changes were important to the factory, he admitted, because they "ensure the speed of construction and production demanded by our country." But because of insufficiencies in technical and administrative plans, production was rushed, and goals were not met. He also wrote that the labor process was dominated by shock work and that productivity was in constant fluctuation. Ri Kyedŭk's letter is not a simple complaint but a detailed criticism of two groups: first, the factory managers, who needed to better accommodate the changes in the production plan; and, second, the state planning specialists, who needed to correctly specify the items required by mines and construction sites. Although the planning agencies and factory management were supposed to communicate closely with each other, there was often little discussion prior to creating new orders, resulting in products needing further modifications. An example of this mismanagement was the production of "fifteen-meter-long conveyor belts that could not be used without modifications."

According to Ri Kyedŭk, the lack of coordination between planning agencies and factory management was not the only cause of low efficiency in equipment use. Another problem was the production process in the factory. First, there was an imbalance between the production of main parts and the production of secondary parts. And second, too much time was spent on polishing old tools: time could be better managed, argued Ri, if a different work team took on the task of polishing. At the end of the letter, Ri proposed to set up a central warehouse at the factory *and* to streamline the storage and distribution of parts and tools, with the ultimate aim of increasing the efficiency of machine use.

Ri Kyedŭk's letter is typical of the period and the magazine. Almost every issue of *Kŭlloja* printed a few letters from readers. As in others, Ri's letter addressed a general issue faced by the industrial sector and how the problem specifically took shape in his factory. Ri described problems (miscommunication between planning agencies and factory management) using examples (conveyor belts needing modification) and proposed possible solutions for all responsible parties. As a shop chief, he did not exclude himself from blame and proposed setting up a central warehouse. The letter shows a glimpse of a normal workspace: full of problems but nonetheless a part of the larger production regime. However, what the description of the labor process further reveals is contention. The normal, everyday work was a world of constant criticism and choice. The state's demand for innovative, efficient, and productive work in fact created a labor process full of choices, a process that depended on these choices to function. Mass movements and propaganda to increase production had the inevitable consequence of leaving much room for the workers' own innovations and improvisations (Ri's factory warehouse, Myŏngsuk's fish farm). Such actions were not outside the plan but precisely necessary parts of it. At every turn, the workers were asked to evaluate, criticize, choose, and solve.

The everyday of North Korean workers presented a reality in which ideological and hegemonic elements as well as elements of agency conflate in the construction of the subject, to the point of erasing the observable boundaries between them. The acts of distancing, appropriation, and resistance were indeed crucial actions of the ordinary people in the face of state power, but what complicated this reality was the field of state power that depended on individual choice and criticism for its functioning. One significant aspect of distancing and appropriation was that even individuals living in a harsh, oppressive environment chose what was best for their survival and fulfillment. A remarkable aspect was thus the capacity to choose, although in everyday life the origin of this capacity was ambiguous. Did this choice come from free will or from an ideologically programmed domain? Was the choice of the shop chief different from the choice of the fish farm champion? Are the choices of these two socialist workers fundamentally different from the choices of capitalist workers? Conceptually, there is surely a difference between free choice and not-so-free choice, between what is ideological and what is not, but this difference is difficult to know and experience in everyday space. Each step in the infinite process of intention and action contains elements of domination and freedom. Their simultaneous, dialectical presence in the everyday is what gives categories such as choice ambiguous origins and boundaries.

After the war, choice came to be programmed into the North Korean state's ideological, hegemonic projects. The actual functioning of mass movements for productivity, beyond slogans and rallies, took place on the shop floor, with workers at all levels engaged in the evaluation and criticism of their labor process. The workplace required the workers to make choices. These choices were certainly within prefigured limits of the ruling ideology, but they were nevertheless real choices that had real effects on the worker's life. A glimpse of the everyday of North Korea in the decade after the Korean War is both limiting and revealing, mundane and extraordinary, full of oppositional and dialectical elements. Such a glimpse shows a historical reality that is a confluence of subjective and dominating forces, effecting, on the one hand, moments of agency through categories such as choice and, on the other hand, conditions of hegemony by aligning individuals' interests and needs with the state's interests and needs.

Representing/Prescribing Life:
Aesthetics of Socialist Realism

The artistic products considered in this chapter share the style of socialist realism. After its official adoption by the Soviet Union in the 1930s, socialist realism became the orthodox style of art and literature in the state socialist world. In North Korea, the authority of defining and deploying socialist realism has lain with the Federation of Literature and Arts Unions of Korea (FLAUK). Closely tied to the party, FLAUK does not sanction cultural production outside its boundaries, although the actual content of North Korea's art and literature often contradicts the principles of socialist realism.[12] This section is about what postwar socialist realism tried to represent and prescribe. This question is germane to the investigation of the everyday because socialist realism entails artistically capturing lived reality. As an overarching style of all socialist art forms, socialist realism is the lens through which reality is interpreted. The reality represented in socialist art is thus always mediated by socialist realism. This mediation, however, is not necessarily a limitation because any reality is at all times mediated. There is no primordial reality lying below mediation: reality as historical construction is always mediated—by language, culture, ideology, and so on. Socialist realism is merely one type in the sea of mediation.

In the fall of 1957, at an arts festival celebrating both the twelfth anniversary of Korea's liberation and the fortieth anniversary of the Russian Revolution, Han Sŏrya (1900–1976), the chairperson of FLAUK and minister of education and culture,[13] expressed disappointment in the play *Majimak pae* (The last boat). The play is set during the colonial period and is about an old oarsman who kills a Japanese policeman. The actors were from the community theater of the Fifth Cooperative of North Hamgyŏng Province, but the play was directed by professional artists of the North Hamgyŏng Provincial Theater. Han's disappointment was not with the cooperative actors but with the professional artists. "In directing the play," Han Sŏrya wrote, "they artificially exaggerated and distorted the truth of simple life as depicted in the original work. . . . They made up a *sinp'a* style scene out of the events surrounding the killing of a Japanese policeman." For Han, *sinp'a* (short for *sinp'agŭk*, "new school theater"), a theater style that began in Japan in the late nineteenth century and gained popularity in Korea during the colonial period, was unfit as socialist art—too melodramatic, without revolutionary content, incapable of capturing the experience of the working people. "They do not know that true dramaturgy is found within life, and only life is the topic for a vivid dramaturgy," Han commented.[14]

Han Sŏrya's criticism of the play was part of an essay on the situation of art in North Korea in the late 1950s. The construction of socialism was bringing great changes to life, the essay stated, and, accordingly, these changes were demanding new aesthetic content. The play directed by the Hamgyŏng Provincial Theater was not truthfully reflecting the new life and therefore not meeting this demand. Han specified what this demand was: "The new life is giving rise to new rhythm, new speech patterns, new bodily movements, new colors, new breath, and new gestures. . . . The people themselves are appearing on the scene as the very creators of new aesthetics and art. . . . The great changes in our life at the moment demands corresponding change in artistic content."[15] He was talking about the task of socialist realism. Economic and social changes were producing new aesthetics and rhythm of life, and all artistic production had the task of capturing and representing the new aesthetics and rhythm. At the same time, the whole process had to consistently refer to the revolutionary significance of socialist construction. The other side of representing life was hence *prescribing* life—the right thought and action for the masses.

Socialist realism was not new in the arts of North Korea in the late 1950s. As in other socialist states, art and culture were important for the North Korean state from early on. Charles Armstrong notes that culture was emphasized from the beginning of North Korea as a physical entity to be consciously constructed, similar to industry.[16] In fact, as the art critic Igor Golomstock writes, the view of culture as an object to be molded was a common feature of all types of totalitarian states, from the Soviet Union to fascist Germany.[17] In North Korea, FLAUK possessed the authority over how socialist realism would be practiced. Founded in March 1946, FLAUK set out to establish a national art and culture based on the principles of "progressive democracy," as a movement for the creative development of the masses.[18] Ten years later Han Sŏrya echoed FLAUK's original aims at a meeting held by the Literature and Arts Propaganda Publishing House: "Our socialist realist literature, which truthfully represents our revolutionary reality with historical concreteness, has created numerous forms of optimistic and party-minded human beings who are models for our people, contributing to the education of the masses into invincible heroes and new socialist beings."[19] The double function of socialist realism is outlined here—the representation of revolutionary life and the prescription of such a life for the masses. In practice, however, North Korea's artistic creations, especially literature, were marked by certain nonsocialist tendencies: ethnocentric pastoralism, antiurbanism, and antiindustrialism.[20] As Sunyoung Park points out, the application of socialist realism in Korea had been debated ever since it had been introduced to writers and critics during the colonial period, with its proponents, such as the poet and critic Im Hwa, upholding it as the solution to Korea's bleak reality, but with others, such as the writer Kim Namch'ŏn, seeing it as an idealistic project.[21]

What were the aesthetics of socialist realism? The term *socialist realism* first appeared in a Soviet literary magazine in May 1932, and, supposedly in a private meeting between Stalin and Soviet writers at Maxim Gorky's apartment in October, socialist realism was adopted as the foundation of socialist art.[22] Two years later, at the first All-Union Congress of Soviet Writers in August 1934, Andrei Zhdanov, a member of the Communist Party Central Committee and a founder of the Soviet Writers' Union, gave socialist realism its official definition. Socialist realism, according to Zhdanov, is an artistic method of faithful and historically concrete depiction of life "in its revolutionary development," charged with the task of "ideologically refashioning the education of the toiling people in the spirit of socialism." He called the literature produced with such a method "revolutionary romanticism," which portrays the "supreme spirit of heroic deeds and magnificent future prospects."[23] Zhdanov's definition is similar to Han Sŏrya's given more than twenty years later, both involving the double function of truthful representation and ideological prescription for the people. Much like the new life created in the revolutionary environment, socialist aesthetics had to be entirely new, as a rejection of the existing aesthetical categories, beauty and the sublime.[24] Socialist aesthetics were not to be metaphysically produced through imagination but rooted in the ideological space produced by history in its revolutionary course.

More specifically, socialist realist aesthetics can be approached in reference to three interconnected concepts: "ideological commitment," "party-mindedness," and "national/popular spirit." As summarized by Leonid Heller, "ideological commitment" means the "uncovering" of the dominant idea in opposition to self-sufficient formalism; "party-mindedness" means the production of an "active effect" of Communist ideas; and "national/popular spirit" means the expression of "expectations and will of the whole people" in opposition to "cosmopolitanism" or "bourgeois nationalism." What was and what was not deemed socialist realist in its application, however, were often unclear. "Socialist realism was normative," Heller writes, "but only negatively so: it gave practical instructions on what could not be done, but its positive applications and its theorizing . . . remained highly nebulous."[25] Distinguishing what was socialist realist art was a situational process, often personal and political.

In May 1956, North Korea's influential literary figure Yun Sep'yŏng wrote an essay criticizing Im Hwa's poem "Uri oppa wa hwaro" (My older brother and the brazier).[26] Published in 1929 when Im Hwa was active in the leftist literary movement in Korea as a key member of the Korea Artista Proleta Federatio, an organization of Marxist writers with its official name in Esperanto, the poem was considered at the time a fine example of proletarian literature. However, looking back upon it in 1956, Yun considered it to be filled with "antirevolutionary ideology of defeatism."[27] Yun provided the following excerpts as examples of defeatism, but it should be noted that the excerpts are only parts of the first two stanzas of a ten-stanza-long narrative poem:

My beloved older brother
The turtle-patterned brazier, which you greatly cared for, cracked
    yesterday
A pair of fire-tongs now hangs neatly on the wall
Just like siblings who have lost a beloved a brother, like poor me
    and Yŏngnam[28]

"My Older Brother and the Brazier" is about three siblings living in colonial Korea, written from the perspective of the second sibling, a young woman recently laid off from work. The poem is her letter to her older brother, who is imprisoned for anti-Japanese activities. Yun Sep'yŏng began his criticism by saying Im Hwa's creative origin was "Dadaism, the direct product of bourgeois decadence." He then offered a crude metaphorical analysis: the cracked brazier is a metaphor for the imprisonment of the older brother, and the pair of fire tongs represents the younger siblings left behind. He saw the poem as a defilement of a revolutionary family, while mentioning that only Im Hwa was able to evade arrest when Korea Artista writers were rounded up by the Japanese. As a final remark, Yun depicted Im Hwa's poetry as a "poison well of defeatism."[29]

Intentionally left out of Yun Sep'yŏng's criticism of the poem are precisely its revolutionary elements, found in lines such as

Since leaving the spinning machine, I break my nails on envelopes
    that pay one *chŏn* for a hundred

Yŏngnam, too, reaches for the envelopes since being fired from the
    tobacco stench pit

The brazier is cracked, but the fire tongs remain like a flagpole

You are gone, but the little pioneer Yŏngnam is still here[30]

The reasons Yun gave for designating "My Older Brother and the Bra-zier" antirevolutionary and defeatist were beyond poetic analysis in refer-ence to socialist realism. When the entire poem is read, it satisfies socialist realism's double function of truthful representation ("I break my nails on envelopes that pays one *chŏn* for a hundred") and ideological education ("You are gone, but the little pioneer Yŏngnam is still here"). However, the absence of specific instruction on how socialist realism ought to be practiced allows the poem to be analyzed as antirevolutionary. The meta-phorical potential of the cracked brazier is large, but Yun's analysis reduced it to represent defeat and hopelessness. The most important fac-tor was thus the political mood of the moment shaped by a certain ideo-logical frame. Once the former members of the South Korean Workers' Party came under the persecutory scrutiny of Kim Il Sung's faction, Im Hwa's poems, too, became a target of political attack. The socialist and proletarian content of his poems was not enough to offset this force. Socialist realism was both flexible and restrictive according to political and ideological factors.

What made a poem (or artistic works in general) *not* socialist realist thus had little to do with tone or topic. A romantic and insouciant poem could be regarded as a suitable work of socialist realism—for instance, the short, delightful poem "Yŏngbyŏn agassi" (Young woman from Yŏngbyŏn) by Chŏng Sŏch'on published in 1958:

Her heart is kind, I tell you, having drunk the clear waters of Yak
  Mountain
She is naturally shy, I tell you, because she is fond of azaleas
I spoke to her once, taken by her weaving of Yak Mountain silk
Don't touch the Ch'ŏrong Castle in my heart, she told me, her love
  lying elsewhere[31]

On its own, the poem is a little gem (especially when read in Korean), but it is largely short on meeting the needs of socialist realism. Where is the truthful representation of reality? Where is the ideological prescription for the masses? The theme is one person's infatuation of a woman, and although she is a producer of silk, there is no suggestion of how socialism has cre-ated a new model person for the masses. Even Ch'orong Castle is not nec-essarily related to socialist history; it is a citadel built during the Koryŏ period (935–1392), famous for withstanding numerous battles against the Liao Empire in the tenth century. Immediately perceivable are the sense of provincialism and the importance of virtue. Brian Myers is right when he says that in North Korea's socialist realist works the protagonists possess the characteristic Korean naïveté, *sobakham*.[32]

"Young Woman from Yŏngbyŏn" is more about the beauty of purity and simplicity than about socialist construction and industrial progress, although it was published by the Korean Writers' Union during the period of nationwide industrial drive. But was not revolution precisely about purity and simplicity—the final, pure expression of class struggle and the abolition of deceptive practices of capitalism, a return to the simple, transparent relationship between humans, products, and surplus? Another poem, "Pangjik'kong ch'ŏnyŏege" (To the young woman weaver), by Chŏng Ch'ŏnrye and published by FLAUK in 1964, at the end of the Ch'ŏllima Movement period, is similar to "Young Woman from Yŏngbyŏn" in its focus on purity and simplicity but entirely different in its message:

> The fatherland today has again put you in charge of two weaving
>   machines
> Happiness has filled your eyes, which look upon the sea of weaving
>   machines
> Your body, lightly wrapped in apron, seems floating
> A thousand, ten thousand strands, and each moving strand sings
>   for you[33]

The poem has an uplifting tone from the beginning ("How happy I am!") and directly addresses the protagonist by name. *I am happy, and it is because of you*, the poem seems to say—as a kind of untampered happiness. "To the Young Woman Weaver," too, is an innocent admiration of a woman and her skills at making a product, but, unlike "The Woman from Yŏngbyŏn," it clearly projects elements of socialist realism. The protagonist is in a working environment created by state socialism ("in charge of two weaving machines"): she is unbound from the domestic space and placed within a modern production system. Her representation on the shop floor is particularly significant in its prescriptive elements. She is an exemplary worker, so immersed in her work that she blends in with the system (in the "sea of weaving machines"). The machines come alive, and human and machine achieve a balance ("each moving strand sings for you"). In her condition of labor, she is more than human. She is a part of the great new machine of socialism, transcending ("floating") above any limitations; she is sublime.

The designation of an artwork as socialist realist was dependent largely on the artist's political and ideological position, as judged by the state. The artist came before the artwork. Once an artist was considered suitable for socialist realism, he or she was allowed a broad artistic field of subject matter, tone, and message. The opposite was true, too. For an artist who was judged antirevolutionary, it was almost impossible to produce artwork that stood alone as an example of socialist realism. For those whose works were reinstated, as in the case of Han Sŏrya, the reinstatement occurred only after the restoration of the artist's name as politically and ideologically suitable. In practice, the artistic content managed by FLAUK was diverse, allowing the portrayal of life as complex. Perhaps the presence of diverse representations was a sign of the state's inability to control socialist realism's negative normativity. But socialist realism should not be easily pronounced another failure of the state-led ideological program, for it reveals once again the fundamentally ambiguous quality of the everyday and the inherent difficulty of its representation.

I conclude this discussion with two paintings by Chŏng Kwanch'ŏl (1916–1983), a highly regarded painter who served as a member of the Supreme People's Assembly and earned the title "people's artist."[34] These paintings (see figures 4.1 and 4.2), included in an anthology of his art published by FLAUK in 1999, are approved works of socialist realism, yet they seem to elude such a designation. Both were created during the second half of the 1950s. The first, *Kyŏul p'unggyŏng* (Winter landscape, 1955), is a scene of postwar Pyongyang, near the Taedong Gate. Unlike many other artworks from the postwar period, this painting does not have banners or revolution motifs. The second, *Poch'ŏnboesŏ* (At Poch'ŏnbo, 1959), is a street scene of the village Poch'ŏnbo, where in 1937 Kim Il Sung and his partisans clashed with a Japanese police garrison. The Battle of Poch'ŏnbo is one of the most celebrated battles of Kim Il Sung's partisan days. Yet the painting is without any reference to the battle or the famous partisan.

Figure 4.1 Chŏng Kwanch'ŏl, *Kyŏul p'unggyŏng* (Winter landscape), oil on canvas, dimensions unavailable, 1955.
Source: Chŏng Kwanch'ŏl, *Chŏng Kwanch'ŏl chakp'umjip* (The art of Chŏng Kwanch'ŏl) (Pyongyang: Munhak Yesul Chonghap Ch'ulp'ansa, 1999).

Figure 4.2 Chŏng Kwanch'ŏl, *Poch'ŏnboesŏ* (At Poch'ŏnbo), oil on canvas, dimensions unavailable, 1959.
Source: Chŏng Kwanch'ŏl, *Chŏng Kwanch'ŏl chakp'umjip.*

Figure 4.3 A painter at work, Mansudae Art Studio, Pyongyang, May 2014.
Source: Photograph by the author.

Unevenness of Work

The state–party project of increasing productivity through mass campaigns was beset with conflicting outcomes. Behind the claims of a 2,000 percent increase in industrial output, a 683 percent increase in national income, and a 539 percent increase in labor productivity between 1946 and 1960,[35] daily life was marked by scarcity and counterproductivity, which included a nationwide food crisis in 1955 (see chapter 3). Kim Il Sung was particularly troubled by unruly workers who seemed out of reach of mass campaigns. In May 1957, he spoke to the workers at the Railroad Management Office of Ch'ŏngjin City: "Among the railroad workers, we are finding signs of neglect toward state properties, indifference toward subordinate workers, dishonesty, and debauchery of drinking." Kim asserted that the workers were drinking excessively, frequently missing work, treating their freight carelessly, and stealing state property because the level of discipline among them was low.[36] However troubling the worker's unruly behavior was, it was less alarming than the inconsistencies in productivity, which occurred even at the best production sites. In September 1959, at Hwanghae Iron and

Steel Works, an emblematic factory of North Korea, Kim Il Sung lamented as a "grave problem" the fluctuating steel output at the factory, from 800 tons a day in March to 500 tons in September. "If we compare the [fluctuation] to an individual," Kim Il Sung said, "this means we have not become a normal person."[37]

The everyday work process was characterized by unevenness—unevenness in daily job attendance, job retention, and (most distressing for the state) productivity. This section looks at work as it was performed by the workers themselves. This means considering work in its unevenness—in its own rhythm—separate from some idealized version of how it should be performed. This approach is not so much about *bad* work, the unruliness of North Korean workers, or the weakness of state control, as it is about the conflicts, problems, and difficulties within the labor process as well as in the workers' own attempts to resolve these things. The everyday is again the space of this rhythm. Both categories of work—as a state project and as an individual practice—are differently but intimately tied to everyday space. The relationship between the categories "work" and "everyday life" is dialectical, with both categories supporting an everyday reality that is always inseparable from ideology. A look at a particular factory and its circumstances provides a good illustration, as told in the essay "Ŭijiŭi him" (The power of will), about the labor hero Pak Pongjo, and summarized here (maintaining the essay's use of present tense for its immediate effect).[38]

The way things are unfolding, the year 1955 is going to be rough for the workers of the Sulfur Shop at the Hŭngnam Fertilizer Factory.[39] The young worker Yang Hŭisŏk, who recently transferred to the repair team of the Sulfur Shop, is thinking about quitting the factory and becoming a farmer. His former post was with the furnace team, but he made the transfer because he could not tolerate the fumes of the furnace. For this, he was openly belittled by a senior worker, Old Man Toil, who thought Hŭisŏk's action was cowardly and unacceptable for the proud workers of the Sulfur Shop. Hŭisŏk was deeply humiliated in front of others and feels he can no longer work at the factory. Old Man Toil is on a forced leave at a rest center to treat his colitis. He is a smelter, one of a tough group of industrial workers who endure high heat, heavy loads, and dangerous gases. Since the colonial period, his job is roasting sulfide ore, which involves the unintended act of breathing in the noxious sulfur dioxide. He has seen, during the colonial period, his coworkers die from sulfur poisoning, and, despite the improved safety and health measures, his job has taken a toll on his body.

Stopping the leakage of sulfur dioxide is thus a pressing issue for the Sulfur Shop. The worker who takes up the task of eliminating the leak is Pak Pongjo. He is a mechanic at the shop, and since the prewar period he has been trying to rebuild the opening of the furnace, through which sulfide ore, around 30 tons per week, is loaded for treatment at 800°C (1,472°F). Pongjo is a respected worker at the shop, dedicated to making sulfur roasting less dangerous. The opening of the furnace is where the leak occurs, which is severe enough to kill a rabbit kept near the furnace to warn the workers of toxicity. Pongjo's idea is a two-tiered hatch, which would allow the ore to fall in but prevent sulfur dioxide from escaping. He is not successful; once, while fixing the leak on-site, he loses consciousness and is rescued by his coworkers. The mechanical problem is one concern, which Pongjo is sure he can fix; another is human related. Pongjo's team leader is trying to take all the credit for Pongjo's work, even boldly asking Pongjo if the two-tiered damper can be announced as his invention, as he once did in the past with another invention.

The year moves on for the better, however. Yang Hŭisŏk decides to go back to his former post at the roasting furnace, determined to become an honorable worker of the nation. Old Man Toil returns in the fall, having recovered his health at the rest center. As for the team leader, he leaves Pongjo alone to do his task. Pongjo eventually builds a two-tiered hatch, which functions without a hitch, sealing in the gas for the first time in the factory's history. For reducing the dangers of the Sulfur Shop and contributing to the increase in productivity, Pak Pongjo is awarded the title "labor hero" in March 1957.

The essay "Ŭijiŭi him" is a narrativization of the vicissitudes of a factory shop in a given year. It dramatizes the events, especially those related to Pak Pongjo, but they were real events and real problems faced by the shop. The Hŭngnam Fertilizer Factory was, and still is, an important enterprise in North Korea, for both propaganda and production, but the details of the everyday at the factory given in the essay show workers quitting, unhealthy settings, and technological shortcomings. The problems of the shop are resolved, as expected in such an essay. As part of an edited volume, this essay was used mainly for workers' education (only 10,000 copies were printed).[40] But it can be assumed these problems were always present, with constant attempts to solve them. The essay "Ŭijiŭi him," therefore, presents the complex situation of the workers' own troubles and triumphs coexisting with the state's hegemonic project of increasing production and building model workers. The shop floor presents a micro-cosm of the totality of human agency and state power.

Fiction was written for mass education as well as for entertainment. The short story "Chikmaeng panchang" (Union chief), written by Yu Hangrim (1914–1980) and published in the popular magazine *Kŏnsŏl ŭi Kil* (The path of construction), is about a diverse group of workers at a cement factory in the immediate postwar period.[41] It received much attention for its detailed portrayal of workers' daily life—revealing both its conservative and its progressive elements and yet blurring the boundaries between them.[42] The cement factory in "Union Chief" is unnamed, but based on its location in Mandal Mountain, it is likely the Sŭngho Precinct Cement Factory, east of central Pyongyang.[43] The story centers on the workers of Lime Kiln Shop Number Four, where limestone (abundant in the area) is heated to a temperature of 1,000°C (1,832°F) to produce quicklime (calcium oxide), which is a main ingredient of cement. The kiln shop is situated some distance away from the main factory. The protagonist is Ch'oe Yŏnghŭi, a twenty-six-year old worker whom the party orders to transfer to the kiln shop and improve its morale and productivity. Yŏnghŭi is high-spirited and diligent, quickly becoming the shop union chief. The shop, however, is in disarray. Here is an inventory of all the problems she faces:

- Workers on overnight guard duty are often asleep.
- The shop dormitory is unfinished due to a lack of building material.
- Work begins long after the start whistle is blown.
- Work is frequently interrupted because the workers are constantly joking with each other.
- Only three workers are working at the push cart when six are assigned.
- Upper management treats women workers as inferior.
- Production is at 30 percent of the plan, the worst in the country.
- The temperature of the kiln is unsteady, producing low-grade quicklime.
- Workers start leaving before the workday is over.
- Work absence is frequent.
- Records of clocking in and clocking out are irregularly kept.
- The shop does not have a party representative and thus lacks solidarity.
- The former union chief has run away after embezzling the supplies.
- Strict work rules are making the workers quit and earn a living at the roadside market.
- The vice shop chief is prone to cursing and yelling.

- Workers are quick to blame each other.
- The record keeper has been lying about certain workers' attendance records.
- The record keeper has been inflating the status of dormitory construction to the manager.
- The record keeper has been manipulating the workers to despise the shop.
- The record keeper collaborated with the former union chief in an embezzlement case.

As in other stories, in "Union Chief" the many problems at the kiln shop are resolved by the end of the story: the workers become more punctual, devoted, and trusting of each other, and it is revealed that the record keeper may have been carrying out sabotage and espionage. The point, however, is not simply to say that everything is resolved; rather, it is to illustrate the complex and contradictory world of the factory shop floor. Ideally, the shop floor is where loyal workers are engaged in the honorable activity of production—which is another way to say the shop floor is where the workers' labor is subsumed by the production regime, presumably without antagonism. But even in socialist realist fiction, the shop floor is far from an ideal place. It is a place of contention between what should be and what should not be. The shop floor is an expression of humanness: workers are often lazy; bosses are irritating; records are occasionally falsified; supplies are periodically low; and some workers do not like each other. "Union Chief" is a typical socialist realist story about heroic workers, but as the plot unfolds, a detailed picture of everyday work emerges.

The everyday happenings on the shop floor have their own rhythm, which cannot be mitigated into uniformity. The kiln shop workers' reasons for being late, being absent, or quitting are various. One worker, referred to as "Kidŏk's Mother," is repeatedly late, even though she lives nearby, because she has to do laundry before work. Another worker, Ch'unsil, is absent for a few days without notice because she is furious after the vice shop chief scolds her in front of a male worker. Yi Talsu is a heavy smoker, and one day he finds a scathing statement about his smoking habit on the notice board. Titled "A Math Problem for Comrade Yi Talsu," it reads: "Comrade Yi Talsu smokes forty-five cigarettes in an eight-hour working day. From eight hours, how many work hours are left after smoking forty-five cigarettes? Comrades, let every single one of us ask Comrade Yi Talsu for the answer."[44] Disgraced and angry, Talsu quits the factory a few days later. Here is a glimpse of the complex human effort to balance duty, enjoyment, dignity, and authority. It shows everyday work as a product of neither resistance nor domination but as a confluence of both and more.

Figure 4.4 shows images of people working during the period of the Ch'ŏllima Movement. They come from the documentary film *Charyŏk kaengsaeng ŭi chŏngsin* (The spirit of independent rebirth), made in the late 1990s during a time of great economic hardship to help the people endure and to keep them working by evoking the transformative era of the 1950s.[45] These images are from exemplary work sites. The top-left image is of Kangsŏn Steelworks in South P'yŏngan Province, the birthplace of the Ch'ŏllima Work Team Movement in 1959. The top-right image is of a small machine factory in Kyŏngsŏng County of North Hamgyŏng Province, which became famous for creating ingenious machine tools for railroad construction in the region. The bottom two images are of the nationwide project to expand irrigated farmland, which began at the end of 1958 once the cooperativization of agriculture was complete. The working conditions at these locations were better than at others, and the workers were highly mobilized and motivated. Nevertheless, it is not difficult to see that working at these sites was not easy. Work was repetitive and intense—two conditions that make it difficult to enjoy work. A normal workday for the furnace workers of Kangsŏn Steelworks entailed many hours of intense heat, mental focus, and physical exertion. To maintain this kind of work day in and day out for a number of years would have been a challenge. But the demand made of workers was even greater: consistent work attendance had to be attended by a consistent increase in productivity. Even the best workers pondered quitting or transferring. The majority of workers were inconsistent in attendance and production, as they rightly should have been in such an environment.

The repetitive and intense work environment was infused with meetings and propaganda, which were formal sources for motivation and ideological readiness. The team meeting was a space of self-criticism and resolution, but not everyone was willing to criticize himself or herself or others. Such a stance is found in the story "Union Chief." When Yŏnghŭi tells Yongsik, whose productivity has fallen low, to undergo self-criticism, Yongsik says, "Please, just spare me the self-criticism. I cannot stand it."[46] Self-criticism was a key device in the evaluation of workers, but it was often

Figure 4.4 Scenes from the documentary *Charyŏk kaengsaeng ŭi chŏngsin* (The spirit of independent rebirth).
Source: *Charyŏk kaengsaeng ŭi chŏngsin* (Seoul: Nambuk Munje Yŏn'guso, n.d. [c. late 1990s]).

a humiliating act. Visual propaganda took the shape primarily of banners hand drawn by the workers. Newspapers, posters, magazines, fiction, and poetry were not equally available everywhere. The top-right image of a machine factory in North Hamgyŏng in figure 4.4 is an example of the extent of propaganda at places far from the capital. The banner on the left states, "The Practice and Result of Comrade Kim Il Sung's On-Site Instruction to Boldly Think and Boldly Act." The banner on the right states, "Steel and Machine Are Kings of Industry," which was a popular slogan in the late 1950s. As in other state socialist countries, propaganda was an essential part of work in North Korea for its potential ideological effect. In fact, propaganda is one element that makes actual socialist work different from actual capitalist work. However, the socialist work setting was not constantly and comprehensively enveloped in propaganda. Propaganda was limited by geography (cooperatives and factories in remote areas received less of it) and resource availability. For instance, the most popular books saw 100,000 prints (as in labor hero Kil Hwaksil's memoir [1961]), but the number of prints for most books was much lower: the collection in which the story about the Sulfur Shop (Sŏ Ch'ŏng's essay "The Power of Will" [1957]) was included saw 10,000 prints.

A final remark to be made about the unevenness of work is based on the image on the bottom right in figure 4.4. In the documentary *The Spirit of Independent Rebirth*, the contraption shown is extolled as an example of workers' ingenuity. It is a hand-cranked conveyor belt made out of straw rope and unhewn timber. The documentary shows the conveyor belt in operation, moving dirt up the hill. In a place and time when motorized equipment was scarce, such a contraption was undoubtedly a testimony to workers' ingenuity and dedication, befitting the nationwide call for collective innovation. This wooden conveyor belt, however, was far from being a practical industrial tool. It likely took many hours to construct it, and it probably could not endure long hours of use. Its worth was in its birth, not in its use. Such was the predicament for the workers' own innovations at production sites.

Work was marked by unevenness—unevenness in the degree of workers' dedication, in the strength and spread of propaganda, and in productivity. The state's attempt at shaping and controlling work—from ethics to production—was incomplete. In the face of difficult work settings and meager material existence, while wanting a dignified life as well as comfort and enjoyment, the workers in their everyday space strove for happiness as practical beings and as proper citizens. The two ontological positions were sometimes antagonistic to each other. Everyday work can be immediately perceived as a contested area, as a place of neither resistance nor repression, as a place of constant negotiation between the state and community and between agency and ideology. What does such contestation further indicate? The everyday hints at the workings of social possibility. From the state's perspective, work was an object of ideological and political control implemented in the space of everyday life. But this very space was marked by unevenness that could not be fully systematized. The unyielding quality of everyday life—evident even in the heavily managed space of work—is also its possibility, the possibility of the everyday as a space of real change.

A World of Struggle: A Reading of
The Furnace Is Breathing

The blast furnace is simple and robust equipment. It melts iron ore, limestone, and coke. Heated air is blasted into the furnace at temperatures between 900 and 1,300°C (1,652–2,372°F) to melt the three ingredients into liquid metal, a process called smelting. The furnace itself does not melt because it is lined with firebrick, which has a melting point of higher than 2,000°C (3,632°F). Liquid metal is about 5 percent carbon and is cooled in a cast to make iron ingots, or pig iron. The term *pig iron* derives from the traditional casting process in which liquid metal, tapped from the furnace, runs into small ingot molds, giving an impression of piglets suckling on a sow. Owing to its high carbon content, pig iron is too brittle for industrial use, so it is further smelted to burn off the carbon and other impure elements. This step results in the production of steel, which has less than 2 percent carbon. Alloy elements of steel include chromium, manganese, and nickel, but the simplest form of steel is made up of iron and carbon.

The blast furnace is thus the first step in producing the most essential material for industrialization—steel. "If corn is the king of field crops," Kim Il Sung said, "then steel is the king of industry. Without steel, industry cannot develop, and the overall economy cannot move forward; even national defense cannot be well managed."[47] The use-value and exchange-value of iron and steel, as well as their symbolic value, were indeed great in postwar North Korea. (This was also true in other state socialist countries, for the progress of socialism was measured largely by its industries. In the Soviet Union, as Stephen Kotkin writes, "steel, as the basis of the state's power and identity, held a kind of magic aura."[48])

In principle, one role of heavy industry was to transform the means of production. This required producing machines that would produce other machines, a process in which iron and steel were indispensable. In 1960, North Korea produced 853,000 tons of pig iron and 641,000 tons of steel, which were 279 times and 127 times the amounts produced in 1946, respectively.[49] The export of metal was also a significant part of North Korea's economy because it was a straightforward way of generating foreign currency. By 1960, ferrous and nonferrous metals made up 43.7 percent of all exports from North Korea.[50] The products born from the belly of the blast furnace were undoubtedly important for the economy, so one emblem of North Korea's industrial transformation was the blast furnace. The leadership spoke about it; writers composed prose and poetry about it; and painters depicted it and its workers on canvas—for instance, Chŏng Kwanch'ŏl' painting of a furnace worker, *Yonghaegong* (Smelter), in which the worker's name, Mun Chaech'ŏl, is written on the lower left (figure 4.5).

Figure 4.5 Chŏng Kwanch'ŏl, *Yonghaegong* (Smelter), oil on canvas , dimensions unavailable, late 1950s.
Source: Chŏng Kwanch'ŏl, *Chŏng Kwanch'ŏl chakp'umjip.*

When the Korean War ended in the summer of 1953, none of the five blast furnaces existing in North Korea was in operation due to damage by bombing and lack of use. They had been built by Japanese enterprises during the colonial period. The two largest blast furnaces in North Korea were at Kim Ch'aek Iron and Steel Works in Ch'ŏngjin City of North Hamgyŏng Province.[51] Each furnace was capable of producing 175,000 tons of pig iron per year.[52] The other three blast furnaces were at Hwanghae Iron and Steel

Works, located in Hwangju County of North Hwanghae Province.[53] The furnaces at Hwanghae had a total capacity to produce 350,000 tons of pig iron a year.[54] The reconstruction of blast furnaces began soon after the war, but it was a slow process. The earliest to be rebuilt was one of the two furnaces at the Kim Ch'aek factory, completed in mid-1955. It took three more years to reconstruct the next blast furnace, and another one was repaired before the decade was over, bringing by 1960 the total number of blast furnaces in operation to three. The least-mentioned aspect of this situation was the assistance of German and Russian workers. In January 1954, highly trained workers from Germany and Russia were already at Hwanghae Steel, participating in the rebuilding of the Steel Manufacturing Shop, the Rolled Steel Shop, the Refractories Shop, and the Main Power Station.[55]

In 1956, North Korea produced 231,000 tons of pig iron.[56] All of it came from the lone furnace at the Kim Ch'aek factory (exceeding the furnace's production capacity). Kim Il Sung called this blast furnace the "only son" of North Korea's iron and steel industry. Thus, in early 1957, as the Five-Year Plan began with the goal of establishing the foundations of a state socialist economy, there was only one functioning blast furnace in the entire country. Its emblematic stature notwithstanding, the amount of pig iron it produced was not enough to meet the state's grand goals. The need to activate more blast furnaces was desperately felt by both the leadership and the workers engaged in reconstruction.

This predicament is the setting of the quintessential novel of the Ch'ŏllima Movement period: *Yonggwangno nŭn sumshinda* (The furnace is breathing), written by Yun Sejung and published in 1960.[57] The story begins in the year 1957, and the workers are in their fourth year at a site. They are the workers of the Reconstruction Department of a factory that remains unnamed, but the readers soon find out it must be based on Hwanghae Iron and Steel Works because the workers in the novel pledge to rebuild a blast furnace by May Day of 1958, just as the workers of Hwanghae factory did in real life. Their task is great—to make the factory fully operational before the end of the decade as part of the Five-Year Plan. They have already rebuilt the rolling mill, the Sheet Steel Shop, the Wire Shop, the power plant, the transport facilities, and the Machine-Manufacturing Shop. The factory is ready to transform pig iron into various forms of steel, but there is no pig iron because the blast furnace is still inoperative. The project of rebuilding the blast furnace is mired in conflicts between the

Figure 4.6 Kim Ch'aek Iron and Steel Works, 1990s.
Source: Chosŏn Hwabosa (Korean Pictorial Agency), *Kim Ilsŏng chusŏk kwa onŭl ŭi Chosŏn* (Premier Kim Il Sung and North Korea today) (Pyongyang: Oegukmun Chonghap Ch'ulp'ansa, 1993).

central planners, the department chief, Kim Il Sung's mandate, and the ordinary workers of the Reconstruction Department.

The Furnace Is Breathing presents a world of work filled with struggles among elements that in the ideal socialist state should not come into conflict with each other. What the novel shows is a working world vastly different from the one commonly thought to exist in state socialism, where one class claims dictatorship over others, where the leadership seems to have absolute power over the people, and where the economy is prescribed by a centralized plan. In the everyday workspace represented in the novel, the plan to rebuild the furnace is in constant conflict with both the workers and the factory's material situation. The implementation of the central plan entails persistent moments of anarchy—from procuring materials to installing parts—that cannot be predicted by the plan. In other words, the plan is carried out amid struggle.

As the novel opens, the equipment-installation team is falling behind on its spending goals. The team is not spending enough money on new parts, and the installation of new parts is occurring slowly. The chief of the Reconstruction Department, O Ilbyŏk, believes that the installation workers are working hard for the wrong reason: "For the next five days," Ilbyŏk says to the engineer of the installation team, Ri Sangbŏm, "make them go on shock-work mode. Why can't we spend the money we have? Also, starting tonight, do not allow them to collect scraps anymore."[58] Sangbŏm knows why his team is coming up short. Not enough shops are ready to be installed with new parts. Moreover, the central planning office has not provided them with detailed blueprints. The overall plan for reconstructing the factory is available, but the blueprints for each piece of equipment have yet to arrive. There is also a reason for the collection of scrap parts at night, which the chief sees as an unfocused act. The workers of the installation team are highly motivated people who have experienced colonialism and war. They are heeding the call by the party to build the blast furnace on their own, through innovation and prudence. Collecting scraps is an act mindful of this call: "A specific construction plan by the ministry has not been directed. The workers were restless. All their free time was spent on preparing for the furnace reconstruction. Even a single broken part could not be wasted! Let us save and collect! But the new chief O Ilbyŏk did not know the feelings of today's workers."[59] The postwar period gave rise to a mass culture of work centered on the notion of the infallible worker: once properly educated and motivated, ordinary workers were supposed to know what was best for the nation. (The ideological side of this notion was, of course, the precondition of subsumption of labor under the production regime.) The workers in their everyday work setting were active and productive in their own ways, often coming into conflict with other systems (such as the state plan) and upper managers.

The one entity the workers of the novel do not struggle against is Kim Il Sung. They are always united with him, even if this unity puts them in opposition to the system around them. Kim Il Sung makes an appearance in the novel (he appears frequently in North Korean literature), remembering the workers' faces and their life stories. When he visited the factory soon after the Five-Year Plan began, he addressed the workers individually and gave the following advice: "We should reuse whatever we can. If it can't be reused now, save it and use it later. When we reuse whatever we can, then planning gets easier and the speed of reconstruction increases. We can save materials and money."[60] And so the workers collect scraps. But given the factory's current situation, their following Kim Il Sung's advice is actually disturbing the monthly spending plan (by encouraging frugality) and constraining the development of blueprints for furnace reconstruction.

There are two ways to rebuild the blast furnace. The first is to import all new parts, including a larger, more advanced furnace, and assembling them at the site. The second is to recover the old furnace and expand it by using salvaged parts. The first method would take the least amount of time, but it would make all existing equipment obsolete, not to mention breaking the spirit of veteran workers. The second method would uphold Kim Il Sung's advice and galvanize the workers, but the technical skills required of the workers could be a challenge because in addition to rebuilding the furnace, the team would have to build a scale car, an air blower, and a winch. Furthermore, by choosing to rebuild the old furnace, the pledge to start operation by May Day of 1958 may be unfulfillable.

The chief planning engineer of the factory, Kim Tongsŏn, is sleeping at the office most nights, trying to come up with a solution to the dilemma. In desperation, he approaches the installation engineer, Ri Sangbŏm, with his problem. Sangbŏm soon assures him of the workers' capacity and determination to rebuild the old furnace: "Make the blueprints boldly. We will make adjustments as we go. I can say this confidently, from the experience of all the workers. The reconstruction work lies in front of us. Whether it can be done or not rests in our hands now, so boldly make the blueprints."[61] Encouraged by Sangbŏm's words, Tongsŏn convinces the planners to proceed with the project of recovering the old furnace.

As a representation of the workers' spirit and as a prescription of socialist life, the story of how the final blueprint is made is in line with socialist realism, especially in the depiction of the workers taking on the challenge on their own, if in a headlong manner. However, considering that the blast furnace is one of the most symbolic and realistically important means of industrial development, the story's depiction of how the plan is made ultimately compromises the central-planning system. The plan is a sacred feature of socialism: the planned economy is one monumental distinction between the socialist system and the capitalist system. The plan is the result of a negotiated calculation of need, capacity, and growth—the negotiations taking place between the specialists of the central planning board and the specialists of the production site. A plan should not be developed spontaneously based on the workers' resolve and pride, no matter how high their spirit is. At the same time, the novel shows the workers' participation in the planning process, especially during moments of dilemma when they make decisions on the ground. The workers' spontaneous participation is an inadvertent recognition of the inherent anarchy of the plan, the anarchy arising from the gap between the knowledge of central planners and the will of workers. The anarchy must be concealed, however, and this is done through the portrayal of the workers' unified spirit.

The workers' strong-willed attitude is, for instance, demonstrated in the assembling of the air blower, a crucial machine in the blast furnace system (it "blasts" air into the furnace). The planners have decided to purchase a new air blower from overseas but are allowing the workers to recover the existing blower until the new blower arrives, the date of which unknown. Kim Chinyŏng, who is in charge of the recovery, is slighted twice: first by a visiting foreign engineer who is shocked to learn that Chinyŏng has not received university training and second by the chief, O Ilbyŏk, who does not allocate extra workers to help Chinyŏng. Chinyŏng thinks to himself: "'I will accomplish it alone. If you want to help me, then help me. If you don't, then don't. Do whatever you wish.'"[62] He and his fellow workers mobilize themselves and rebuild the air blower during their spare time.

After many tribulations—including torrential rain, which almost knocks down the furnace, and a spy who tries to convince the workers that the US military is returning to Korea to occupy the entire peninsula—the workers complete the reconstruction of the blast furnace system ahead of the promised date, May Day 1958. Their self-determination is heavily stressed at the end of the novel: "The working class who built the blast furnace—they are ordinary workers. Ordinary workers and ordinary people! They are the owners of the furnace. They are ordinary Korean workers existing in ordinary settings everywhere." Finally, "the furnace is breathing. . . . The furnace rises and breathes by May Day, as *he* had wished. Some engineers and specialists had shaken their heads, saying it would be difficult, but the workers and technicians, loyal to the leader, pulverized the old myth with their burning passion."[63]

The novel is ultimately about the unstoppable force of history, which takes the human form of the worker. In terms of historical materialism, the workers are members of the proletarian class, but in North Korea the worker's proletarian identity is weak. Instead, the worker is identified as a member of the masses, *taejung*, which also includes farmers, office workers, and students. Class distinction among the masses is not important: they are generally poor and simple people with a shared experience of loss from colonialism and the war. It is the masses who play a central role in North Korea's socialist construction. Their unity is a negative identity based not on what they have but on what they lack, which is expressed as poverty and hardship. The negative identity of their unity conceals the antagonism

Figure 4.7 Illustration of the final scene in the novel *The Furnace Is Breathing*.
Source: Yun Sejung, *Yonggwangno nŭn sumshinda* (Pyongyang: Munye Ch'ulp'ansa, 1960).

among the masses, and so the North Korean people appear harmonious and conflict free.

What Yun Sejung's novel shows, above all, is the contentious working world beneath the surface of the apparently ideal socialist state. The workers struggle against many elements (including inclement weather and self-doubt), but the most critical target of struggle is the socialist system itself. In portraying the undying spirit of the masses, the novel reveals the reality of constant struggles between the masses and the state system in North Korea, with the system represented in the novel by the planning board and its elite specialists. The workers come into conflict with the planning board throughout the novel: they feel as if the planners deny the wisdom of veteran workers and reject the possibilities of the masses' own innovations. The reconstruction workers persistently go against the plan; the only directive they adhere to comes from Kim Il Sung. Moreover, the struggle of the masses takes place in the everyday, where the workers rely on individual experience, spontaneous innovations, and solidarity among themselves. The continuous struggle between the masses and the socialist system is both how the masses retain their sense of self-determination and how the socialist system is in the end reproduced.

Life in Labor, Labor in Life

In late summer of 1961, a few weeks before the Fourth Congress of the Korean Workers' Party (September 11–18), the chief of the Machine Shop at Tŏkch'ŏn Automobile Factory was approached by a complaining apprentice.[64] The apprentice had been temporarily stationed at a steel-plate machine normally handled by Kim Hakjun, who had gone home for vacation a few days earlier. But the apprentice wanted a new station because he was not able to gain any work time at the current station: Kim Hakjun was back at that machine, the apprentice said. Indeed, the shop chief found Hakjun working away even though the record book indicated that he was supposed to be on vacation. Hakjun had cut his vacation short upon hearing that the factory was organizing a shock-work team for the Fourth Party Congress. The shop chief was perplexed.

SHOP CHIEF: What about your vacation time?
HAKJUN: I will spend it here.

SHOP CHIEF: Spend it here? This is not a vacation. This isn't allowed.

HAKJUN: What do you mean it's not allowed? The workers at Pyongyang and Pukch'ang factories are foregoing their vacation and instead working to increase production. As owners of this factory, why can't we?

SHOP CHIEF: Then let's postpone your vacation. You can start your regular shift tomorrow.[65]

The next day the shop chief noticed that although Kim Hakjun was back at work, his time card was not punched. His status was still "on vacation."

The account of Kim Hakjun is about the best workers of the period, those who aspired to become labor heroes. Most workers, in contrast, needed rest from the intense and repetitive work. Guaranteed paid vacation, after all, was part of North Korea's progressive labor laws, of which the workers were proud. In practice, all leisure time—vacations, weekends, after-work hours, and holidays—was potential free labor time, especially for large public projects such as land expansion. Daily life was filled with all types of work besides regular wage work—for example, road construction work, party organization work, and weekend volunteer work, not to mention the patriarchal practice of reserving household work for women. Individuals who participated in diverse types of work were awarded, and those who did minimal work were targets of criticism and conversion (a topic discussed in the next section). The focus here is the collapsing divide between life and labor in the space of the everyday. On the one hand, the collapse is about the infiltration of work into the private sphere of home life. On the other hand, it is about the existence of multiple structures of domination—not only work but also private structures such as marriage. The *formal* collapse in the division of life and labor is easily observable, as in the case of Kim Hakjun, but the detection of the *real* collapse of the division between life and labor requires a dialectical critique of everyday life.

The analysis here can start with the film *Sinhonbubu* (The newlyweds).[66] Released in 1955 during the heady period of postwar reconstruction, *The Newlyweds* is a movie that follows the codes of socialist realism, but through its plot and characters it offers insight into postwar everyday life. The film presents the concrete elements of the everyday as mode of production as well as the ambivalent elements of the everyday as multiple structures of domination—in this case, the state, work, and marriage. The story develops around a newly married couple—Ŭnsil, the wife, and Yŏngch'ŏl, the husband. The Korean War has recently ended, and the entire country is fervent with the mission of reconstruction: the ground is dug, buildings are rising, and machines never stop running. The backdrop is the city of Pyongyang. A few years after the war, the city shows that only little remains of the destruction. The urban landscape is covered with plant life, and the Taedong and Pot'ong Rivers winding through the city are yet to be banked with concrete; Pyongyang in the film is strikingly different from what it would look like in just ten years.[67]

Upon marriage, Ŭnsil quits her job as a machinist at the local railroad machine factory, where train parts are inspected and replaced, to devote herself to household work, not an unusual career path for North Korean women at the time. Yŏngch'ŏl is a motivated train engineer, driving his train farther and faster than anyone else on the team. His ambition to be the best engineer is equally matched by his insistence on Ŭnsil staying at home. Although she is ashamed for "not carrying a single brick," they are relatively happy; their affection for each other hides the guilt they feel. Ŭnsil feels guilty for being idle while her fellow women workers participate in the grand plan of socialist construction, and Yŏngch'ŏl feels guilty for being tyrannical in keeping Ŭnsil, formerly an exemplary worker at the factory, at home.

The everyday activities of maintaining their house and preparing meals keep Ŭnsil's guilt from affecting her life, and Yŏngch'ŏl's guilt is suppressed through long hours of work and his desire to become the best train engineer in the country. However, these are temporary shields; the everyday is both dormant and volatile. The eruption finally occurs in a mundane setting. They go shopping for face powder at Central Department Store Number Two. It is the weekend, and the department store is filled with shoppers like Ŭnsil and Yŏngch'ŏl. On their return home, they pass by a construction site lively with women and men at work. One woman worker notices Ŭnsil and runs toward her. She is Ŭnsil's friend Aesŏng, and she is working at the construction site together with her husband: "Everyone would ridicule me if I ran away from the factory just because I got married," she tells Ŭnsil. The encounter with Aesŏng is the moment of eruption, and an argument ensues between Ŭnsil and Yŏngch'ŏl about Ŭnsil's desire to return to work:

ŬNSIL: Two or five years from now, you will be proud of yourself. But how can I welcome such happiness when I have not carried a single brick?

YŏNGCH'ŏL: Don't you think helping me is like working *with* me?

ŬNSIL: It won't be as honest as actually working.

YŏNGCH'ŏL: What's more important? My work for the state or your wish to feel proud?

ŬNSIL: Both are important . . .

YŏNGCH'ŏL: If we both work, then our home will become a mess.

ŬNSIL: If we both work, our home will get better, not worse.

YŏNGCH'ŏL: You still don't know how we men feel. . . .

ŬNSIL: Oh, I think I do. You want to chain us to the house, don't you?

YŏNGCH'ŏL: Damn it! Women just don't want to stay inside anymore!

ŬNSIL: That's true, too, but both are not right.

YŏNGCH'ŏL: That's enough. Let's not talk about these things ever again.

Multiple forces of domination can be discerned in this conversation. Yŏngch'ŏl's chauvinistic language provides a glimpse of the everyday space of marriage that reproduces the condition of male domination: a woman's ambition—Ŭnsil's desire to partake in the national project—is seen as merely a "wish to feel proud." The great enthusiasm generated by the reconstruction efforts seems to lose its grip in this space, and what is exposed is the ideology of patriarchy packaged as men's authentic emotions ("you still don't know how we men feel"). Everyday life of the household indeed offers a partial shield from the direct control of the production regime. It was Ŭnsil's choice to leave the workplace and devote herself to household work, however frowned upon such a choice is. And throughout the film, no incidence of coercion occurs to bring her back to work. This shield, however, is partial because being a good worker begins with being a good family member (which is an ethical formula recognized globally, from industrial capitalism to the Ch'ŏllima Movement). In addition to household work, Ŭnsil's domestic occupation has the function of keeping Yŏngch'ŏl happy, healthy, and motivated to ensure that he can keep on working. The extension of work ideology into the private domain of the household is captured in Yŏngch'ŏl's words: "Helping me is like working *with* me."

The household created by Ŭnsil and Yŏngch'ŏl is a space of control through patriarchy packaged in the form of tradition, the defining method of which is the subordination of women. Conceptually speaking, as one leaves the factory structure of domination, one enters the household structure of domination, and both structures share the everyday as a concrete space of manifestation. This structural situation is identical for Ŭnsil and Yŏngch'ŏl, but the effect on the individual is different: Yŏngch'ŏl may be bossed around at work, but once he is at home, the system of patriarchy provides him with authority; for Ŭnsil, both work and home demand subordination. The style of subordination is warm and even loving. In the dialogue given earlier, Yŏngch'ŏl is caring and smiling when he says, "That's enough. Let's not talk about these things ever again." At the end of the movie, the guilt of not being productive as demanded by the state compels Ŭnsil to return to work. Her biggest barrier is her husband: the everyday space of marriage in which her husband's patriarchal tendency is supported by her own wish to create a happy home. Her announcement of her decision to return to work is strange; it sounds strong in its tone yet is submissive in its message: "I'm going back to the factory. I want to stand proudly in front of you. . . . There is something missing in our love. . . . I've been circling inside this room, playing house, as if this is the extent of our happiness, while so much is happening outside. . . . Your attitude toward me is wrong. You treat me like a plaything. . . . I can be better at household work while I work at the factory. . . . I must return to the factory. I must help you the right way." Ŭnsil's decision to return to work, which opposes her husband's wish, shows a level of self-determination befitting the national call of the period. At the same time, however, her decision acknowledges and reinforces her subordinated position: her work of fixing machine parts is only to "help" Yŏngch'ŏl's work of driving the train built with those parts. The ambivalence regarding Ŭnsil's subjectivity is demonstrated toward the end of the film when she has prepared dinner after returning home from work and is happily waiting for her husband. The condition of double subordination—at work under the state's call to produce and at home under the traditional institution of marriage—is portrayed as an ideal family situation ("I can be better at household work while I work at the factory").

The ambivalence regarding Ŭnsil's subjectivity is not connected to a flaw in her character but to the general human condition in the situation of multiple dominating structures. Ambivalence enables the subject to maintain a sense of agency within each structure of domination: it prevents the fixation of the subject to any one structure, as much as that structure attempts to do so (in the name of a national plan, for instance). This prevention occurs at the level of the everyday, where one must play various roles and appropriate various ideological forces. The everyday is thus a space where multiple structures of domination exist, but this multiplicity also indicates that no one structure has complete control.

Life and labor exhibit dominating structures with blurred boundaries. What can be noticed in *The Newlyweds* is, first, that the everyday space of multiple structures of domination makes life all the more difficult, especially for women, who often face a condition of double subordination, as wage workers under the production regime and as domestic workers

Figure 4.8 Scenes from *Sinhonbubui* (The newlyweds).
Source: Yun Ryonggyu, dir., *Sinhonbubu* (Pyongyang: Chosŏn Kungnip Yŏnghwa Chwalyŏngso, 1955).

performing unpaid labor determined by patriarchy in the guise of tradition. In a place like North Korea (which is to say in most industrializing or industrialized countries of the twentieth century), women were asked to be wageworkers while at the same time to uphold the traditional order of patriarchy. To be sure, this traditional order applied to men as well—to work hard during the day and then to come home to be a caring husband and father—but men's contribution to household work was regulated by convenience. For women, the double work duty was an obligation for the purpose of establishing an exemplary workplace and a worthy home. Second, in this repressive everyday space, there emerges a remarkable aspect of subjectivity: ambivalence. While playing the assigned roles—worker, wife, husband—the person continues to be subjectively ambivalent. In the formally repressive situation created by the production regime and the patriarchal household, Ǔnsil switches her role from worker to wife and back. The ambivalent subject persists to impart a sense of agency: ambivalence signals possibilities. Multiple forces of domination exist in the everyday, but the subject also remains open in the face of this domination. The structures of domination that must rely on the everyday for their implementation are always partially configured. The everyday is capable of destructuring domination as a space of both its realization and its negation.

I Will Trouble You No More: Conversion and the Ideology of Work

Chang Poil was in the postwar period the most famous worker at the Kǔmsong Agricultural Cooperative of Sangwǒn County in South P'yǒngan Province. Kim Il Sung had praised Poil for convincing a family member to change her ways: "What a wonderful deed," Kim said, "to educate [kyoyang] and change [kaejo] one's mother, as she has done. . . . This comrade has educated and converted a woman who was once a member of the leisured class."[68] Poil was married and lived in a village nearby her mother's village; the two villages belonged to the same agricultural cooperative. One day Poil discovered that her mother was neglecting work at the cooperative and collecting and selling chestnuts at the local market to bring home additional income.[69] She went to her mother's house and waited. Upon seeing her mother with a basket of chestnuts, she scolded her for being selfish at a moment when everyone was working at the cooperative. The mother's reply was unexpected: "You should only be as diligent as I am. Women need to know how to care for the household. Contributing to the household by selling these things is a good deed. . . . I raised you preciously, but now you treat me like a stranger."[70]

Poil regretted her conduct and decided the solution would be to honor her mother, listen to her, and help her to see on her own the importance of collective labor. Her mother, Poil realized, still held onto the outlook she had developed in the past, when she was poor and often had to beg to make ends meet. For her mother, the world was precarious, and a person had to be resourceful—to be able to collect and sell chestnuts, if need be. There was also the pain of losing her son, Poil's older brother, from illness, the treatment for which was limited by the family's poverty. Gradually, with this better understanding, Poil was able to change her mother's attitude, to "convert" her so she could see the benefit the cooperative had on each household. The mother, the essay concluded, went up to the work team leader and apologized a "hundred times for her behavior" and soon became a worker who was "first to arrive and last to leave," attaining the highest marks on her team.[71]

An important part of the socialist everyday was the conversion of people from bad workers to good workers. No one was *born* a "backward element," and such a thought entailed a duty to convert those who did not measure up to socialist standards of collective work and party-mindedness. The conversion began with people closest to oneself—siblings, friends, and parents. As in the case of Poil, conversion was often a violent act of rejecting the other person's essential features. A resourceful mother who had endured great hardship to bring up a family was, in the eye of the state, a backward element. The identity of such a mother had to be destroyed so that a new mother—a socialist mother—could be born. Poil's mother became a worker whose identity was now defined by the ability to create surplus as part of a great collective means of production, where individual identity fades away.

In the postwar years, the notion of conversion would find an official, discursive foothold, as in *The Ch'ŏllima Riders Handbook* published in 1963. It lists five features of the Communist disposition: first, the sense of responsibility for the revolution; second, the collective spirit of embracing all human beings; third, the love for labor; fourth, patriotism and internationalism for the happiness of all workers; and fifth, humanness (*in'gansŏng*) and culture-mindedness oriented toward sacrifice and morality among the people.[72] These features suggest that the Communist disposition, especially for exemplary Ch'ŏllima Riders, was about making everyone *possess* the Communist disposition. Ch'ŏllima Riders, the handbook states, "believe in and embrace the people and must sincerely educate and pull up those who are falling off the path." The technique of pulling up those "falling off the path" was not didacticism but everydayness: "everyday attention to their life, health, and happy future."[73] The handbook provides a real example of everyday technique: a worker at the Pyongyang Train Station named Kim Sinsuk cares for a wounded veteran, Ri Chaesu, even though it is not her job. The veteran has come to the city to receive an overnight treatment, and when his treatment is finished in the morning, Kim Sinsuk escorts him all the way to his hometown, even after having worked the night shift at the station. The textbook asks, What enables her to act in such a way? It is her "overflowing humanness, which cherishes human beings and attempts to give happiness to life."[74] The foundation of conversion was thus everyday humanness, a natural concern for another person.

Perhaps no one was a better model of the practice of conversion and everyday humanness than the legendary labor hero Kil Hwaksil (also, there could not be a better name for someone who served as such a model than "Hwaksil," which means "certainty").[75] A textile worker at Pyongyang Spinning Factory since her teen years, she became a work team leader in October 1958 at the age of twenty-one.[76] Kil Hwaksil was a gifted leader, and within three years she made a mark in history by leading three separate teams to earn the title "Ch'ŏllima Work Team," with two teams earning the title twice. She possessed the ability not only to increase production but also to transform the team members' lives. Kil Hwaksil was a national sensation; Kim Il Sung often mentioned her name (they met several times during this period). Her experience as a work team leader was quickly turned into a book, *Ch'ŏllima chagŏpbanjang ŭi sugi* (A memoir of a Ch'ŏllima Work Team leader), printed in August 1961.[77] It saw 100,000 prints, a quantity reserved only for truly worthy books, as judged by the state. She was twenty-four years old when the memoir was published. It is essentially about the conversion of rowdy workers into model workers through self-realization and acceptance of the call of the party and the leader. Various individuals are encountered in the memoir, each with a special talent or experience, all of whom become ideal socialist workers under Kil Hwaksil's management.

In one entry in the memoir, Hwaksil is concerned about an underperforming worker named Chŏn Ch'aewŏl. It is May 1959, and her work team, Work Team Number Four, has decided to participate in the Ch'ŏllima Work Team Movement sweeping the nation, but they are not yet making any strides in production. The nationwide movement began in March, initiated by Chin Ŭngwŏn's smelting team at Kangsŏn Steelworks. Hwaksil's forty-eight-member team is made up of young women. Their performance is in constant fluctuation, suffering from, as Hwaksil thinks, a "tendency to work only when told to work and a lack of collective awareness." Ch'aewŏl is such a worker:

> Comrade Ch'aewŏl was not good at her job, and her passion for team projects was not high. She was frequently absent and usually did not meet the production quota. She was not comfortable among the comrades. In daily life and at work, her spirit and patience for service were insufficient. However, she sang very well. . . . When we would walk in the factory garden or along Taedong River, she sang almost unconsciously . . . with a fine voice. When she sang, she became cheerful and got along with other comrades.[78]

Hwaksil's plan for transforming Ch'aewŏl into a better worker is to use her singing talent. To encourage Ch'aewŏl to be passionate about collective work, Hwaksil assigns her the task of leading the team choir. Reluctant at first, Ch'aewŏl, a gifted singer, soon becomes a competent choir director and at the same time a responsible worker. As Hwaksil recalls, Ch'aewŏl learns about the importance of collective work through the choir: "She felt firsthand how unfortunate it is when a person acts selfishly or falls behind in a collective setting."[79] In Hwaksil's view, Ch'aewŏl's passion for the choir expanded to work and gradually made collective work enjoyable for Ch'aewŏl, changing her into a leader of the choir as well as a leader in production. In the everyday space, the ethical force of work merges with the passion for singing. "As the days passed," Hwaksil writes, "our daily life became overflowing with song, dance, and innovation. Labor became happiness, and song became life."[80] In the process of converting Ch'aewŏl into a model worker, Hwaksil, too, changes: she becomes a small tyrant who uses another individual's passion and talent as instruments of surplus

Figure 4.9 Legendary labor hero Kil Hwaksil at work. Still from the documentary *The Spirit of Independent Rebirth*.
Source: *Charyŏk kaengsaeng ŭi chŏngsin.*

production. Singing is Ch'aewŏl's true calling, and her passion for it makes her happy and sociable, but instead of helping Ch'aewŏl develop her passion, Hwaksil renders singing into a device of control. Rather than freeing her, singing further binds Ch'aewŏl to the regime of production. Hwaksil's tyranny is not so much the demand of hard work from her team members but the enforcement of the link between individual passion and the state interest of surplus production.

Another worker, Kim Kyŏngja, goes through a similar transformation, according to the memoir. In Kyŏngja's case, a much fuller ideological picture emerges. Kyŏngja was a brilliant student and a good person, staying at the top of her class and always willing to help other people. Kyŏngja's life, however, turned for the worse when she discovered while in middle school that she is in fact an orphan, raised by an aunt whom she had believed to be her biological mother. Now at the age of eighteen Kyŏngja is a wayward worker on Hwaksil's team. She is prone to skipping work, leaving her workstation unattended, and running away from the factory.

The nadir of Kyŏngja's wayward behavior—and the starting point of her transformation—is when she steals a coworker's satin skirt and runs away from the factory. A week later she is found at a department store, disheveled and staring at a display. "I cannot go back to the factory . . . please just leave me as I am," she says to Hwaksil and others who find her. Despite these issues, Hwaksil convinces her coworkers that Kyŏngja's problems stem from not having been loved, which can be resolved through love from comrades. Hwaksil even volunteers to share a bed with Kyŏngja, which enables Kyŏngja to live at the factory. Kyŏngja comes around after realizing she has been hurting not just herself but also the people around her. At one point, Hwaksil tells her, "When people scorn you, and when you don't fulfill your duties, have you thought about how sad our premier would be?" Through work and under the care of her team, Kyŏngja gradually finds fulfillment and recognition. Hwaksil relieves her of duty at the spinning machine and places her in the media team, where she thrives as a correspondent for the factory newspaper. She tells Hwaksil in the end, "Now I don't think I can live away from my comrades. I will trouble you no more."[81]

Kyŏngja's problems—acting carelessly, running away, and stealing—are resolved through the ideological function of work. This resolution, however, entails, first, the misrecognition of Kyŏngja's troubles as originating from a lack of love and, second, the satisfaction of that lack with the sense of fulfillment that is supposed to come from collective labor. The sense of fulfillment masks the hegemonic workings of the production regime in which Hwaksil and other team members participate, willingly or not. Kyŏngja's behavioral dysfunction is related to deep psychological troubles. However, the real trauma is not the fact that she is an orphan, for she has been surrounded by people who love her, including her aunt. Her loneliness and dysfunction are not caused by orphanhood but rather by the fundamental human condition of alienation, the emptiness of any meaning, which has come close to Kyŏngja's consciousness (but never actually surfaces)—a condition initiated by the shock of discovering her orphanhood. Hence, what is consciously recognized is not the condition of alienation but alienation's potential arrival—recognized in language as a lack of love. It is crucial to note that the real alienation of nonsymbolic emptiness is not consciously recognized but rather is misrecognized as a lack of love; the misrecognition is thus necessary for the proper functioning of the symbolic order, not to mention for the health of the individual.

What makes misrecognition possible? It is ideology. In Kyŏngja's case, it is the ideology of work, with its dual function of, first, misrecognizing the origin of trauma as a lack of love and, second, satisfying that lack with a sense of fulfillment arising from collective labor. The hegemony of the production regime is masked in the process. But how does the dual ideological function of misrecognition and satisfaction actually lead a person to work, to enable the person to physically go onto the shop floor and produce? This is a question regarding the ideological process of moving from misrecognition to satisfaction. Before Kyŏngja reaches the stage of actual labor exertion, under the care of her fellow comrades, the solution to her problems begins with guilt—the guilt produced from avoiding the call of the nation and the leader ("Have you thought about how sad our premier would be?"). Guilt has the important role of designating an object that will alleviate the guilt, which in this case is labor. In this sense, guilt is essentially the same as desire in relation to the object. Labor becomes the object *and* the cause of both guilt and desire. Labor is the object toward which desire sets its course, and at the same time labor is the cause of that desire. As ideology, labor is more than a means of production; it is the object-cause of desire hiding the workings of power. The object-cause nature of labor prevents the complete satisfaction of desire. Like its ultimate product—surplus—labor should not have a limit (there's always more work to be done!). Labor in real life is a finite human activity with physical limitations, but as an ideology it must detach itself from any limitations. (Labor as an ideological form is a prime example of Lacan's *objet petit a*—the object-cause of desire that has broken away from the subject, around which desire moves without clinging to it.[82]) The Ch'ŏllima Movement, with its feature of never-ending work, is thus precisely about labor as an object-cause of desire. Thus, one conclusion is that the ultimate aim of the ideology of work is the desire to work.

The underperformance or failure of two women, Ch'aewŏl and Kyŏngja, as proper workers reveals another dimension of everyday life in postwar North Korea. For every Hwaksil, there were hundreds of Ch'aewŏls and Kyŏngjas who belonged to the middle section of the workforce demographic, the area of the ordinary. And it was not workers like Hwaksil but ordinary workers who actually performed the jobs and produced surplus for the national economy. The practice of conversion was a crucial but overwhelming task of the production regime. Its emphasis on the humanistic approach (through passion, love, and comradeship) made conversion one of many noncoercive methods of creating a more productive work-force. Like other noncoercive ways, conversion took place in the everyday space of work and leisure (through conducting choir practice, by sharing a bed). And as in other hegemonic systems, in the socialist state conversion based on humanism was an ideological process, with the ultimate aim of creating the desire for work, the desire that can never be satisfied. The desire for work designates labor as an object as well as the cause, and the double structure of object-cause makes full arrival at the object impossible. The ideological aim of creating the desire for work signals the impossibility of that desire's full realization.

The relationship between the everyday and state power is asymptotic. The two do not converge, and yet they depend on each other for their continuation. Just as much as state power manipulates the everyday for the purpose of meeting its needs (extracting surplus, political monopoly, ideological education), the people appropriate state power for survival and happiness. What is this asymptote? As an aspect of reality, the everyday is represented and mediated by language and practice—two expressions always entailing moments of ideological workings of power, whether it is state politics, the production regime, or patriarchy disguised as tradition. In such a situation, agency is a thorny problem: it does not exist in and of itself but as practice within structures of power. The novel *The Furnace Is Breathing* is about the complexity of agency in relation to the state. Dedicated workers such as Ri Sangbŏm struggle with other workers over planning, finance, and materials to build the blast furnace. They undoubtedly struggle in the name of the nation and the leader, but the process involves choices and struggles that have genuine consequences to their lives. In a world where the plan and command should reign supreme, the novel instead shows an everyday reality where historical actors contend for choices. To be sure, their struggles are not outright resistance against the system. The question of agency is not about resistance or freedom but about choices and actions within a subjugating system, which have real consequences in life.

However much the North Korean state wanted to portray its citizen workers as potential labor heroes, the vast majority of wageworkers did not quietly submit to the demands of modern industrialism. Within the fervor of socialist transformation, they were simultaneously malleable and obstinate; sometimes they were lazy, full of complaints, drunk, and troubled by living—in a word, normal. The rhythm of life was sometimes in line with and sometimes in opposition to the demands of the state. What determined this rhythm was a confluence of state power and the quest for happiness. The terrain of everyday work presented in this chapter makes understanding the everyday no less difficult, but it does point to moments of possibility. Whether successful or not, the everyday was a space of possibility for both the production regime and the communal life of workers. State projects such as mass movements were possible only through their translation into everyday activity, while the everyday space was where the workers' struggles and choices took on meaning and led to real consequences.

CHAPTER 5

Vinalon City

Industrialism as Socialist Everyday Life

At one end, raw, telluric matter, at the other, the finished, human object; and between these two extremes, nothing; nothing but a transit, hardly watched over by an attendant in a cloth cap, half-god, half robot.

—ROLAND BARTHES, *MYTHOLOGIES*

On the night of April 1, 1961, a spring snowstorm blew into Hamhŭng. All outdoor construction was ordered to be halted, but the workers of Ri Hŭisang's construction team could not stop now, not when they had only 5 more meters go to complete a 40-meter (130-foot) smokestack.[1] The smokestack would be a vital part of the new Vinalon Factory, funneling away the toxic gas produced when making the compound polyvinyl alcohol, the fiber form of which is *pinallon* (vinalon). The ten-person construction team, calling themselves the Phoenix Shock Troop, had been working furiously for two weeks, and with only 5 meters left they were not about to stop because of a snowstorm.[2] Earlier that day, Kim Il Sung had visited the factory, for the second time since construction had begun in early June the previous year. After having watched from the unfinished smokestack Kim Il Sung touring the factory grounds, Hŭisang's team resolved to "not come down until a red flag is flying from the top."[3] The night was so cold their clothing froze and light bulbs burst, and it was so windy molding plates blew away.[4] But the concrete continued to flow, and when the sun arose the next day, a red flag flew from the top. The 40-meter smokestack was built by hand in thirteen days.

The Vinalon Factory (officially called the February Eighth Vinalon Factory Complex) was where the revolutionary elements of North Korea's state-led socialism came together to produce extraordinary results, the construction being completed in just fourteen months. As the Five-Year Plan wound down, as the state nationalized all industries and farmland, and as the Ch'ŏllima Work Team Movement swept the across the land, the Vinalon Factory came to symbolize the new dawn of socialist economic progress determined largely by industrialization. The completion of the factory was part of the birth of an industrial narrative in postwar North Korea, a narrative forging a unity between socialist revolution, national independence, and productivity in factory work.

The most extraordinary element was vinalon itself: a purely Korean product produced in a factory built from the toils of Korean workers. "Vinalon" was the name given in North Korea to the synthetic fiber spun from the common chemical compound polyvinyl alcohol. The first successful production of vinalon was carried out by a research team at Japan's Kyoto (then Imperial) University in 1939, as the Japanese Empire waged war in China. A principal member of this team was a Korean chemist, Ri Sŭnggi. In 1950, as the Korean War broke out, Ri Sŭnggi was recruited by North Korea, where he became a national hero as the inventor of vinalon. Located in Hamhŭng City of South Hamgyŏng Province, the factory, too, had colonial origins. Built in 1936, it was a fertilizer factory owned by Nihon Chisso, the largest Japanese chemical company and one of the largest investors and builders in colonial Korea. Furthermore, Hamhŭng was the location of post–Korean War reconstruction efforts led by East Germany.

The history of vinalon is thus a confluence of at least five historical trajectories. The first was the colonial industrial system driven by market-imperial motives of profit and resources from the colonies. The second was the merger of science and technology with Japan's imperial discourse and practice, which, as Hiromi Mizuno writes, unified and controlled research programs toward a new order of "science–technology" in the empire.[5] The third was the postliberation nationalist ideology of state building, in which the recruitment of scientists and engineers, especially from South Korea, became an important mission of the young socialist state. The fourth was the dynamics of multinational postwar reconstruction, which saw the state socialist countries of eastern Europe and China leading and assisting the infrastructural recovery of major cities of North Korea. And the fifth was the command over production and politics by Kim Il Sung and his faction, eliminating competing political groups and erasing the truly international history of North Korea's beginnings. Vinalon City, as the immense factory was called, was a transnational object par excellence, but at the same time it was immutably localized for ordinary North Korean people, replete with work heroes who achieved superhuman levels of productivity.

This chapter is primarily about the history of the factory's construction and the function of vinalon in relation to the everyday reality of postwar North Korea. The everyday in this relationship is the concept and space where practice and ideology meet. The ideological force of vinalon is sustained in everyday life as a concrete object—produced by the workers and worn by the public. Workers such as Ri Hŭisang and his team, who built the factory and labored within it, emerge in the everyday as dialectical beings who through their extraordinary acts anticipate the negation of the planned system from which they are born. The labor hero and vinalon are essentially indeterminate in their function. The very moment the extraordinary worker represents the ideal socialist being is also the moment of the breakdown of the central plan, which must depend on individual workers' spontaneous acts. Similarly, vinalon is both the object of labor and its cause, supporting the ideology of work, whose aim is not so much the satisfaction of need but the reproduction of work itself. The ambiguity of their function is precisely what Michael Burawoy sees as the ideological effect of the industrial labor process generating the "complicity of workers in their own subordination."[6] Ambiguity is thus not only an abstract characteristic but a concrete practice embedded in the everyday: ambiguity as practice upholding a certain ideological activity—in this case, industrial work.[7]

Turning labor power and its products into ideological means for the regeneration of labor power, the only real source of surplus, was, of course, a worldwide phenomenon highlighted by industrialism in its global scale since the nineteenth century. Factories analogous to the Vinalon Factory existed in cities throughout the world—from Magnitogorsk in the Soviet Union and Anshan in China to Gary, Indiana, in the United States and Pohang in South Korea—all symbolizing the industrial might of their times. North Korea's attempt at controlling work was therefore part of the code of industrialism that overwhelmed the entire modern world. Regardless of how surplus was appropriated (by the state in state socialist countries or by private domains in existing capitalist countries), the principle method of producing surplus was the same. Industrial work was the universal ground on which North Korea's particular style of work culture exerted its hegemonic force. The critique of industrialism is thus how the particular analysis of vinalon is brought into the general critique of modernity. As such, in this chapter, the critique is aimed both at the particular historical condition of postwar North Korea, from which much of its current authoritarian qualities are born, and at the universal condition of industrialism, which has ordered a great deal of modern everyday life.

Colonial Beginnings

The origin of Korea's chemical industry and the origin of the Vinalon Factory are tied to one person: Noguchi Jun (1873–1944), the Japanese engineer turned entrepreneur who in 1908 founded Nihon Chisso Hiryō Kabushiki Kaisha (Japan Nitrogenous Fertilizer Company) in Minamata, Japan's Kyushu region.[8] By the mid-1920s, Nihon Chisso was a dominant chemical company in Japan possessing a large capital accumulated from selling fertilizer as well as stock shares. With capital in hand, Noguchi sought expansion into Korea after recognizing a rise in demand for his products and after a policy change had made investment in the colony easier.[9] First, following Japan's Rice Riots of 1918, rapid agricultural development took place in colonial Korea to produce low-priced rice for Japan, which in turn created a high demand for chemical fertilizer. Second, the abolishment of the Corporation Law in 1920 lifted many business regulations and made investment in Korea easier. In addition, Korea had cheaper labor, lower taxes, less competition, and greater availability of resources (and their intensive use)—all made possible by the colonial system.

In 1927, Noguchi established Chōsen Chisso Hiryō Kabushiki Kaisha (Korea Nitrogenous Fertilizer Company). Chōsen Chisso was the largest and most-invested business enterprise in colonial Korea, with more than twenty subsidiary companies in diverse industries, including not only chemical but also power, steel, mining, and food processing. Nihon Chisso acquired Chōsen Chisso in 1941, so this chapter treats the two as the same company. One subsidiary of Nihon Chisso was a soybean-processing factory located in the town of Pon'gung. In June 1936, the Pon'gung soybean factory was turned into a chemical fertilizer factory, which would become in 1961 the Vinalon Factory. The Pon'gung Chemical Fertilizer Factory grew to be one of the largest factories in colonial Korea: by 1943, it had 6,800 employees (of which around 2,000 were Japanese) and produced 30 percent of the fertilizer ingredient carbide consumed in the Japanese Empire.[10]

What happened to the Pon'gung Factory when the empire dissolved? (One person who never got to find out was Noguchi, who died in February 1944.) With liberation on August 15, 1945, and with another foreign occupation of the peninsula by the end of September—this time the Soviet Union in the northern half and the United States in the southern half—North Korea inherited a colonial industrial system made up of more than a thousand enterprises. The recovery and operation of these enterprises became a priority of the Soviets as well as of the nascent government of North Korea, made up of numerous People's Committees.[11] The resumption of operation began immediately, with Korean, Soviet, and Japanese workers, technicians, and administrators working together. But the process was uneven. According to one Soviet source, in September 1946 only 16 percent of the iron and steel industry and 21 percent of the mining industry were in operation, whereas the chemical industry was working at 83 percent capacity.[12]

As part of the Hŭngnam Area People's Factory, the Pon'gung Factory resumed operation at the end of August 1945. In its first few years, the factory's production level remained at about half of what it was during the colonial period: in the summer of 1947, it produced 700 tons of ammonium sulfate a day (versus 1,500 tons in 1944) and 300 tons of carbide a day (versus 500 tons in 1944).[13] The Pon'gung Factory suffered from lack of expertise and shortage of raw materials, but it had retained its equipment and capacity to become part of the postcolonial state socialist world. Removed from the expansive industrial network of the empire, where input and output were determined by global market forces as well as by a costly war, the factory found a new role determined by a different set of forces, one of which was the central plan and another the ideological force of national independence.

Rebuilding Hamhŭng

Vinalon City was built (and rebuilt) as part of the development of the entire Sŏngch'ŏn River Delta—more broadly known as the Hamhŭng Plains—as the center of Korea's chemical industry.[14] The Hamhŭng Plains occupy the southeastern region of Hamgyŏng, which in 1896 split into north and south provinces. During the Chosŏn period (1392–1910), Hamgyŏng was considered a frontier, a rebellious place far from the administrative, economic, and cultural influence of the capital at Hanyang (modern-day central Seoul north of the Han River). At the same time, Hamgyŏng held a sense of mystique as the birthplace of Yi Sŏnggye (1335–1408), the founder of the Chosŏn dynasty who was born in the town of Yŏnghŭng. After founding the new dynasty, Yi Sŏnggye built a palace with a shrine for his ancestors just south of Hamhŭng on the eastern bank of the Sŏngch'ŏn River. In 1398, the aging Yi Sŏnggye, distraught by his sons' bloody fight for the throne, briefly retired to a life of Buddhism at the shrine. Because the palace was occupied by the dynasty's founder, it was called *pon'gung*, "main palace." The term eventually came to denote the area itself.

After the Japanese colonial period, another major development of the Hamhŭng Plains took place during reconstruction after the Korean War. As one of five original industrial sites targeted by US Strategic Air Command (along with Wŏnsan, Pyongyang, Ch'ŏngjin, and Rajin), Hamhŭng's Hŭngnam District was hit with both incendiary and demolition bombs from the beginning of the war. According to a report by the then industry minister Chŏng Ilryong, most factories critical for export-oriented products, including the Pon'gung Chemical Fertilizer Factory, stopped their operation by the end of 1950.[15] The overall output of North Korea's chemical industry for 1953—the war ended in July—was 22 percent of the prewar level: South Hamgyŏng fared slightly better than the national average, at 36 percent of the level at 1949.[16]

The reconstruction of Hamhŭng City officially began in 1954 with Cabinet Decision Number 42, which also included the cities Ch'ŏngjin, Wŏnsan, Sariwŏn, Kanggye, and Namp'o—all important industrial cities heavily damaged during the war.[17] The basic city plan approved by the cabinet had the following items: a balance of educational, cultural, and welfare facilities; a living space of 6 to 9 square meters (65 to 97 square feet) per person; a green space of 7 to 12 square meters (75 to 130 square feet) per person; and the erection of administrative buildings, a plaza, a park, and a sport stadium in the center.[18] In cities such as Hamhŭng, the plan resulted in the construction of a large plaza near a train station with main roads radiating from the plaza. On the main roads were usually multistory administrative buildings and apartment complexes. Housing, an urgent problem in the postwar period, was based on standardized design, materials, and construction.[19] Prefabricated housing thus became the standard housing style, whether apartments in urban centers or tract houses in the countryside.

A vital part of urban and industrial reconstruction was the assistance received from other socialist countries. Toward the end of the war, the Korean Workers' Party recognized the urgency of obtaining foreign assistance and passed a plan to accept a vast amount of material aid from "brotherly" states.[20] Hungary took part in the reconstruction of Pyongyang; Poland played an important role in planning the merger of Ch'ŏngjin and Ranam into the larger Ch'ŏngjin City, where Romania built a pharmaceutical factory and Czechoslovakia built a hospital; Sinŭiju, in the Northwest, is where the Chinese military helped to build around 100,000 houses before withdrawing from North Korea in 1958; and Bulgaria built the provincial hospital of Sinŭiju.[21]

The feel-good story about East Germany's assistance in the reconstruction of Hamhŭng involves Kim Il Sung's thankful letter, on July 6, 1954, to the East German prime minister Otto Grotewohl to tell him of the selection of Hamhŭng in response to Grotewohl's willingness to help rebuild a city of North Korea's choosing. Another story, more in tune with the socialist hierarchy of the time, is that East Germany's assistance was part of its World War II reparation to the Soviet Union, forced by Stalin. In addition to making East Germany disassemble its factories and railways and send them to the Soviet Union, Moscow ordered it to participate in North Korea's postwar reconstruction.[22] East Germany's involvement officially lasted until 1962, and through four agreements East Germany's assistance entailed constructing the urban infrastructure of Hamhŭng as well as setting up an engine factory, printing factory, textile factory, and steel factory.[23]

An investigation team from East Germany arrived in Hamhŭng at the end of 1954, and actual planning and construction began in mid-1955 under the agency Baustab Korea (Construction Staff of Korea). Baustab Korea comprised numerous teams, including road construction, waterworks, bridge construction, drainage and irrigation, and public works.[24] The first joint effort between North Korea and East Germany led to the erection in 1955 of 400 housing units arranged in four-story apartment complexes in the city center.[25] By the end of 1958, this site was expanded and providing housing for 100,000 residents of Hamhŭng.[26] Just outside the city, in 1957 an entire community rose up from 170,000 square meters (200,000 square yards) of previously rural land, complete with a school, daycare center, and cultural facilities.[27] The most symbolic structure of this joint effort was Wilhelm Pieck Avenue, the wide street running through the center of

Figure 5.1 Hamhŭng's Chŏngsŏng Avenue today, formerly called Wilhelm Pieck Avenue, May 2014. The apartments along the street were originally built jointly with East Germany.

Source: Photograph by the author.

Figure 5.2 South Hamgyŏng House of Culture, Hamhŭng, May 2014. The Bauhaus influence is visible.

Source: Photograph by the author.

Hamhŭng, named after the first president of East Germany. As for industrial sites, East Germany helped to bring in new equipment for practically all the factories in the area, including the Pon'gung Factory.[28] Education and training were also part of the assistance. In 1956, there were 938 different lectures for 17,750 North Korean workers, with topics ranging from agricultural and construction to chemistry and physics.[29]

Within a decade, East Germany's involvement propelled the Hamhŭng area into the center of North Korea's chemical industry, whose size and capacity were among the largest in the world. The migration of workers and their families to Hamhŭng turned the area into the second-largest metropolitan area in North Korea, and in the 1960s its administrative districts came to encompass the entire Sŏngch'ŏn River Delta. With the technology gained from the reconstruction experience, urban development continued at a rapid pace in Hamhŭng after the East Germans left. For instance, in 1962 and 1963 the Hamhŭng Housing Construction Enterprise built, without any foreign assistance, 7,000 apartment units in the Sŏngch'ŏn District, supposedly at a rate of 24 units a day.[30] With further development, however, modern Hamhŭng's international past gradually disappeared from its urban surface. Wilhelm Pieck Avenue, the symbol of North Korea's joint effort with East Germany, now goes by the name "Chŏngsŏng Avenue" (figure 5.1).[31] The memory of that past is gone for most of the city's residents, but the structures are still there. Walking the city, one will constantly come across buildings designed in the linear and functional Bauhaus style (figure 5.2).

Ri Sŭnggi: A Man Saved by the Nation

In July 1950, during the initial phase of the Korean War, when the North Korean military had occupied 90 percent of South Korea, the chemist Ri Sŭnggi began working as a technical expert at a chemical factory in Hamhŭng.[32] Ri Sŭnggi had only recently come to North Korea, a place that evoked both admiration and fear among the intellectuals of South Korea. But it was a place of opportunity. That summer, when the war broke out, he left his post at the fledgling Seoul National University (formerly the Kyŏngsŏng Imperial University), where he was a professor in the Chemistry Department and once had been the dean of the College of Science and Engineering. He crossed the border not alone but with some of his students, whose future depended on his success in the new country.[33]

Ri Sǔnggi's northward movement (*wŏlbuk*) was part of the third and last wave of movement of scientists and engineers from South Korea to North Korea that took place in the postliberation period. The first wave was from July to December 1946, when the plan to build Kim Il Sung University was announced (July 8) and when the first crisis in the plan to create a single national university in South Korea left many scholars jobless and angry (August to December).[34] This group was generally sympathetic of North Korea's emphasis on science and technology and was curious about the adaptation of these fields to education and industry.[35] The second wave— made up of individuals who were more ideologically aligned with North Korea—lasted until 1948, when two separate states were established, and overlapped with the second crisis of South Korea's national university plan.[36] The third wave took place during the war and was made up mostly of scientists and engineers whose main interest was in the continuation of their work, without much ideological motive or sympathy toward North Korea's system.[37] Ri Sǔnggi belonged to the third group, and this perhaps explains his employment at the chemical factory in Hamhǔng, far from Pyongyang and its new university—a job that was certainly a step down from his former post.

There was another, more important reason for Ri Sǔnggi's placement at Hamhǔng, though, and it had to do with the overall industrial development of the area. A critical part of development was the setting up of education and research facilities. In September 1947, North Korea established its first college of science and technology at Hǔngnam, the Hǔngnam College of Technology. By the end of 1948, the college had forty-five faculty members, twenty-eight of whom had come from South Korea.[38] In addition, in June 1948 the old factory laboratories of Nihon Chisso, some fifty of them, were turned into the Hǔngnam Research Institute, with Yŏ Kyŏnggu, the Waseda-educated engineer and the nephew of the independence activist Yŏ Unhyŏng (assassinated the previous year), serving as its first director.[39] Once the college and the research institute were in place, the Hamhǔng–Hǔngnam area became North Korea's center of science and technology. In July 1950, Ri Sǔnggi began a new life in Hamhǔng, which had not only the infrastructure for research but also his peers from the South, who, along with Ri, were thrown into a new world that brought them both fame and misfortune.

Figure 5.3 Ri Sŭnggi, 1961.
Source: Chunggongŏp Wiwŏnhoe (Heavy Industry Committee), *Pinallon Kongjang kŏnsŏl* (The construction of the Vinalon Factory) (Pyongyang: Kungnip Kŏnsŏl Ch'ulp'ansa, 1961), xix.

Born in 1905 in Tamyang, located in the South Chŏlla Province of the southwestern region of the peninsula, Ri Sŭnggi received his undergraduate and graduate education from Kyoto Imperial University, specializing in high-polymer chemistry, a field he was able to study in English, German, French, Italian, and, of course, Japanese.[40] In the spring of 1938, Ri joined the synthetic fiber research laboratory headed by the chemist Sakurada Ichiro (1906–1986) at the Institute for Chemical Fibers Research, Kyoto University. Motivated by the usefulness and need of synthetic fibers—as Japan prepared for war and as DuPont discovered nylon in February 1938—Sakurada's laboratory carried out experiments to create synthetic fibers from polyvinyl alcohol.[41] In 1939, the laboratory succeeded in obtaining a water-insoluble synthetic fiber from polyvinyl alcohol and named it "Synthesis Number One" (*gosei-ichigo*).[42] Ri Sŭnggi was one of the main researchers in the project, and it is he who in the fall of 1939 made the announcement of a new synthetic fiber to the public. The patent for the fiber (Japan patent number 147,958) is held by, in the order listed on the patent document, Sakurada Ichiro, Ri Sŭnggi, and Kawakami Hiroshi.[43] In 1948, Japan's scientific community gave the fiber the generic name *biniron* (*vinylon* in English; *pinillon* in Korean), a name that is a combination of *biniru* (vinyl) and *nairon* (nylon).[44] The fiber took on a different name in North Korea, however. The official story told is that in 1957 Kim Il Sung gave it the name *pinallon* (*vinalon* in English) to include the Korean word *nal*, which means "thread."[45] In North Korea, the English term for the substance is never spelled with a *y*, *vinylon*, but rather *vinalon*, and the North Korean term for it is never *pinillon*, but *pinallon*.

The industrial development of vinalon in North Korea began in June 1952, when the state officially called for the mass production of synthetic fibers. Ri Sŭnggi was transferred from Hamhŭng to Ch'ŏngsu in North P'yŏngan Province, where there was another large chemical factory, formerly part of the Nihon Chisso Fuel Company. He set up a small experimental shop within the Ch'ŏngsu factory, and two years later he and his team processed the first 20-kilogram (45-pound) batch of vinalon.[46] When the production capacity reached 200 kilograms (440 pounds) a day in 1957, the potential for industrialization was confirmed, and Ri Sŭnggi returned to Hamhŭng and participated in the planning of one of the largest vinalon factories the world had ever seen. He advised the entire process, from the design of the blueprints to the installation of equipment, receiving the title "labor hero" for this work in the fall of 1961.

After that, Ri Sŭnggi's life story was treated with a heavy dose of nationalism in North Korea's system of hagiography. Foremost, the invention of vinalon took on a nationalistic (not to mention patriarchal) purpose: "Feeling the sorrow as a colonial intellectual, he resolved to develop a new synthetic fiber, which can relieve Korean women from the burden of spinning and weaving," one biography reads.[47] Moreover, his interest in synthetic fibers became an anti-Japanese act, and he is portrayed as having been defiant toward the empire's demand for military research toward the end of his time in Japan: "The Japanese military police kept his movements under surveillance, and he was imprisoned for refusing to do research in military science. He greeted the August 15 liberation from a Japanese military prison," this same biography continues.[48] In the postliberation world, the sense of nationalism in Ri Sŭnggi's life story was further reinforced by the reflective glory of Kim Il Sung. His worth as a scientist was fully realized when he came under the leader's care: "Only when he entered the northern republic during the war and was embraced by the great leader Kim Il Sung did his talent bloom and was he able to realize his long-cherished desire."[49] Ri consented to this rhetoric in exchange for resources, fame, and comfort for his family. As the Vinalon Factory was being built, he wrote: "Such care and happiness were unthinkable . . . in not only Japan but also in South Korea. . . . Under the warm care and leadership of our party, the scientific project moved forward. . . . Whenever we faced difficulties in our research, we thought about Comrade Kim Il Sung's advice to boldly pave the road of our chemical fibers."[50] It is not known, however, how he was really treated in Japan. In general, Korean intellectuals in Japan experienced some discrimination and felt the pressure to conform to imperial policies,[51] but at least within the scientific community at Kyoto University Ri does not seem to have suffered. From the time he joined Sakurada's laboratory in 1938 until liberation in 1945, he published at least eight journal articles, four with him as the only author; he even published in postimperial Japan in 1946, around the time he left Japan and joined the faculty at Seoul National University.[52]

The recognition of Ri Sŭnggi's work in Japan was miniscule in comparison to how it was received in North Korea. In 1952, for his two-year work at Hamhŭng, he was admitted to North Korea's Academy of Sciences—thus earning the highest academic title, "councilor of academy" (wŏnsa), and in August 1957 he became a member of the Supreme People's Assembly.[53] In 1959, he was given the People's Award for his service to improve the people's livelihood.[54] Ri Sŭnggi's final influential post, beginning in February 1961, was the directorship of the Hamhŭng branch of the Academy of Sciences. He went on to receive the Kim Il Sung Medal of Honor. On Ri's ninetieth birthday in 1995, Kim Jong Il gave him a special birthday celebration.[55] When he died four months later, in February 1996 at the age of ninety-one, he was given a state funeral and buried at the Cemetery for Patriotic Martyrs in Pyongyang. Ri Sŭnggi lived a long time and witnessed epochal changes in the fall of an empire, the division of a nation, a bloody war, and the rise of two antagonistic states. He took part in the rise of the socialist state in important ways, and in the process he saw himself transformed within the discourse of nation building from a hapless colonial intellectual to a national hero whose knowledge and hard work improved the lives of millions of people and raised the international stature of a young state. In official history, he is depicted first as a man saved by the nation and then as a man who saved the nation.

From Coal to Clothes: Making and Using Vinalon

Since the early the 1970s, in North Korea the vinalon fiber has been called the "cotton of self-reliance" (*chuch'e ŭi som*) because, as Ri Sŭnggi explained, it was "miraculously created in a short amount of time, with our own strength, with our own technology, and with our resources. . . . [It is] a great creation of our *chuch'e* period and a fine fiber replacing cotton."[56] It is also known as the "king of fibers," "universal fiber," and "*chuch'e* fiber." Vinalon made up more than half of all fibers (natural or synthetic) produced in North Korea, and at least until the mid-1980s North Korea was one of the largest producers of this fiber.

The postwar North Korean economy was rife with shortages, among which fabric was a particular problem, enough so that Kim Il Sung said to the politburo of East Germany's Socialist Unity Party on June 8, 1956: "Currently, 40 million meters [44 million yards] [of fabric] are produced, but this is not enough for the people. Including the imported amount, domestic production is at 5 meters [5.5 yards) per person per year." Before ending his remark, he said, "When it comes to relieving the people's hardship, what is lacking more than anything else is textile goods."[57] One important reason for the shortage was that North Korea at the time could not spare large tracts of flat, arable land to grow anything other than food. At the end of the 1950s, North Korea had 5 million acres of arable land, and it would take 10 percent of that land to produce enough fabric for its 10 million people, which was at least 150 million meters (165 million yards) of fabric annually.[58] The same amount of fabric could be produced from 20,000 tons of vinalon, a realistic output for a single factory.

There are two types of chemical fibers: cellulose fibers and synthetic fibers. Cellulose fibers are made from the cellulose of plants—from the pulp of corn or reed, for example. The best-known type of cellulose fiber is rayon (*ingyŏn*); the oldest cellulose fiber, rayon was first patented in 1855, and its first commercial production began in 1905 in Europe. In the 1930s, Japan was the largest producer of rayon in the world.[59] North Korea was interested in cellulose fibers, too, but its dependence on plant and agricultural materials for food shifted the focus toward synthetic fibers. Synthetic fibers are made chiefly from chemical compounds extracted from petroleum, natural gas, and coal. The most abundant synthetic fibers are nylon, acrylics, and polyesters, with nylon accounting for nearly half of all synthetic fibers produced in the world. Whereas nylon and polyesters are made from petroleum-derived compounds, acrylics are made from natural-gas derivatives. Synthetic fibers made from coal include polypropylene (used to make packaging, ropes, containers, and furniture) and vinyl fibers. Vinyl fibers are further categorized into vinyon fibers and vinal fibers. Vinyon fibers are made from vinyl chloride and are used mostly as binding agents, whereas vinal fibers, produced in greater quantities than vinyon fibers, are made from vinyl alcohol.[60] To be more specific, vinal fibers are polyvinyl alcohol fibers, the generic name of which, given in 1948 in Japan, is "vinylon." Only in North Korea is the polyvinyl alcohol fiber called "vinalon."

Polyvinyl alcohol was discovered by German chemists W. Haehnel and W. O. Herrmann, and the patent for it was registered in 1924. Fifteen years later it was first successfully turned into fiber by Sakurada's team. Polyvinyl alcohol originates in Germany, but the majority of polyvinyl alcohol production in the world takes place in Japan, China, Taiwan, Singapore, South Korea, and North Korea. The Japanese company Kuraray was the first commercial producer, starting in 1950, and is the single largest producer today, with an annual capacity of 194,000 tons.[61] China has the largest vinylon industry today, born in 1963 when the Japanese manufacturer Kuraray—as part of the first trade agreement between Japan and China, the Liao-Takasaki Trade Agreement—signed a deal with Beijing to provide a 30-tons-a-day vinylon plant.[62] The American company DuPont also produces a large amount of polyvinyl alcohol under the trade name Elvanol but does not produce any significant amount of polyvinyl alcohol fibers. The size of the global polyvinyl alcohol market in 2001 was around US$1.2 billion.[63]

The making of vinalon requires three main raw materials: coal (sŏkt'an or muyŏnt'an), limestone (sŏkhoesŏk or sŏkhoeam), and salt (sogŭm). North Korea does not produce any petroleum or natural gas, but it has large deposits of coal and limestone and produces abundant amounts of them. North Korea also produces enough salt for domestic use. First, the coal is baked in an oven at a temperature of 2,000°C (3,632°F) to drive off water and gas. The result is coke, an important industrial compound used, for instance, as fuel in smelting iron ore. Limestone, which is made up mostly of calcium and carbon, is also baked, which turns the limestone into lime, or calcium oxide. Coke and lime are mixed in a furnace at a temperature of 2,000°C to produce calcium carbide (CaC_2). Carbide is basically carbon with a metallic element. Calcium carbide is the most common carbide metal used in North Korea due to its large limestone deposits. It is used in making various industrial products, including steel and fertilizer. Salt—sodium chloride (NaCl)—is electrolyzed in water and turned into a base: sodium hydroxide (NaOH), also called "caustic soda." Sodium hydroxide is essential in the later stage of making vinalon.

The next stage in vinalon manufacture is the treatment of carbide with water—hydrolysis—to produce the highly combustible acetylene gas (C_2H_2), which is then hydrated using a mercury catalyst to make acetaldehyde (CH_3CHO). Acetaldehyde, a widely used compound in making drugs and perfume, is oxidized into an acetic acid (*ch'osan*; CH_3COOH). Acetic acid is another widely used compound, from rubber to pharmaceuticals. It is also the main acid of vinegar. In the next step, acetic acid is catalyzed with a zinc chloride compound to form vinyl acetate (*ch'osan pinil*; $CH_3COOCH = CH_2$), which is the monomer that undergoes polymerization (*chunghap*). Polymerization occurs in a methanol solvent containing the compound azobisisobutyronitrile, commonly known as AIBN (*abin*). AIBN decomposes to release radicals that initiate the polymerization of vinyl acetate. Polyvinyl acetate ($C_4H_6O_2$) is then mixed with sodium hydroxide (NaOH) and methanol in the hydrolytic process of saponification to produce the final compound, polyvinyl alcohol, a chain of C_2H_4O molecules. The process of turning polyvinyl alcohol into fiber starts with purification through filtering and washing. Polyvinyl alcohol is then dissolved in hot water to achieve a certain level of viscosity. After furthered filtration, the solution is sent to a spinning machine, where the solution is extruded through spinnerets—each hole between 0.07 and 0.1 millimeter wide—into either a coagulating bath or dry spinning tubes. The process using a coagulating bath is called the "wet spinning process," and the process using dry spinning tubes is called the "dry spinning process." In North Korea, wet spinning is used exclusively. Fiber extraction through the wet spinning process—not the discovery of vinalon—is what Ri Sŭnggi and the Sakurada team accomplished in 1939. To prevent breakdown in water or melting in high temperature, the fibers are treated with heat, formalin

(CH_2O), and acid. Once the fibers are washed and dried, they become the final product, vinalon fibers.

Vinalon is a remarkable compound. The fiber is able to absorb more moisture (hygroscopicity) than any other synthetic fiber. It has high resistance against sunlight, ultraviolet light, solvents, oils, and salts.[64] The vinalon fiber is lighter than cotton and yet three to four times stronger.[65] It has many industrial uses due to its high strength, low elongation tendency, and high resistance to chemicals. In the rubber industry, vinalon is used as reinforcement in belts, hoses, and tires; in the agriculture and fishing industries, it is used as shade cloth (to protects vegetables), fishing nets, and ropes for ships; in the sewing industry, it is used as sewing threads for leather materials such as shoes and bags; and in the paper industry, it is used to improve paper strength and make paper alkali (base) resistant.[66] In the manufacture of clothing, polyester is the most common synthetic fiber in the world, but the vinalon fiber is extensively used in North Korea to make everything from suits, shirts, work clothes, and dresses to underwear, sweaters, towels, and socks.[67] To most of the rest of the world, however, due to historical and market reasons vinalon is known mostly for industrial purposes. And today in North Korea, circumstances have changed, so vinalon is no longer the main fiber used for clothing.

Vinalon is also completely biodegradable, leaving only water and carbon dioxide.[68] It is a nonhazardous material and has a very low order of toxicity, thus finding a wide use in construction as a replacement for asbestos.[69] In North Korea, vinalon is also used as an absorbable surgical suture.[70] However, vinalon's biodegradability and nontoxicity do not mean that it is pollution free. From the raw material carbide to the various solutions required in making vinalon, harmful gases are released into the air, including carbon monoxide, formaldehyde, and gaseous acids. Nevertheless, for the North Korean state in the postwar era, vinalon was an answer to the dire problem of textile shortage. It required coal, limestone, and salt, the three items North Korea possessed in abundance. The country already had the industrial infrastructure to produce carbide and acetylene, although that infrastructure was in need of repair after bombings and abandonment during the Korean War. And North Korea had scouted the top expert in polyvinyl fiber manufacturing. Diversification was not an option for a country lacking hard currency, raw materials, and time. All bets were on vinalon.

Figure 5.4 Vinalon fiber.
Source: Chosŏn Hwabosa (Korean Pictorial Agency), *Kim Ilsŏng chusŏk kwa onŭlŭi Chosŏn* (Premier Kim Il Sung and North Korea today) (Pyongyang: Oegukmun Chonghap Ch'ulp'ansa, 1993).

Constructing Vinalon City

A popular saying about the construction of the Vinalon Factory is that if the earth removed during its construction were piled in cubic meter blocks, the height of the pile would be 150 times the height of Mount Paektu, the tallest mountain on the Korean Peninsula at 2,744 meters (9,003 feet). That would be 256 miles high. As it originally stood in colonial Korea, it was spatially a medium-size plant, at 2 square kilometers (0.8 square mile). But the Pon'gung Chemical Fertilizer Factory was the largest chemical factory, and its reconstruction was the most ambitious and publicized in the postwar period.

The Vinalon Factory sits on flat land on the eastern bank of Sŏngch'ŏn River, halfway between Sŏhojin Bay and central Hamhŭng, on the grounds named after the palace built by the founder of the Chosŏn dynasty, as part of Sap'o County, where many East German workers paved roads, raised apartments, and laid pipes in the late 1950s. According to an official account in 1961, the fifty large and small buildings of Vinalon City had a total floor space of 130,000 square meters (1.4 million square feet), 15,000 production machines, and 1,700 container tanks. *And* they were connected by 500 kilometers (310 miles) of piping, enough to make a round trip to and from Pyongyang. The annual production capacity in 1961 was 20,000 tons of vinalon fiber, enough to make 25 million suits.[71] The factory was also capable of making synthetic rubber for tires and herbicides to kill weeds. The editors of the Heavy Industry Committee wrote, "Our ancestors suffered the cold and heat without much clothing, and they broke their backs fighting against weed. Their pain has forever become history."[72] Vinalon had a historical mission.

The most publicized aspect of the factory's construction was speed, which came to be known as "vinalon speed." The length of time from the planning to the completion of the factory was fourteen months, from March 1960 to May 1961. The first announcement of the construction was made in 1957. Around the time when Ri Sŭnggi and his team were manufacturing 200 kilograms (440 pounds) of vinalon per day, Kim Il Sung visited Hamhŭng in March 1957 and announced the plan to build the factory.[73] In October 1958, the cabinet ordered the mobilization of workers and the preparation of floor plans, budget, and construction equipment. The Ministry of Chemical Industry sent numerous trucks, compressors, bulldozers, and excavators; and the Kiyang Machine Tools Factory and the Ragwŏn Machine Tools Factory sent twenty tower cranes. But the fervor of construction was not felt until the first voluntary group of workers—1,300 of them—arrived on January 20, 1959. They were a team of young women and men (*ch'ŏngnyŏn*) and held a rally on the factory grounds, resolving to act as "vanguards" and "shock workers" in the construction project. By end of June, there had assembled a motley construction crew of 11,000 people made up of not only construction workers but also farmers, students, and soldiers.[74]

The Vinalon Factory Construction Planning Committee, the state agency overseeing the project, was officially formed in January 1960, sending the message that it was formed only after the masses had already heeded the state's call and begun to organize themselves as shock workers. Thus, the willful action and ingenuity of ordinary people are heavily emphasized in the official history of the Vinalon Factory's construction. One early instance of workers rising to the challenge involved making blueprints. This was the task of Design Team Number Five of the Heavy Industry Committee, which had forty undertrained but devoted engineers. The committee reported that beginning in March 1960 the design team

Figure 5.5 The Spinning Shop, Vinalon Factory, 1961.
Source: Chunggongŏp Wiwŏnhoe, *Pinallon Kongjang kŏnsŏl*, xiii.

Figure 5.6 Kim Il Sung's visit to the Vinalon Factory construction site, August 28, 1960.
The thin, bespectacled person to the right of Kim Il Sung is Ri Sŭnggi.
Source: Chunggongŏp Wiwŏnhoe, *Pinallon Kongjang kŏnsŏl*, vi.

made 12,000 blueprints in six months, an amount that would normally have taken "three hundred engineers two to three years."[75] The notion of "vinalon speed" began with the design team.

The tallest building was the Acetic Acid Shop. It was 32 meters (104 feet) in height and included the 40-meter smokestack built by Ri Hŭisang's Phoenix Shock Troop; the vertical windows of the building exemplified the modern style of the entire factory complex.[76] The largest building was the Spinning Shop (figure 5.5). Situated in the western part of the factory site, near the river and the railway, the Spinning Shop turned polyvinyl alcohol into vinalon fibers and shipped them out to textile factories. It was 160 meters long and 117 meters (560 by 410 feet) wide, with 35,000 square meters (377,000 square feet) of floor space. One-third of the floor space is said to have been dedicated to the workers' nonproductive time, including break rooms, toilets and showers, and recreational facilities. Outside, there was a water fountain, a flower garden, and a wide green area lined with trees. The Spinning Shop represented what Vinalon City was all about—a "workers' palace" supporting a healthy, productive culture.[77] On the eastern edge of the factory, a culture center was built, which still shows movies today.

The ceremony for the completion of the Vinalon Factory took place over two days on May 6 and 7, 1961, with Kim Il Sung in attendance both days, the first ceremony on factory grounds and the second in central Hamhŭng. After fourteen months of planning and construction, the factory was ready for operation. It had taken a great deal of materials, technical ingenuity, and, above all, hard work by the people. With respect to the latter factor, the aggrandized account of the Vinalon Factory is not wrong: the factory was an enormous toiling ground of tens of thousands of volunteer workers made up of students, soldiers, farmers, fishers, medical workers, office workers, artists, homemakers, and workers on vacation from their formal jobs. In this situation, a new historical memory was born and took effect in the everyday.

Vinalon Heroes and Sublime Danger

The winters in this region were especially hard for the workers constructing the factory because the ground and water stayed frozen for months, but work had to continue if the May Day deadline was to be met. One winter day the sand necessary in making cement had stopped arriving at the site. The boat carrying the sand stood still in the frozen Sŏngch'ŏn River. The work team held an urgent meeting but could come up with no practical solution, at which point the vanguard worker Chang Kyech'ang got up and said, "How can we, who have inherited the spirit of anti-Japanese partisans, give in to this small obstacle? Don't worry, my comrades."[78] Then he walked to the boat, broke the ice, jumped into the freezing water, and freed the vessel.

As workers from all over the country, a large portion of them volunteers, gathered at Pon'gung and pledged to execute the will of the party, the site became a mass movement within a mass movement. The nationwide momentum of the Ch'ŏllima Work Team Movement, in which a half-million workers were participating, was carried to the Vinalon Factory. In the course of fourteen months, the Vinalon City project gave rise to more than two hundred shock-work teams, including the August Eighth Shock Troop, the April First Shock Troop, the Mount Paektu Young People's Shock Troop, the Poch'ŏnbo Torch Shock Troop, and the Phoenix Shock Troop.[79] These teams were made up mostly of nonskilled workers, and what they essentially did was a great amount of nonmechanized work in a short amount of time and in a difficult environment. For example, the Mount Paektu Young People's Shock Troop made a name for itself by shoveling and hauling 15 cubic meters of dirt (57,000 pounds) from the frozen ground in the span of a night in a temperature of −20°C (−4°F).[80]

As a mass movement of its own, the construction site was a stage for labor heroism. Three months after construction was complete, the Supreme People's Assembly awarded twenty-two people who had participated in the construction of the Vinalon Factory with the title "labor hero," a group including ordinary workers, technical experts, soldiers, and a certain famous chemist; one soldier, Ri Insik, was awarded the title "hero of the republic" (see table 5.1 for the complete list). The most celebrated labor hero was, of course, Ri Sŭnggi, but his story at the construction site is not dramatic, although his life certainly is; he did not become a hero because of a single superhuman act, as other labor heroes had done. Stories about these individuals are indeed heroic, and, like true heroic tales, they fall on the verge of being tragic. Two individuals deserve a mention: Ko Tuman, a boiler worker, and Ri Insik, a private in the People's Army. No human being should go through what they did. One criticism about mass movements is

TABLE 5.1

People Recognized for Their Contribution to the Construction of the
Vinalon Factory, 1960–1961

Name	Title	Occupation
Ri Insik	hero of the republic	soldier, private
Ri Sŭnggi	labor hero	chemist
Ko Tuman	labor hero	boiler worker
Kim Yunhyŏp	labor hero	welder
Kim Ikro	labor hero	department chief
Ri Kyŏngha	labor hero	shop chief
Ri Yŏngsu	labor hero	shop chief
Ri Ch'ŏnbaek	labor hero	department chief
Pak Chuhwan	labor hero	design engineer
Pang Kyesun	labor hero	assembler
Chŏn Charyŏn	labor hero	Ch'ŏllima Work Team leader
Cho Sun'gyu	labor hero	industrial worker
Kim Myŏngsŏ	labor hero	soldier, officer
Kim Ikgyo	labor hero	soldier, officer
Ryuk Chonghyŏn	labor hero	soldier, officer
Ri Myŏngsŏn	labor hero	soldier, officer
Pak Sŏnhwan	labor hero	soldier, officer
Pak Hŭijin	labor hero	soldier, officer
Son Inp'il	labor lero	soldier, officer
Cho Tonghŭi	labor hero	soldier, officer
Kim Tŏkpong	labor hero	soldier, petty officer
Ha Ch'angju	labor hero	soldier, private
Ham Ch'unbong	labor hero	soldier, private

Source: *Chunggongŏp Wiwŏnhoe* (Heavy Industry Committee), *Pinallon Kongjang kŏnsŏl* (The construction of the Vinalon Factory) (Pyongyang: Kungnip Kŏnsŏl Ch'ulp'ansa, 1961), xix–xx.

that their aestheticization of work led to the tolerance of atrocious work conditions.

Ko Tuman was the boiler team leader of the Materials Shop (figure 5.7). One morning in February 1961 he confronted a problem.[81] The boiler pressure was going down because the boiler smokestack was clogged with ash. To remove the ash, the boiler would have to be shut down for a few

Figure 5.7 The labor hero Ko Tuman, 1961.
Source: Chunggongŏp Wiwŏnhoe, *Pinallon Kongjang kŏnsŏl*, xix.

days, which would also shut down the production of construction materials. But the shop could not stop production at a moment when many buildings were in the final phase of completion. Kim Il Sung had said that the making of construction materials had to continue under any circumstance. So Ko Tuman's answer to the problem he discovered was to clean the smokestack while the boiler was running. He put on cotton-padded winter clothing, a hat, a mask, and a pair of goggles. He then drenched himself in cold water and entered the smokestack. The temperature inside the smokestack was 300°C (572°F). "Life is valuable," he thought to himself, surrounded by heat and ash, "but it's not as valuable as the future of the fatherland. . . . I have but one life, but what greater happiness is there than giving my life to the fatherland?"[82] Ko had been born on Cheju Island and was a good swimmer: he held his breath inside so he would not inhale the toxic gas. After he made five trips to the inner chamber of the smokestack, each trip requiring a soaking of his clothes, the smokestack began to emit smoke.

The story of how Ri Insik earned the title "hero of the republic" is just as incredible. On an off day in March 1961, Ri Insik, a twenty-year-old private in the army, was thinking about how to speed up the installation of columns supporting the floors of the Acetic Acid Shop. The reason his squad took forty minutes to install one column, he noticed, was that the crane held the column as it was being welded into place, when the crane could be bringing another column to the next slot. The column could be supported by ropes while it is being welded. He presented the idea to his squad leader, who implemented it immediately. The idea worked, and by the end of the day the squad had installed three times the daily average number of columns. Just before the shift ended, the wind picked up and

Figure 5.8 Illustration of Ri Insik wrapping the rope around his body.
Source: Chunggongŏp Wiwŏnhoe, *Pinallon Kongjang kŏnsŏl.*

shook the one column still not welded. If the column were to fall, it would injure many workers and damage what had already been built. Ri Insik acted quickly and grabbed a loose rope from the slowly falling column, which was 12 meters (40 feet) high and weighed nine tons. As the column leaned, he wound the rope around his body and felt the ligaments in his hands and arms being torn. At the moment, the will to save the factory overwhelmed the pain he felt all over his body. The resistance of his body stopped the column's leaning, but he soon lost consciousness, and his squad rushed in to take control of the situation (see figure 5.8).[83]

The official history of the Vinalon Factory entails the glorification of dangerous and risky actions through stories of labor heroes. Dangerous actions were tolerated as long as they were done for the completion of state goals—the means to an end corresponding to the expansion of state power. What was this danger attached to the notion of heroism? Was there some kind of aestheticization of danger that allowed the state and community to accept what should be considered, to say the least, an atrocious violation of human and labor rights? A heroic deed is one of sublime danger—danger transcending place and time and falling upon any person, whether a guerilla soldier in Manchuria or a worker at Pon'gung. The danger faced on the battlefield and the danger faced on the construction site were the same: a stage for a greater cause—the supraindividual aim of the state.

Sublime danger, with its supraindividual consequences, is the aestheticization of what is arduous, painful, and often life threatening. In the discourse of labor heroes, what is perilous becomes beautiful ("What greater happiness is there than giving my life to the fatherland?"), and this beauty is often tied to the nationalist sentiment. (To be sure, nationalism as an aesthetic category is a universal phenomenon of the twentieth century, especially in postcolonial countries, whether socialist or not.) A central component of danger as a sublime category is the body: the sensual body in practice with an abstract cause. The soldier Ri Insik certainly felt the pain of his torn ligaments, but he did not let go—not so that he could become a hero, for that itself could never be the goal, but so that he could repay his debt to the nation that had given him a new life. The destruction of his body was therefore not the giving up of what was expendable (not strictly a sacrifice) but the making up for what had been due from him, as a worker and citizen of North Korea, all along. The offering of the body evens out what is owed. Susan Buck-Morss, looking at labor heroes of the Soviet Union, talks about the heroic body in a similar way: "The physical suffering that hollows out the individual for the sake of the collective is the ecstasy of the Soviet sublime. The triumph of the body is its destruction as well."[84]

The construction site of the Vinalon Factory was a frenzied environment of tens of thousands of mostly nonskilled workers from different regions and backgrounds working under multiple chains of command and various plans. The other side of blinding speed and ingenuity was therefore disorder. Burawoy has conceptualized this phenomenon as the "anarchy of the socialist plan," which requires a constant reorganization of the labor process.[85] After all, the brave builders of the 40-meter smokestack, who finished it in a snowstorm, made a name for themselves for refusing to come down when they were ordered to do so. And the day when the work hero Ri Insik pitched his new idea and saved a falling column had been his day off. The heroic work of ordinary people emerged essentially from everyday disorder, in which state power—represented by the central plan—was ineffective.

Extraordinary acts of ordinary workers were thus symptoms of an ineffective central plan, whose goal was reached not so much by systematic adherence to the plan but by the unplanned actions and creativity of ordinary nonskilled workers in everyday space who played no part in making the plan. It was nothing other than frenzied work that kept the plan functioning. But, of course, the planners were not blind to the necessity of spontaneous knowledge and actions. For instance, as Deborah Kaple writes, the Chinese Communist Party authorities considered the system of labor heroism the most rational tool for the success of an enterprise.[86] When the labor-hero system was functioning, it did so while undermining the central plan, the hallmark of socialist economy.[87] The destruction of the body in becoming a hero was simultaneously the dissolution of the plan. Labor heroes and the system from which they were born existed in a dialectical relationship of negation.

Industrialism as Everyday Life

The completion of Vinalon City in May 1961 was part of North Korea's great industrial narrative rooted in real economic transformation. This moment coincided with the proclamation of a socialized economy (January 1961) and the preparation for the Fourth Korean Workers' Party

Congress, known as the "Congress of Victors" (September 1961). At the dawn of a new decade, North Korea had proletarianized its citizens and nationalized all forms of production, thereby establishing a centralized system of appropriating total surplus. Furthermore, the emphasis was on the achievements of the North Koreans themselves. The industrial narrative for the new socialist era entailed an origin story that excludes international involvement. The transnational history of Vinalon City became immutably localized and took on the dimension of everyday reality. In the everyday, vinalon exerted its ideological force. As Sheila Fitzpatrick remarks about everyday life in the Soviet Union of the 1930s, where tremendous change occurred in people's lifetimes, the "utopian vision" was "part of everyone's everyday experience."[88]

Ri Sŭnggi once said, "Please don't treat the vinalon fabric irreverently. And please don't think it was made by one scientist. . . . When your children ask about how vinalon came to be, tell them not of a scientist's name but of the history of the Workers' Party."[89] Ri's statement is precisely about the ideological effect of vinalon as a common product. By linking the history of vinalon with the history of the Korean Workers' Party, Ri was revealing an all-too-familiar ideological moment: the fetishism of the product. The everyday aspect of vinalon encompasses the fetishism of vinalon and the factory not because they are glorified emblems of North Korea but because they are misrecognized—in their glorification—as something they are not but something they appear to be.

Everyday life supports the fetishism of vinalon by making it appear to be the product of an extrasocial entity, the Korean Workers' Party. Misrecognized in the fetishism are the historical and collective aspects of vinalon. First, the complex, transnational history of vinalon—bringing together the Japanese colonial industry, North Korea's postliberation effort to start a chemical industry, and East Germany's reconstruction assistance—is sublimated in the national narrative. Second, the enormous amount of collective labor used to start up the factory and to produce the fiber is misrecognized as something originating from the party and the state. Vinalon as a historical and collective product is characterized as a product that justifies the hegemonic relationship between the state, the party, and the workers. The fetishism of vinalon supports its appropriation by an extrasocial entity, the state.

Two years after the Vinalon Factory went into operation, a team of writers from the popular magazine *Ch'ŏllima* visited the factory. Upon arriving at the Spinning Shop, they saw a "truly mysterious" sight: "From each spinning machine, the golden silk strips were flowing out like a seven-colored rainbow, as if to envelop our entire country in it."[90] The exaltation of vinalon is understandable because by this time the factory was producing 20,000 tons of vinalon fabric a year and beginning to satisfy the population's fabric needs. This was still only 15 meters (16.5 yards) of fabric per person per year, but it was a major improvement from 5 meters (5.5 yards) of fabric per person per year in the mid-1950s. Here is the magazine's account of the Aldehyde Shop: "What surprised us while walking up to the fifth floor is that nobody was in sight. There was only the sound coming from the myriad pipes . . . as if we were in a fantastic world of science."[91] The factory was a symbol for the new socialist era in which the workers were liberated, through mechanization, from dangerous and difficult work (although dangerous and difficult work was exactly how the factory was built). The magazine also wrote about a song sung by the spinning workers:

The golden star of *ch'ŏllima* shines on,
as we, the spinning workers, create fireworks.
Forever tended by our leader,
each work hand flows with excitement.[92]

The spinners' song leads to the final point of this chapter: the connection between vinalon and the ideology of work. The meaning of vinalon, as an everyday product of labor consumed by the public ("as we, the spinning workers, create fireworks"), has a dimension of fetishism: vinalon as a manifestation of the state. The collective labor contained in vinalon is misrecognized as the materialization of the state's capacity ("The golden star of Ch'ŏllima shines on"). The everyday dimension is situated precisely where ideological power is hidden. It begins with the misrecognition of the product—vinalon as a product not of collective labor but of state capacity. Specifically, the misrecognition is a process in the ideology of work in which work becomes the *object-cause* of desire. Vinalon supports the ideology of work by connecting work with desire ("each working hand flows with excitement").

Work is the object toward which desire sets its course; at the same time, work is the cause of that desire. And the conceptually circular movement prevents the satisfaction of desire. Desire moves around the object but never attains it, and so the object-cause does not have a limit (Lacan's *objet petit a*). In the labor process, whether socialist or capitalist in appearance, the circular movement of work as an object-cause takes on the characteristic of ambiguity, sustaining the complicity of workers within the unstable labor process while masking the subjugating reality of industrial production. The production of vinalon is the object-cause of workers' desire, which, like vinalon itself flowing out like a rainbow, can never be satisfied. The everyday is the concrete space where practice and ideology meet, ultimately sustaining the desire to work. For ideology to take effect, it must exist in everyday life as practice. Fetishism, misrecognition, and object causation are not merely concepts: they are essential stages in the production and consumption of things such as vinalon. What is more, in industrial work in general, they constitute the process by which the workers become, at least temporarily, complicit in the reproduction of their own working condition. Everyday life remains opaque as domination and subjectivity are enmeshed within it, neither of them fully arriving at its intent.

By the late 1960s, Hamhŭng boasted, along with the Vinalon Factory, the full operation of a half-dozen large factories, employing tens of thousands of workers and supporting the livelihoods of 500,000 people. Some thirty years later, however, Hamŭng's industrial production came to a standstill. Raw materials, supplies, and power began dwindling by the early 1990s, but, more than that, the workers stopped going to work in search of food and money, the two things the factories and the distribution system could no longer provide.[93] Stripped machine parts as well as pure nickel and copper taken from wires and pipes began to appear at local markets.[94] At the end of the twentieth century, the industries of Hamhŭng Plains suffered the same predicament as the rest of the country, but they were once the pride of North Korea's economy and some of the largest chemical factories in the world.

In his work on Magnitogorsk, the largest steel factory of the Stalin era, Stephen Kotkin writes that heavy industry was "pursued zealously by the Soviet leadership as the key to modern civilization." The paradox in the pursuit of Stalinist industrialization, as Kotkin points out, was the involvement of leading capitalist firms in the form of advice and aid.[95] For both existing socialism and existing capitalism of the twentieth century, industrialism was the road to their particular destinations. Whether the goal was to change the mode of production or to accumulate capital, the essential ingredient was the production of surplus, and nowhere was this production more effective and massive than in industrial work. The Vina-lon Factory, Magnitogorsk Iron and Steel Works, Gary Works (United States), and Pohang Iron and Steel Company (South Korea)—all emblem-atic of their national situation—were fundamentally the same in subsum-ing life under work in order or pump out surplus from the worker. At the heart of modernization (the socialist or any other kind) was the logic of industrialism treating work as sacred and productivity as the measure of human character, with the heroicization of exceptional workers in social-ism finding its equivalent in the idolization of self-made entrepreneurs in capitalism.

One aim of this chapter has been to contribute to shaping a critique in the study of North Korea that builds upon the routine method of search-ing out the failures and deviances of North Korea in relation to ideal imag-inations of socialism, capitalism, and democracy. To be sure, it is important to criticize North Korea's practice of patriarchy as a vast contradiction to the law on gender equality, the religion-like glorification of the nation's leader as a serious impediment to democracy, the expansion of militarism as a debilitating barrier to human emancipation, and the notion of sacred work as a thin veil of exploitative labor.

A glaring problem in such a style of critique, however, is that all the problems found in North Korea are also found in all other countries, nations, cultures, and traditions. The demand for improvements in human rights in North Korea, for example, illustrates this exact situation: Can a

Figure 5.9 The main entrance of the Vinalon Factory, May 2014. The smokestack alludes to the one built by Ri Hŭisang's team in 1961.
Source: Photograph by the author.

government or organization effectively condemn and demand changes in North Korea's human rights practices when it, too, violates these rights? The same logic can be applied to other issues. A way out of this quandary is to place the critique of the particularities of North Korea (its failures and deviances) within the general critique of modernity (capitalist modernity). The universal condition of the modern world can be critiqued by using particular, historical situations. The transnational history of the Vinalon Factory, the analysis of it in relation to industrialism, and the investigation of everyday work, all presented in this chapter, are such an attempt.

CONCLUSION

The Negation of Work and
Other Everyday Maneuvers

A sign was painted said Private Property,

but on the back side it didn't say nothing—

—WOODY GUTHRIE, "THIS LAND IS YOUR LAND" (ORIGINAL LYRICS)

For the vast majority of the North Korean people in the postwar period, their experience as citizens and subjects was one of neither coercion nor consensus, of neither repression nor reciprocity. In and through the space of the everyday, the abstract and concrete forms of state control (patriotism and production, for instance) contended with individuals to create a reality where both the state's and its citizens' choices and actions relied on each other for real effects. Everyday space brought about a lived experience, which *un*differentiated various forms of hegemony from subjective existence. Even during the demanding periods of shock-work campaigns, the people of North Korea experienced life as a whole. This is a crucial starting point for addressing the ambiguous practice of contention against the state. Contention is indeed an important action of ordinary people in the face of state power, but what complicates the matter is that the field of state power often depends on this very practice for proper functioning. In North Korea, contention was one way the shop floor organized and operated its production process. Such an interaction is represented in the novel *The Furnace Is Breathing*, where *what* and *how* things are made are the result of struggle among the workers as well as of the workers' struggle against the central plan's directives. The workers' improvisations, innovations, and contention on the shop floor are not outside the state's hegemonic boundaries. They are not in opposition to the greater milieu of state socialism. In the North Korea of the postwar period, the workers' individual experiences and improvisations were essential to realizing the grand plan as indispensable parts of mass campaigns to unify the workers and increase production.

For the North Korean state during the postwar period, the decisive domain of control was work. Work as a mode of hegemony stemmed from the need to accumulate surplus through industrialization. The industrial drive was a common trait in state socialist countries, and as far as *form* is concerned, industrial work was identical in socialism and capitalism. In the industrial situation, wage labor became the principle method of compensation, and productivity became a measure of human character. As a concept, work was not only a source of happiness and fulfillment but also a collective duty for all citizens. As practice, work was an activity through which the workers were politically organized and ideologically educated while engaged in production. And typical of state socialism, surplus value that came from work (always unpaid labor) ended up entirely in the possession of the state.

Postwar factory management in North Korea had a troika structure consisting of management, party, and union at each level: for example, at the first level of production the work team's management consisted of a work team leader, a party-cell delegate, and a union chief. The presence of the party in all aspects of production was to ensure that production occurred in correlation with not only national and industrial needs but also the party's ideological and political needs. Labor was both an economic and political act. Increasing production and productivity was a multidimensional effort of party involvement in production, mass campaigns, and ideological education, with the additional aims of promoting militancy in the workplace and linking production goals with loyalty to the state. The system of bestowing the title "labor hero" on workers was the pinnacle of ideological education because the title brought honor and material benefits and carried the message that ordinary workers possessed extraordinary potential. The attributes of work as simultaneously a source of collective happiness *and* a domain of control point to the ideological side of modern industrial work.

Along with ideological and moralistic means, monetary and calculative measures of increasing productivity and efficiency, too, were important. The preferred wage type in North Korea was piecework wage, where wage was determined by the quantitative expression of labor—the number of products actually produced at a certain level of quality. The measures to increase efficiency entailed the standardization of workload, work time, and work space; they were methods of improving productivity without the workers' own effort or innovation. Wage and efficiency calculations are not unique to socialism: they are universal industrial measures. In the same way, piecework wage is a universally practiced form of wage. Nevertheless, at least in principle, in the postwar period the socialist wage had to be defined as radically different from the capitalist wage. It could no longer be the quantified expression of labor value. Instead, the socialist wage was to be a fair return of the total surplus back to the worker after a certain amount was kept by the state for public needs. The irony of piecework wage was that it was also the preferred wage system in capitalist production, where the workers could be persuaded by the earning potential to produce more without concern for the intensity of exploitation.

The relationship between work and ideology can be questioned in a similar manner. Is the ideological side of work, as represented through mass campaigns, propaganda, and morale, exclusively a socialist phenomenon in countries such as North Korea? Is ideological education in the workplace unique to state socialist countries? To begin with the latter, what was unique about socialist work management, including North Korea's, was the direct involvement of the party at all levels of the factory for the purpose of workers' education. Such political party involvement may be unimaginable in a so-called capitalist country, but the occurrence of workers' education in the capitalist setting is quite common. One role of a human resources department is precisely ideological—that is, to praise the firm and its workers while masking the fact that all wage work is exploitative. What else is corporate culture but ideological propaganda ("employee of the month," "casual Fridays," and "company happy hour") that enables the workers to accept their condition as a means of production for the owner? The market (like the party) is the ever-present guide in the capitalist firm, and the unquestioned belief in market logic shapes the firm's process of management, including the justifications for layoffs and antiunion campaigns.

Regarding the first question, on work ideology, all types of wage work are necessarily ideological, for the unmistakable reason of surplus, which is produced only through unpaid labor and has to be appropriated by owners without making the workers feel completely cheated. This condition of appropriation is identical in existing capitalism and existing socialism. The condition of appropriation, which keeps the workers producing, is created and sustained in large ways by the ideology of work, which should not be treated as a mere frame of mind. Every moment in the processes of production and exchange can undergo an ideological turn, the transformation from a non-ideological moment to an ideological one. For instance, a mass movement to increase production is nonideological if it plainly organizes volunteer work in order to produce surplus without compensating the workers. In this case, the workers are aware that there is no compensation, but they may still participate because resisting the movement could be more troublesome for them. However, a mass movement *is* ideological if volunteer work is organized in the name of the nation. The workers are still aware of the noncompensatory nature of the work they perform, but they willingly participate because the volunteer work may bring some benefit to the nation. The ideological turn is thus the inclusion of the nation in the process of organizing volunteer work, which still does not change the fact that the labor is unpaid. What is misrecognized within the ideology of work is not the fact of unpaid labor—the workers may know well their work begets no compensation—but rather the exploitative practice of the state dissimulated as the call of the nation. What is both plain and disturbing is the ideological subjugation happening while the workers know very well they are not getting paid.

If every element of production and exchange can undergo the ideological turn, then it goes without saying that the state also shifts between being a nonideological entity and an ideological entity. The state is an ideological entity involved in organizing work and controlling surplus. This role of the state is more apparent in state socialism, but even in capitalism the state directly participates in the control of labor and surplus through, for example, labor laws, government procurements, and trade agreements with other states. Capital and labor are always framed—mediated—by the state. One function of the state lies within the process of surplus appropriation and redistribution, whether this process takes place in socialism or in capitalism. The state, in this function, is a type of exchange, which is the philosopher Kojin Karatani's original assertion. Karatani opposes the long-held view of the state (and of the nation) as a superstructure determined by the economic base: "The world organized by money and credit is rather one of illusion." Karatani also sees it limiting to consider the state as a political expression of the nation or an ideological apparatus of hegemony. These traits are observations of the state from only within the state. Rather, Karatani stresses seeing the state as "existing in relationship with other states" because "absolutist states appeared amid the competition with each other in world capitalism, and are still amid the same competition."[1] Socialist states are no different.

Karatani's observation of the state is based on the exchange principle of plunder and redistribution or, more specifically, the institution of redistribution "in order to plunder continuously." Such an exchange relationship began in the feudal ages between the state and independent agrarian communities, when peasants paid various taxes in return for the overseers' protection and public projects: "That is to say that plunder takes the guise of reciprocity. This form of redistribution was essentially consistent with that in absolutist monarchies as well as nation-states. By redistributing the tax it levies, the state apparatus seeks to resolve class conflicts and solve unemployment problems. And again all of these are represented as the state's gift."[2]

The state's role, especially salient in state socialist countries such as North Korea, is found in exchange *and* in the organization of that exchange. The process of appropriating (plundering) surplus and redistributing it for the survival of the population is necessarily an ideological process because how the surplus is returned is uneven—uneven according to class, status, geography, and gender. Moreover, for Karatani, the exchange-type state is different from the exchange-type market, where exchange occurs through money. The state is a unique type of exchange separate from the market. Whatever name a modern state takes on ("liberal democracy" or "socialist state"), the essential mechanism of plunder and redistribution remains the same in the type of exchange it practices.

Karatani's concept of the state as a specific exchange type poses a radical question for this study on everyday work. Is genuinely useful and fulfilling work possible under the existing form of the state? Any kind of labor organized within the state, whether in state socialism or so-called capitalism, inevitably enters into an unequal exchange with the state. The practice of honorable work, common across the world, is an ideological treatment masking the exploitative exchange type of the state. As long as the state engages in the exchange of plunder and distribution, no type of work will be free of ideological mechanisms concealing the exploitative relationship. The workers remain a means of surplus production for someone/something whose final interest is the preservation of this condition. The ideological mechanisms of work are not easy to dispose of: they are parts of everyday life. The mundane and repetitive characteristic of everyday life sustains the exchange relationship between the state and the workers.

What is to become of work and everyday life? Now is a moment to consider Lefebvre's view of Marx as a "thinker of the negative."[3] In Marx's designation of wage workers as revolutionary beings, he is also referring to the possible negation of their identity as labor commodities. Negative reasoning is thus behind Marx's claim that labor must return to life so that life—not labor—can become honorable. The final step of communism, too, is seen in such a light: communism is the "complete return of man to himself as a social (i.e., human) being—a return accomplished consciously and embracing the entire wealth of previous development."[4] Lefebvre speaks about how this final step can be reached: "Workers . . . have as their historical mission the negation of work."[5] It is the rejection of commodified labor—the collective negation of work—that fosters the imagination of a new kind of work. But, of course, the process of negating work also involves everyday life because the abstract and concrete ideological elements of work are always caught up in the everyday. Here, I turn to Lefebvre one last time. Real change, he famously said, is not just a change in personnel or institutions: "it must change everyday life."[6] Changing everyday life must happen from within by fundamentally changing the labor market and the state organizing it. This is a double movement of dissolving both the capital-commodity economy and the competitive state-form economy existing across the world.

Creating a detailed map of this movement is an ongoing project. A useful source on the matter is, once again, Karatani. First, on the aim of abolishing the capitalist economy, Karatani emphasizes resistance outside production. Because of the ideological pull of the modern production process to make the workers' interest the same as that of the owner, the workers feel the need to preserve the very system operating to commodify their labor and organize them hierarchically and unequally. Within the production process, "workers are apt to adopt the same position as capital," Karatani says, which makes universal struggle that transcends particular interests very difficult. But once the workers' concurrent role as consumers is also recognized, the sphere of resistance becomes larger. The location of resistance is now outside the production process and within circulation, where capital finds itself "placed in a relation of servitude to worker-consumers." The recognition of the proletariat as consumers is an important step in widening the methods of resistance against the capitalist system because within the process of circulation, capital is unable to control the proletariat: "capital has the power to force people to work but not to make them buy." From this position, Karatani proposes the boycott as the primary method of resistance by the proletariat: the refusal to buy commodities and the refusal to sell the labor commodity. As capital profit decreases, a noncapitalist economy would arise through the expansion of consumer–producer cooperatives, local currencies, and local credit systems.[7] Labor movements based on unions are still the most powerful kind of resistance, but they are partial and thus need to be augmented by worker-consumer movements.

Second, on the aim of abolishing the state, Karatani envisions a world without sovereign states. As states exist today, all are hegemonic entities with the purpose of maintaining sovereignty through the method of plunder and distribution, while competitively engaging with other states for resources—competitions inevitably leading to military expansion and aggression. States, in other words, exist in a situation of constant antagonism with each other (there are no permanent allies). For Karatani, this antagonism cannot be alleviated through military means. He says, "A true resolution of this hostility is only possible through the elimination of economic disparities between states." Economic disparities can be eliminated when the source perpetuating the disparities is eliminated—that is, when states are eliminated. A new world system without states would be a federation of nations. And the exchanges among the states would be grounded on reciprocity, which is further based on the principle of gift. Karatani stresses that reciprocity based on gift is not like today's foreign aid: "what would be given under this [system] are not products but the technical knowledge (intellectual property) needed to carry out production." Furthermore, reciprocity is not limited to property and extends to practices such as voluntary disarmament to abolish weapons posing a threat to others.[8] A global structure of reciprocity—of ideas, technologies, and practices of peace—would therefore have the force of undermining and replacing the unequal world system of states.

I am in support of Karatani's vision. In the introduction, I wrote that North Korea has all the same problems humanity faces in this world. Yes, North Korea is a place suffering from state oppression, poverty, food shortage, economic inequality, militarization of culture, negligence of labor and human rights, personality worship, party despotism, lack of artistic freedom, lack of freedom of information, lack of freedom of association, economic restrictions, joblessness, bans on travel and migration, and international derision. But these problems, as egregious as they are in North

Korea, exist everywhere. The fact that 24 million children experience hunger each day in the United States, the wealthiest and most abundant country in the world, is just as appalling and unacceptable as the problems of food shortage and malnutrition in North Korea. Political imprisonment is also a serious problem in the North Korean state, but the United States has the highest number of incarcerated people in the world.

The proper and practical stance is to recognize North Korea's problems as universal problems. This stance is to be critical of the North Korean state but not to be naive about the ubiquity or the causes of these problems. My task is to adapt the double movement of overcoming the commodity system and realizing global reciprocity to my own life as an academic working in the United States. From my position, I can construct my everyday maneuvers in the following ways. First, in classrooms, talks, and conferences, I can foster discussions about the world that move beyond the logics of market, security, and sovereignty—a rhetorical maneuver particularly important when discussing North Korea. Second, I can be rigorous in critical, historical, and transnational research that contributes to the body of knowledge useful for countering the forces of capital and state. Third, I can build lasting exchanges between students and scholars from the United States and North Korea, with sufficient public funding to alleviate financial disparities between them. And fourth, I can help to redress the university's market practices by advocating for free public education. These activities are not new, nor are they necessarily radical. People all over the world do them in everyday life, which always has the potential to supersede various forms of domination.

Notes

Introduction: Postwar North Korea, the Era of Work

1. Vinalon is North Korea's version of the synthetic fiber pulled from polyvinyl alcohol. It became an important fiber for textile manufacturing in postwar North Korea because polyvinyl alcohol could be made from the coal that was abundant there and because its invention was attributed to a colonial Korean scientist, Ri Sŭnggi. Chapter 5 is about this fiber.

2. Chunggongŏp Wiwŏnhoe (Heavy Industry Committee), *Pinallon Kongjang kŏnsŏl* (The construction of the Vinalon Factory) (Pyongyang: Kungnip Kŏnsŏl Ch'ulp'ansa, 1961), 318; all translations from Korean to English are mine unless otherwise noted.

3. Chunggongŏp Wiwŏnhoe, *Pinallon Kongjang kŏnsŏl*, 321.

4. See Cheehyung Kim, "Total, Thus Broken: *Chuch'e sasang* and North Korea's Terrain of Subjectivity," *Journal of Korean Studies* 17, no. 1 (2012): 69–96.

5. Leon Trotksy, "How to Begin" (August 8, 1923), in *Problems of Everyday Life: And Other Writings on Culture and Science* (New York: Monad Press, 1973), 72.

6. Leon Trotksy, "Vodka, the Church, and the Cinema" (July 12, 1923), in *Problems of Everyday Life*, 32.

7. Suzy Kim, *Everyday Life in the North Korean Revolution, 1945–1950* (Ithaca, NY: Cornell University Press, 2013), 240.

8. Kim, *Everyday Life*, 11–12.

9. Kim, *Everyday Life,* 124.

10. Kim, *Everyday Life*, 41.

11. Kojin Karatani, *The Structure of World History: From Modes of Production to Modes of Exchange*, trans. Michael K. Bourdaghs (Durham, NC: Duke University Press, 2014), 1–11, esp. 9.

12. Karatani, *Structure of World History*, 10.

13. Karatani, *Structure of World History*, 273.

14. Karatani, *Structure of World History*, 250.

15. Yun Ŭisŏp and Ch'a Sunhŏn, *Konghwaguk'ka esŏŭi imgŭm chojik kwa rodong ŭi kijun-hwa* (The standardization of wage and labor in the republic) (Pyongyang: Kung-nip Ch'ulp'ansa, 1955), 55–56.

16. Karatani, *Structure of World History*, 249.

17. Karatani, *Structure of World History*, 256–257.

18. Karl Marx, *Capital*, vol. 1 (London: Penguin, 1976), 509.

19. Marx, *Capital*, 1:530–533.

20. Marx, *Capital*, 1:532.

21. Marx, *Capital*, 1:544.

22. Marx, *Capital*, 1:533, 536.

23. Michael Buraowy, *The Politics of Production: Factory Regimes Under Capitalism and Socialism* (London: Verso, 1985), 51–52.

24. Buraowy, *Politics of Production*, 54.

25. See Kimura Mitsuhiko and Abe Keiji, *Chŏnjaengi mandŭn nara: Pukhan ŭi kunsa kongŏphwa* (The country made by war: The military industrialization of North Korea), trans. Ch'a Munsŏk and Pak Chŏngjin (Seoul: Mizi, 2009).

26. Yun Sejung, *Yonggwangno nŭn sumshinda* (The furnace is breathing) (Pyongyang: Munye Ch'ulp'ansa, 1960).

27. Hyun Ok Park, *The Capitalist Unconscious: From Korean Unification to Transnational Korea* (New York: Columbia University Press, 2015), 3, 209.

28. Park, *Capitalist Unconscious*, 13, 7, 289.

29. Park, *Capitalist Unconscious*, 15.

30. Hwang Changyŏp, *Sahoe palchŏnsa* (The history of societal development) (Pyongyang: Chosŏn Rodongdang Ch'ulp'ansa, 1956).

1. The Historical Concept of Work

1. Kim Il Sung, *Kim Ilsŏng chŏjakchip* (The works of Kim Il Sung), 47 vols. (Pyongyang: Chosŏn Rodongdang Ch'ulp'ansa, 1979–1997), 2:168. The Hŭngnam Fertilizer Factory, the largest chemical fertilizer factory in North Korea, was rebuilt from the Japanese-owned Nihon Chisso factory in Hŭngnam, which began production in 1930. At its peak during the colonial period, it employed 7,918 workers (2,402 of them Japanese) and had the highest production of ammonium sulfate in the empire, at 500,000 tons a year, or 26 percent of the Japanese Empire's total ammonium sulfate production. On the early industrial system of North Korea, see Kimura Mitsuhiko and Abe Keiji, *Chŏnjaengi mandŭn nara: Pukhan ŭi kunsa kongŏphwa* (The country made by war: The military industrialization of North Korea), trans. Cha Munsŏk and Pak Chŏngjin (Seoul: Mizi, 2009).

2. On Nakchung (1901–?) was in Pyongyang to attend the historic North–South Joint Conference, April 19–23, 1948, for which 695 representatives from fifty-six organizations (including political parties) gathered at Moranbong Theater to

discuss the possibility of a unified Korean state, the hope for which was dimming by early 1948. The conference was a final push for a single governing body in Korea, especially in response to the United Nations' plan to guide a "nationwide" election, which would take place only in South Korea (on May 10). The conference also led to the famous meetings of the Four Kims on April 26 and 30: nationalist leaders Kim Ku and Kim Kyusik of South Korea and Communist leaders Kim Il Sung and Kim Tubong of North Korea. On Nakchung was attending as a reporter for the newspaper *Chungang Ilbo*, and based on his experience there he wrote *Pukchosŏn kihaeng* (Travels to North Korea) (Seoul: Chosŏn Chungangilbo Ch'ulp'anbu, 1948), published later that year in South Korea.

3. On, *Pukchosŏn kihaeng*, 6, 7, 8.
4. Charles K. Armstrong, *The North Korean Revolution, 1945–1950* (Ithaca, NY: Cornell University Press, 2003), 76.
5. Central Statistical Board, *Statistical Returns of the National Economy of the Democratic People's Republic of Korea, 1946–1960* (Pyongyang: Foreign Languages Publishing House, 1961), 57.
6. Central Statistical Board, *Statistical Returns*, 57–58.
7. On North Korean law, see Ch'oe Chonggo, *Pukhanpŏb* (North Korean law) (Seoul: Pagyŏngsa, 2001).
8. Kimura and Abe, *Chŏnjaengi mandŭn nara*, 234.
9. Kimura and Abe, *Chŏnjaengi mandŭn nara*, 234.
10. Kim Il Sung, *Chŏjakchip*, 2:344–345.
11. Central Statistical Board, *Statistical Returns*, 36–37.
12. Kuksa P'yŏnch'an Wiwŏnhoe (National Institute of Korean History), *Pukhan kwan'gye saryojip* (Historical material on North Korea), vol. 30 (Kwachŏn: Kuksa P'yŏnch'an Wiwŏnhoe Ch'ulp'ansa, 1998), 201.
13. Kuksa P'yŏnch'an Wiwŏnhoe, *Pukhan kwan'gye saryojip*, 297–299.
14. Kuksa P'yŏnch'an Wiwŏnhoe, *Pukhan kwan'gye saryojip*, 299.
15. Kuksa P'yŏnch'an Wiwŏnhoe, *Pukhan kwan'gye saryojip*, 299.
16. Kim Sango, "Kisa" (The engineer), in *Pukhan munhak* (The literature of North Korea), ed. Sin Hyŏnggi, O Sŏngho, and Yi Sŏnmi (Seoul: Munhak'kwa Chisŏngsa, 2007), 1223–1224.
17. Ri Chŭngok, "Roryŏk hubi yangsŏng saŏp ŭi palchŏn" (The development in the training of reserve labor power), *Rodong*, no. 9 (1958): 26–31.
18. Ri Chŭngok, "Roryŏk hubi yangsŏng."
19. Ri Chŭngok, "Roryŏk hubi yangsŏng."
20. Kim Il Sung, *Chŏjakchip*, 6:24.
21. Ch'a Munsŏk, "Han'guk Chŏnjaeng sigi Pukhan ŭi chŏnsi saengsanch'eje: Kongjang sogae wa chŏnsi saengsanjŏngch'aek ŭl chumgsim ŭro" (The wartime production system of North Korea during the Korean War: A look at the factory relocation project and wartime production policy), *T'ongil Munje Yŏngu* 39 (2003): 79.
22. Ch'a, "Han'guk Chŏnjaeng sigi," 79.
23. Kim Tongch'an, "Roryŏk poch'ung sa'ŏp ŭi palchŏn" (The development of reserve labor power), *Rodong*, no. 8 (1958): 8.

24. *Rodong Sinmun,* "Chŏnsi ŭimu roryŏkdongwŏn e kwanhayŏ" (On wartime compulsory labor mobilization), July 28, 1950.
25. *Rodong Sinmun,* "Chŏnsi ŭimu roryŏkdongwŏn e kwanhayŏ."
26. Kim Tongch'an, "Roryŏk poch'ung sa'ŏp," 8.
27. Sŏ Tongman, *Pukchosŏn sahoechuŭi ch'eje sŏngnipsa, 1945–1961* (The formation of state socialism in North Korea, 1945–1961) (Seoul: Sunin, 2005), 451.
28. Ch'a, "Han'guk Chŏnjaeng sigi," 81
29. Ch'a, "Han'guk Chŏnjaeng sigi," 81.
30. Kuksa P'yŏnch'an Wiwŏnhoe, *Pukhan kwan'gye saryojip,* 438.
31. Pak Yŏngja, "Yugio chŏnjaeng kwa Pukhanyŏsŏng ŭi nodongsegye: P'agoe wa pisaengsan ŭi ch'angjo wa saengsan ŭi chuch'e yŏttŏn yŏsŏng yŏn'gu" (War of June 25 and the working world of North Korean women: A study of women who were the subjects of creation and production from a war of destruction and antiproduction), *Asia Yŏsŏng Yŏn'gu* 45, no. 2 (2006): 65.
32. Pak Yŏngja, "Yugio chŏnjaeng kwa Pukhanyŏsŏng," 70.
33. Kim Soryŏn, "Hambukdo nae tasunyŏnsŏngdŭl soksok saengsanjikjang e chinch'ul" (Many women of North Hamgyŏng enter production facilities), *Rodong Sinmun,* July 27, 1950.
34. Kim Soryŏn, "Hambukdo."
35. Pak Yŏngja, "Yugio chŏnjaeng kwa Pukhanyŏsŏng," 67–68.
36. Kuksa P'yŏnch'an Wiwŏnhoe, *Pukhan kwan'gye saryojip,* 427.
37. Kim Il Sung, *Chŏjakchip,* 7:136–137.
38. Kim Il Sung, *Chŏjakchip,* 6:243.
39. Kim Il Sung, *Chŏjakchip,* 6:526.
40. Chosŏn Chungang T'ongsinsa (Korean Central News Agency), "Che ilhoe Choguk Pogwi Pokkwŏn Ch'uch'ŏm Wiwŏnhoe kusŏng" (The first Fatherland Restoration Lottery Drawing Committee established), *Rodong Sinmun,* November 25, 1951.
41. Chin Hŭigwan, "Pukhan ŭi kyŏngje wa kyŏngjekwalli pangsik" (North Korea's economy and economic management), in *Rodongsinmun ŭl t'onghae pon Pukhan pyŏnhwa* (Changes in North Korea as observed through *Rodong Sinmun*), ed. Ko Yuhwan (Seoul: Sunin, 2006), 288.
42. Chin Hŭigwan, "Pukhan ŭi kyŏngje," 288.
43. Kimura and Abe, *Chŏnjaengi mandŭn nara,* 293. The authors cite a letter from Kim Il Sung and Pak Hŏnyŏng to the Russian ambassador on February 3, 1949, in which North Korea requested a loan of US$30 million, the repayment to begin in 1951 for three years.
44. Kimura and Abe, *Chŏnjaengi mandŭn nara,* 252–288.
45. Kimura and Abe, *Chŏnjaengi mandŭn nara,* 263.
46. Kimura and Abe, *Chŏnjaengi mandŭn nara,* 267–268.
47. Kim Il Sung, *Chŏjakchip,* 6:134.
48. Kim Il Sung, *Chŏjakchip,* 6:134.
49. Ch'a, "Han'guk Chŏnjaeng sigi," 89.
50. Ch'a, "Han'guk Chŏnjaeng sigi," 91.
51. Ch'a, "Han'guk Chŏnjaeng sigi," 91.

52. Giorgio Agamben, *State of Exception*, trans. Kevin Attell (Chicago: University of Chicago Press, 2005), 4, 29.

53. Kim Tubong, "Sinnyŏnsa" (New Year's address), *Rodong Sinmun*, January 1, 1953.

54. Kim Tubong, "Sinnyŏnsa."

55. Agamben, *State of Exception*, 31.

56. Agamben, *State of Exception*, 5, 2.

57. Hwang Changyŏp, *Sahoe palchŏnsa* (The history of societal development) (Pyongyang: Chosŏn Rodongdang Ch'ulp'ansa, 1956), 7, 14, 16–17. Hwang Changyŏp was educated in Japan and the Soviet Union. In 1965, he became the president of Kim Il Sung University, where he taught the young Kim Jong Il. From 1972 to 1983, he served as chair of the Standing Committee of the Supreme People's Assembly. In the early 1970s, he devoted himself to turning Kim Il Sung's idea of *chuch'e* (self-reliance, subjectivity) into a coherent thought system and ultimately the national philosophy of North Korea. In 1997, however, he defected to South Korea, where he was an outspoken critic of North Korea's ruling class.

58. Hwang, *Sahoe palchŏnsa*, 126, 130, 133, 134–135. The phrase Hwang used in his text contradicts the quintessential socialist maxim "From each according to one's ability, to each according to one's need," in which the crucial point is that what a person receives should be based not on labor output but on personal need.

59. Kim Il Sung, *Chŏjakchip*, 21:464, 465.

60. Kim Il Sung, *Chŏjakchip*, 13:346–347.

61. Karl Marx, "*The German Ideology*," in Karl Marx and Friedrich Engels, *The Marx–Engels Reader*, ed. Robert Tucker (New York: Norton, 1978), 159, 176, 193, my emphasis.

62. Karl Marx, "Wage, Labor, and Capital," in Marx and Engels, *Marx–Engels Reader*, 204.

63. Shlomo Avineri, *Social and Political Thought of Marx* (London: Cambridge University Press, 1968), 85–86.

64. Avineri, *Social and Political Thought of Marx*, 85, 89.

65. This definition comes from Engels's footnote to the fourth German edition of *Capital*. See Karl Marx, *Capital*, vol. 1 (London: Penguin, 1976), 138 n.

66. Karl Marx, *Value, Price, and Profit* (London: ElecBooks, 1998), 53.

67. Herbert Applebaum, *The Concept of Work: Ancient, Medieval, and Modern* (Albany: State University of New York Press, 1992), 7–8.

68. Applebaum, *Concept of Work*, 579.

69. Applebaum, *Concept of Work*, 579.

70. Applebaum, *Concept of Work*, 579.

71. Aristotle, *The Nichomachean Ethics* (Cambridge, MA: Harvard University Press, 1934), 615, 617.

72. The notion of work in the Christian Bible comes from this tradition. As punishment for eating the fruit of knowledge, Adam and Eve are bound to a life in which survival depends on their toil on the ground. Physical work, in other words, is God's punishment.

73. As discussed in Applebaum, *Concept of Work*, 582.

74. Applebaum, *Concept of Work*, 582.

75. As discussed in Applebaum, *Concept of Work*, 584.

76. Applebaum, *Concept of Work*, 584.

77. Applebaum, *Concept of Work*, 584.

78. Karl Polanyi, *The Great Transformation: The Political and Economic Origins of Our Time* (Boston: Beacon, 2001).

79. V. I. Lenin, "The State and Revolution," in *Essential Works of Lenin* (New York: Dover, 1987), 342.

80. V. I. Lenin, "From the Destruction of the Old Socialist System to the Creation of the New" (April 11, 1920), Marxists Internet Archive, http://www.marxists .org/archive/lenin/works/1920/apr/11.htm.

81. Jay B. Sorenson, *The Life and Death of Soviet Trade Unionism, 1917–1928* (New York: Atherton Press 1969), 140. Sorenson's now classic work on Bolshevik domination of workers shows the development of the modern socialist concept of work under Lenin.

82. Sorenson, *Life and Death*, 141.

83. Lenin, "The State and Revolution," 345, 348, emphasis in original.

84. Ch'a Munsŏk, *Pannodong ŭi yut'op'ia* (The utopia of antilabor) (Seoul: Pak Chongchŏl Ch'ulp'ansa, 2001), 16.

85. Kwŏn Tuŏn, "Ch'angjojŏk rodong ŭi him" (The strength of creative labor), *Rodong*, no. 6 (1958): 1.

86. Henri De Man, *Joy in Work* (1927; reprint, New York: Arno Press, 1977), 81–171. Henri De Man (1885–1953), a Flemish Belgian, was a leading socialist intellectual of Europe in the early twentieth century, at one point assuming the presidency of the Belgian Workers' Party. He was critical of Marxism's claims about the spontaneous emergence of workers' revolutionary class consciousness, but he remained devoted to the international socialist movement. His support for fascism and his collaboration with the Nazi Party tainted his life and thought, however. He died in a car accident in 1953, which may have been suicide. The literary theorist Paul De Man is his nephew.

2. Work as State Practice

1. Ch'a Munsŏk, *Pannodong ŭi yut'op'ia* (The utopia of antilabor) (Seoul: Pak Chongchŏl Ch'ulp'ansa, 2001), 271.

2. On the dynamics of the troika system, see Ch'a Munsŏk, "Pukhan ŭi kongjang-gwallicheje wa chŏljŏnggi sŭt'allinjuŭi: Taehan ŭi saŏpch'egye e taehan saeroun haesŏk" (North Korea's factory-management system and High Stalinism: A new interpretation of the Taean Work System), *Pukhan Yŏn'gu Hakhoebo* 3, no. 2 (1999): 227–250, and *Pannodong ŭi yut'op'ia*.

3. On the concept of work in Karl Marx and Adam Smith, see Shlomo Avineri, *The Social and Political Thought of Marx* (London: Cambridge University Press, 1968), and Paul J. McNulty, "Adam Smith's Concept of Labor," *Journal of the History of Ideas* 34, no. 3 (1973): 345–366.

4. János Kornai, *The Socialist System: The Political Economy of Communism* (Princeton, NJ: Princeton University Press, 1992).

5. Kornai, *Socialist System*, 264.

6. Michael Burawoy, *The Politics of Production: Factory Regimes Under Capitalism and Socialism* (London: Verso, 1985), 159, 160.

7. Burawoy, *Politics of Production*, 163.

8. Burawoy, *Politics of Production*, 163, emphasis in original.

9. Central Statistical Board, *Statistical Returns of the National Economy of the Democratic People's Republic of Korea, 1946–1960* (Pyongyang: Foreign Languages Publishing House, 1961), 17.

10. Central Statistical Board, *Statistical Returns*, 123.

11. Central Statistical Board, *Statistical Returns*, 17.

12. Central Statistical Board, *Statistical Returns*, 123.

13. Ch'a, *Pannodong ŭi yut'op'ia*, 130–132.

14. All of the information in this paragraph comes from Kwŏn Hŭiyŏng, "Chosŏn Nodong Kongjehoe wa kongje" (Workers' Mutual Aid Society and *kongje*), *Chŏngsin Munhwa Yŏn'gu* 16, no. 2 (1993): 142, 143–144.

15. Sin Yongha, "Ch'ŏn'gubaekisipinyŏn Chosŏn Nodong Yŏnmaenghoe ŭi ch'angrip kwa nodong undong" (The formation of the Chosŏn Workers' League in 1922 and the labor movement), *Sahoewa Yŏksa* 15, no. 1 (1989): 55–96, esp. 75.

16. Minjujuŭi Minjok Chŏnsŏn (Democratic National United Front), *Chosŏn haebang yŏn'bo* (Annual report on Korea's liberation) (Seoul: Minjujuŭi Minjok Chŏnsŏn Press, 1946), 158, cited in Charles K. Armstrong, *The North Korean Revolution, 1945–1950* (Ithaca, NY: Cornell University Press, 2003), 87.

17. Kwŏn Oyun, "Pukhan ŭi pyŏnhwach'ujin kanŭngseryŏk ŭrosŏ Chigŏp Ch'ongdongmaeng ŭi kŏmt'o" (A study of the General Federation of Trade Unions as a possible agent of change in North Korea), *Taehan Chŏngch'ihak Hoebo* 13, no. 2 (2005): 36.

18. Kwŏn Oyun, "Pukhan ŭi pyŏnhwach'ujin," 38.

19. Sŏ Tongman, *Pukchosŏn sahoechuŭi ch'eje sŏngnipsa, 1945–1961* (The formation of state socialism in North Korea, 1945–1961) (Seoul: Sunin, 2005), 321.

20. Anna Louise Strong, *Inside North Korea: An Eye-witness Report* (N.p.: Self-published, 1949), 32.

21. *Rodong Sinmun*, "Nambuk Chosŏn chikmaeng tanche rŭl t'ongil hayŏ Chosŏn Chigŏp Ch'ongdongmaeng ŭro sinbalchok" (The inauguration of the General Federation of Trade Unions of Korea by uniting the trade federations of South and North Koreas), January 24, 1951.

22. Quoted in Kim Il Sung, *Kim Ilsŏng chŏjakchip* (The works of Kim Il Sung), 47 vols. (Pyongyang: Chosŏn Rodongdang Ch'ulp'ansa, 1979–1997), 12:132.

23. Chŏng Sangdon, "Pukhan nodongjohap ŭi 'chayulsŏng' nonjaeng: Haebang ihubutŏ han'gukjŏnjaeng ijŏnkkaji" (The debate on the autonomy of North Korea's trade unions: From liberation to the Korean War), *Sahoe Kwahak Nonjip* 21, no. 1 (2003): 51–71.

24. Ch'a, *Pannodong ŭi yut'op'ia*, 143.

25. Deborah A. Kaple, *Dream of a Red Factory: The Legacy of High Stalinism in China* (New York: Oxford University Press, 1994), 21–22.

26. Kaple, *Dream of a Red Factory*, 7–9. One of the most unfortunate aspects of state socialism was and is the culture of militarism. How and why militarism came to dominate socialist culture is not addressed in this study, but it is a worthy future project.

27. On socialist factory management, see Joseph S. Berliner, *Factory and Manager in the USSR* (Cambridge, MA: Harvard University Press, 1957); Alexander Vucinich, "The Structure of Factory Control in the Soviet Union," *American Sociological Review* 15, no. 2 (1950): 179–186; Hiroaki Kuromiya, "*Edinonachalie* and the Soviet Industrial Manager, 1928–1937," *Soviet Studies* 36, no. 2 (1984): 185–204; and Ch'a, "Pukhan ǔi kongjanggwallicheje" and *Pannodong ǔi yut'op'ia*. As an additional agency of factory control, Alexander Vucinich includes local voluntary groups, but their actual influence on controlling production seems miniscule. Vucinich's article is very helpful in other ways, though, in that he places factory management within a network of various governmental agencies, including the Central Board of Industrial Management, trusts and combines, cabinet ministries, and the State Planning Commission.

28. Berliner, *Factory and Manager*, 17–24.

29. Berliner, *Factory and Manager*, 15–16.

30. Kuromiya, "*Edinonachalie*," 187, 185.

31. Kuromiya, "*Edinonachalie*," 196.

32. Ch'a, *Pannodong ǔi yut'op'ia*, 194.

33. Kim Il Sung, *Chŏjakchip*, 8:303.

34. Kim Il Sung, *Chŏjakchip*, 8:303.

35. Changes in the line of factory control in North Korea:

    1948–1972: cabinet, ministry, bureau, factory

    1972–1985: administration, department, bureau, factory

    1985–1998: administration, department, factory trust, factory

    1998–today: cabinet, ministry, factory trust, factory

The cabinet and the administration are similar in function. In 1972, with the establishment of the Socialist Constitution of the DPRK, the cabinet–ministry system (headed by a premier) was dissolved and replaced by the administration–department system (headed by a president). In 1998, with the adoption of another constitution, the cabinet–ministry system was brought back. The actual chain of control of factories is more complex, however. The Ministry of Industry directly manages some important factories, such as the Hwanghae Iron and Steel Works, and the military manages its own weapons-making factories.

36. Central Statistical Board, *Statistical Returns*, 36–37.

37. Kim Il Sung, *Chŏjakchip*, 10:30.

38. Kim Il Sung, *Chŏjakchip*, 8:303.

39. Kim Il Sung, *Chŏjakchip*, 8:365.

40. Kim Il Sung, *Chŏjakchip*, 8:387.

41. Ch'a, "Pukhan ǔi kongjanggwallicheje," 237.

42. Kim Ŭnggi, "Kiŏpso, kongjang tŭl esŏ saengsan munhwa ŭi hwangnip ŭl wihayŏ" (Toward establishing production culture in firms and factories), *Rodong*, no. 6 (1958): 6.

43. Sahoegwahagwon Kyŏngjeyŏn'guso Kongŏpgyŏngjeyŏn'gusil (Industrial Economy Research Team of Economic Research Center at the Institute for Social Science), *Sahoejuŭi kyŏngjegwalli esŏ taean ŭi saŏpchegye* (The Taean Work System in socialist economic management) (Pyongyang: Sahoegwahak Ch'ulp'ansa, 1969), 187.

44. Chŏng Ilyŏng, "Kongjang kwallich'eje rŭl t'onghae pon Pukhan sahoe ŭi pyŏnhwa: Tangbisŏ-chibaein-nodongja samgak kwan'gye ŭi pyŏnhwa rŭl chungsim ŭro" (Changes in North Korean society as seen through the factory-management system: Changes in the triangular relationship between the party secretary, factory director, and the worker), *T'ongil Yŏn'gu* 17, no. 1 (2013): 16.

45. Kim Il Sung, *Chŏjakchip*, 16:497.

46. Kim Il Sung, *Chŏjakchip*, 16:500.

47. Sahoegwahagwon Kyŏngjeyŏn, *Sahoejuŭi kyŏngjegwalli esŏ taean ŭi saŏpchegye*, 216, 250, 267, 303.

48. Franz Schurmann, *Ideology and Organization in Communist China* (Berkeley and Los Angeles: University of California Press, 1966), 256, 258.

49. Schurmann, *Ideology and Organization*, 267, 271.

50. Schurmann, *Ideology and Organization*, 285.

51. Kim Chongyŏn, "Rodong kijunhwa saŏp ŭi palchŏn" (The development in the standardization of labor), *Rodong*, no. 8 (1958): 12.

52. Kim Chongyŏn, "Rodong kijunhwa," 14.

53. Kim Chongyŏn, "Rodong kijunhwa," 14.

54. Kim Il Sung, *Chŏjakchip*, 8:46–47.

55. Kim Chongyŏn, "Rodong kijunhwa," 14.

56. Kim Chongyŏn, "Rodong kijunhwa," 14.

57. Kim Chongyŏn, "Rodong kijunhwa," 14.

58. Kim Chongyŏn, "Rodong saengsan nŭngyul ŭi piyak chŏgin changsŏng ŭl wihayŏ hyŏksinchŏk rodong kijunnyang ŭl toip haja" (Let us implement innovative work standards for the rapid growth of work-production efficiency), *Rodong*, no. 12 (1958): 21.

59. Kim Chongyŏn, "Rodong chŏngyang saŏp esŏŭi hyŏksin ŭl wihayŏ" (For the improvement of quantitative labor tasks), *Rodong*, no. 5 (1959): 12–15.

60. Kim Pyŏngch'ŏn, "Rodong sigan riyong e taehan t'onggyejŏk punsŏk" (Statistical analysis of labor-time use), *Rodong*, no. 10 (1959): 31.

61. Kong Chint'ae, "Kongjak kigyedŭl ŭi riyongryul chego rŭl wihan rodong sigan ŭi ch'ŭkjŏng" (Work-time measurement to improve the use rate of manufacturing machines), *Rodong*, no. 8 (1958): 40.

62. Yang Inhyŏk, "Rodong sigan yebi ŭi chŏkbal kwa kŭ ŭi riyong pangbŏp" (The exposure of spare labor time and methods of its use), *Rodong*, no. 4 (1959): 35.

63. Kim Insŏn, "Sŏnjin kisul chagŏp pangbŏp ŭl toip hayŏ sae kijunnyang ŭl ch'angjo" (The creation of new standards by adopting advanced technology and manufacturing methods), *Rodong*, no. 12 (1958): 51–52.

64. Kim Ch'unsang, "Chŏnmunhwa wa hyŏptonghwa e ŭihan chikp'o tagidae chagŏp" (Handling many fabric machines through specialization and collectivization), *Rodong*, no. 7 (1958): 42.

65. Yun Ŭisŏp and Ch'a Sunhŏn, *Konghwaguk'ka esŏŭi imgŭm chojik kwa rodong ŭi kijunhwa* (The standardization of wage and labor in the republic) (Pyongyang: Kungnip Ch'ulp'ansa, 1955), 50.

66. Mun Ch'isu, "Imgŭm chedo ŭi palchŏn" (The development of the wage system), *Rodong*, no. 9 (1958): 26.

67. Central Statistical Board, *Statistical Returns*, 29.

68. Mun, "Imgŭm chedo," 26. Payment-in-kind should be distinguished from state rations such as rice because rations are given along with a wage, whereas payment-in-kind is given in lieu of a wage.

69. Yun and Ch'a, *Konghwaguk'ka esŏŭi imgŭm*, 55–56.

70. Yun and Ch'a, *Konghwaguk'ka esŏŭi imgŭm*, 57.

71. Yun and Ch'a, *Konghwaguk'ka esŏŭi imgŭm*, 57.

72. Yun and Ch'a, *Konghwaguk'ka esŏŭi imgŭm*, 60.

73. Yun and Ch'a, *Konghwaguk'ka esŏŭi imgŭm*, 60.

74. Yun and Ch'a, *Konghwaguk'ka esŏŭi imgŭm*, 41.

75. Yun and Ch'a, *Konghwaguk'ka esŏŭi imgŭm*, 41.

76. V. I. Lenin, *The State and Revolution*, in *Essential Works of Lenin* (New York: Dover, 1987), 342.

77. Central Statistical Board, *Statistical Returns*, 22–28.

78. Hungarian embassy to the DPRK, report, May 10, 1955, Korea Top Secret Documents, box 5, 5/c, 006048/1955, cited in Balázs Szalontai, *Kim Il Sung in the Khrushchev Era: Soviet–DPRK Relations and the Roots of North Korean Despotism* (Stanford, Calif.: Stanford University Press, 2003), 65.

79. Kornai, *Socialist System*, 167–169.

80. Jake Werner, "Global Fordism in 1950s Urban China," *Frontiers of History in China* 7, no. 3 (2012): 421–433.

81. Werner, "Global Fordism in 1950s Urban China," 434.

3. Producing the Everyday Life of Work

1. Henri Lefebvre, "The Everyday and Everydayness," *Yale French Studies*, no. 73 (1987): 10.

2. Kimura Mitsuhiko and Abe Keiji, *Chŏnjaengi mandŭn nara: Pukhan ŭi kunsa kongŏphwa* (The country made by war: The military industrialization of North Korea), trans. Ch'a Munsŏk and Pak Chŏngjin (Seoul: Mizi, 2009), 46–47. This book is the most accurate account of North Korea's industrial system before the Korean War. Originally published in Japanese in 2003, it was translated into Korean in 2009.

3. Kimura and Abe, *Chŏnjaengi mandŭn nara*, 183.

4. Kimura and Abe, *Chŏnjaengi mandŭn nara*, 183.

5. Kimura and Abe, *Chŏnjaengi mandŭn nara*, 189.

6. Archive of the Ministry of Foreign Affairs of the Russian Federation, collection 0102, inventory 6, file 49, folder 22, cited in Kimura Mitsuhiko, "Senkyūhyaku yonjūgo gojūnen no kitachōsen sangyō shiryō" (North Korea's industrial items, 1945–1950), *Aoyama Kokusai Seikei Ronshū* 52 (2000): 156–157, cited in Kimura and Abe, *Chŏnjaengi mandŭn nara*, 298–299.

7. Archive of the Ministry of Foreign Affairs of the Russian Federation, collection 0102, inventory 6, file 49, folder 22, cited in Kimura Mitsuhiko, "Senkyūhyaku yonjūgo gojūnen no kitachōsen sangyō shiryō," (North Korea's industrial items, 1945–1950), *Aoyama Kokusai Seikei Ronshū*, vol. 52 (2000): 156–157, cited in Kimura and Abe, *Chŏnjaengi mandŭn nara*, 298–299.

8. Ministry of Industry, DPRK, "Ch'on'gubaek sasipgunyŏndo taesso such'ulp'um ch'ulha silchŏkp'yo" (The record of export items to the Soviet Union in 1949), in *Pukhan kyŏngje kwan'gye munsŏjip* (North Korean documents on the economy), vol. 2 (Chunch'ŏn: Hallimtaehakkyo Aseamunhwayŏn'guso, 1997), 538–543, cited in Kimura and Abe, *Chŏnjaengi mandŭn nara*, 296–297.

9. Kimura and Abe, *Chŏnjaengi mandŭn nara*, 295. A commonly accepted exchange rate in the mid–twentieth century was four Soviet rubles to one US dollar.

10. Archive of the Ministry of Foreign Affairs of the Russian Federation, collection 0102, inventory 6, file 49, folder 22, cited in Kimura Mitsuhiko, "Senkyūhyaku yonjūgo gojūnen no kitachōsen sangyō shiryō" (North Korea's industrial items, 1945–1950), *Aoyama Kokusai Seikei Ronshū* 52 (2000): 156–157, cited in Kimura and Abe, *Chŏnjaengi mandŭn nara*, 298–299; Kathryn Weathersby, *Soviet Aims in Korea and the Origins of the Korean War, 1945–1950: New Evidence from Russian Archives*, Cold War International History Project Working Paper 8 (Washington, DC: Woodrow Wilson International Center for Scholars, 1993), 25.

11. Conrad C. Crane, "Raiding the Beggar's Pantry: The Search for Airpower Strategy in the Korean War," *Journal of Military History* 63, no. 4 (1999): 893.

12. Jong Won Lee (Yi Chongwŏn), "The Impact of the Korean War on the Korean Economy," *International Journal of Korean Studies* 5, no. 1 (2001): 103.

13. Crane, "Raiding the Beggar's Pantry," 895, 913.

14. Crane, "Raiding the Beggar's Pantry," 919.

15. Ch'a Munsŏk, "Han'guk Chŏnjaeng sigi Pukhan ŭi chŏnsi saengsanch'eje: Kongjang sogae wa chŏnsi saengsanjŏngch'aek ŭl chumgsim ŭro" (The wartime production system of North Korea during the Korean War: A look at the factory relocation project and wartime production policy), *T'ongil Munje Yŏn'gu* 39 (2003): 83.

16. Ch'a, "Han'guk Chŏnjaeng," 83.

17. Ch'a, "Han'guk Chŏnjaeng," 83.

18. Central Statistical Board, *Statistical Returns of the National Economy of the Democratic People's Republic of Korea, 1946–1960* (Pyongyang: Foreign Languages Publishing House, 1961), 36. These are official numbers published by North Korea's State Planning Commission. They raise doubts about their accuracy, as state data do throughout the world, but the general pattern shows North Korea's industrial damage as not total and as varying widely according to sector.

19. Adapted from Central Statistical Board, *Statistical Returns*, 40–41.

20. Adapted from Central Statistical Board, *Statistical Returns*, 44.
21. Adapted from Central Statistical Board, *Statistical Returns*, 44.
22. Adapted from Central Statistical Board, *Statistical Returns*, 45–47.
23. Adapted from Central Statistical Board, *Statistical Returns*, 45–47.
24. Adapted from Central Statistical Board, *Statistical Returns*, 83.
25. This party document is given in Kuksa P'yŏnch'an Wiwŏnhoe (National Institute of Korean History), *Pukhan kwan'gye saryojip* (Historical material on North Korea), vol. 30 (Kwachŏn: Kuksa P'yŏnch'an Wiwŏnhoe Ch'ulp'ansa, 1998), 356–386.
26. Kuksa P'yŏnch'an Wiwŏnhoe, *Pukhan kwan'gye saryojip*, 361.
27. Kuksa P'yŏnch'an Wiwŏnhoe, *Pukhan kwan'gye saryojip*, 363.
28. Kuksa P'yŏnch'an Wiwŏnhoe, *Pukhan kwan'gye saryojip*, 363–367.
29. Central Statistical Board, *Statistical Returns*, 152.
30. Kuksa P'yŏnch'an Wiwŏnhoe, *Pukhan kwan'gye saryojip*, 365.
31. Kuksa P'yŏnch'an Wiwŏnhoe, *Pukhan kwan'gye saryojip*, 366.
32. Kuksa P'yŏnch'an Wiwŏnhoe, *Pukhan kwan'gye saryojip*, 367.
33. Theodore Shabad, "North Korea's Postwar Recovery," *Far Eastern Survey* 25, no. 6 (1956): 87.
34. Kuksa P'yŏnch'an Wiwŏnhoe, *Pukhan kwan'gye saryojip*, 369–370.
35. Kuksa P'yŏnch'an Wiwŏnhoe, *Pukhan kwan'gye saryojip*, 370.
36. Kuksa P'yŏnch'an Wiwŏnhoe, *Pukhan kwan'gye saryojip*, 377.
37. Kuksa P'yŏnch'an Wiwŏnhoe, *Pukhan kwan'gye saryojip*, 377.
38. Yoon T. Kuark, "North Korea's Industrial Development During the Post-war Period," *China Quarterly* 14 (1963): 61.
39. Kuark, "North Korea's Industrial Development," 61.
40. Kuark, "North Korea's Industrial Development," 61.
41. Kim Yŏngsŏng, "Pukhan ŭi kŏnch'uk yangsikdŭl" (North Korea's architectural styles), *Konch'uk* 37, no. 4 (1993): 59.
42. Kim Myŏn, "Pimilmunsŏro pon kudongdok ŭi Hamhŭngsi kŏnsŏlp'urojekt'ŭ: Chŏnhu sahoejuŭi tosi kŏnsŏl ŭi saeroun model" (The reconstruction project of Hamhŭng by the former East Germany as seen through secret documents: A new model of postwar socialist city construction), *Minjok 21*, no. 51 (2005): 95.
43. Kim Myŏn, "Pimilmunsŏro pon kudongdok ŭi Hamhŭngsi kŏnsŏlp'urojekt'ŭ," 96.
44. According to Wada Haruki, Kim Il Sung entered North Korea in 1945 with 133 partisans. See Wada Haruki, *Puk Chosŏn: Yugyŏkdae kuk'kaesŏ chŏnggyugun kuk'karo* (North Korea: From a guerilla state to a military state), trans. Sŏ Tongman and Nam Kijŏng (Seoul: Dolbegae, 2002), 278.
45. Kim Il Sung, *Kim Ilsŏng chŏjakchip* (The works of Kim Il Sung), 47 vols., (Pyongyang: Chosŏn Rodongdang Ch'ulp'ansa, 1979–1997), 8:18.
46. Pak Ch'angok, "Ch'ŏngubaekosipsanyŏn ch'ŏngubaekosipyuknyŏn Chosŏn Minjujuŭi Inmingonghwaguk inmingyŏngje pokgubalchŏn sam kaenyŏn kyehwek e kwanhan pogo" (A report on the Democratic People's Republic of Korea's 1954–1956 Three-Year Plan for recovery and development of the people's economy), *Kŭlloja*, no. 102 (1954): 37–66.

47. Hungarian embassy to the DPRK, report, April 13, 1955, Korea Top Secret Documents, box 7, 5/f, 006054/1955, and Hungarian embassy to the DPRK, report, October 17, 1961, Korea Administrative Documents, box 1, 1/c, 1/25/46–1/1961, cited in Balázs Szalontai, *Kim Il Sung in the Khrushchev Era: Soviet–DPRK Relations and the Roots of North Korean Despotism* (Stanford, CA: Stanford University Press, 2003), 92.

48. *Rodong Sinmun*, "Chŏngubaekosiponyŏn inmin kyŏngje kyehoek" (People's economic plan for 1955), December 14, 1954.

49. Kim Il Sung, *Kim Ilsŏng sŏnjip* (The selected works of Kim Il Sung), vol. 1 (Pyongyang: Chosŏn Rodongdang Ch'ulp'ansa, 1960), 384–385, cited in Sŏ Tongman, *Pukchosŏn sahoechuŭi ch'eje sŏngnipsa, 1945–1961* (The formation of state socialism in North Korea, 1945–1961) (Seoul: Sunin, 2005), 393.

50. Szalontai, *Kim Il Sung in the Khrushchev Era*, 243.

51. Nikita S. Khrushchev, "Speech to the 20th Congress of the Communist Party of the Soviet Union" (1956), Marxists Internet Archive, http://www.marxists.org /archive/khrushchev/1956/02/24.htm

52. Sŏ Tongman, *Pukchosŏn sahoechuŭi*, 535–536.

53. Chosŏn Nodongdang (Korean Workers' Party), *Chosŏn Nodongdang Taehoe charyojip che ilchip* (Documents of the Korean Workers' Party Congress), vol. 1 (Seoul: Kukt'o T'ongilwŏn Ch'ulp'ansa, 1979), 470.

54. Sŏ Tongman, *Pukchosŏn sahoechuŭi*, 217, 550.

55. Sŏ Tongman, *Pukchosŏn sahoechuŭi*, 550.

56. Sŏ Tongman, *Pukchosŏn sahoechuŭi*, 550.

57. Sŏ Tongman, *Pukchosŏn sahoechuŭi*, 550.

58. The ten-member team consisted of Kim Il Sung, Pak Chŏngae (Korean Workers' Party Central Committee), Nam Il (foreign minister), Ri Chongok (chair of state planning), Ko Chunt'aek (Minju Party), Kim Pyŏngche (Ch'ŏndogyo Ch'ŏngu Party), Ch'oe Hyŏn (deputy defense minister), Cho Kŭmsong (president of Kim Ch'aek University), Han Kich'ang (labor hero), and Chŏn Sŏngbok (labor hero). The schedule of the trip in the summer of 1956 was as follows: Soviet Union (June 1–6), East Germany (June 7–12), Romania (June 13–17), Hungary (June 17–20), Czechoslovakia (June 21–25), Bulgaria (June 25–29), Albania (June 29–July 1), Poland (July 2–6), Soviet Union (again, July 6–15), and Mongolia (July 16–18). See Chosŏn Rodongdang (Korean Workers' Party), *Kukjejuŭijŏk ch'insŏn* (International friendship) (Pyongyang: Chosŏn Rodongdang Ch'ulp'ansa, 1956).

59. Szalontai, *Kim Il Sung in the Khrushchev Era*, 95.

60. Szalontai, *Kim Il Sung in the Khrushchev Era*, 95.

61. Andrei N. Lankov, *Soryŏn ŭi charyoro pon Pukhan hyŏndaechŏngch'isa* (The political history of North Korea as seen through Soviet documents), trans. Kim Kwangrin (Seoul: Orŭm, 1995), 217–227. In late July and early August 1956, key individuals in the anti–Kim Il Sung faction (led by Ri P'ilgyu, Choe Ch'angik, Kim Sŭnghwa, Yun Konghŭm, and Pak Ch'angok) met with Soviet embassy officials to discuss their plans to publicly denounce Kim Il Sung.

62. Kuksa P'yŏnch'an Wiwŏnhoe, *Pukhan kwan'gye saryojip*, 780.

63. Quoted in Lankov, *Pukhan hyŏndaechŏngch'isa*, 227.
64. Kuksa P'yŏnch'an Wiwŏnhoe, *Pukhan kwan'gye saryojip*, 785–787.
65. Kuksa P'yŏnch'an Wiwŏnhoe, *Pukhan kwan'gye saryojip*, 796.
66. Chosŏn Nodongdang, *Chosŏn Nodongdang Taehoe charyojip che ilchip*, 72.
67. Sŏ Tongman, *Pukchosŏn sahoechuŭi*, 795.
68. Chosŏn Nodongdang (Korean Workers' Party), *Pukhan Chosŏn Nodongdang Tae-hoe chuyo munhŏnjip* (Essential documents of North Korea's Korean Workers' Party Congress) (Seoul: Tolbegae P'yŏnjipbu, 1988), 236.
69. Sŏ Tongman, *Pukchosŏn sahoechuŭi*, 795–796.
70. Sŏ Tongman, *Pukchosŏn sahoechuŭi*, 798, 961.
71. Sŏ Tongman, *Pukchosŏn sahoechuŭi*, 781.
72. Sŏ Tongman, *Pukchosŏn sahoechuŭi*, 781.
73. Bruce Cumings, *The Origins of the Korean War*, vol. 2: *The Roaring of the Cataract, 1947–1950* (Princeton, NJ: Princeton University Press, 1990), 299–300.
74. Cumings, *Origins of the Korean War*, 2:300.
75. Cumings, *Origins of the Korean War*, 2:303.
76. Philip Rudolph, "North Korea and the Path to Socialism," *Pacific Affairs* 32, no. 2 (1959): 134.
77. Rudolph, "North Korea and the Path to Socialism," 134.
78. Chong-Sik Lee, "The 'Socialist Revolution' in the North Korean Countryside," *Asian Survey* 2, no. 8 (1962): 10.
79. Central Statistical Board, *Statistical Returns*, 36, 84.
80. Kang Chiwŏn, "Nongŏp e taehan kongŏp ŭi pangjo" (The industrial assistance of agriculture), *Kŭlloja*, no. 128 (1956): 47.
81. Kang Chiwŏn, "Nongŏp e taehan kongŏp ŭi pangjo", 46–47.
82. Kang Chiwŏn, "Nongŏp e taehan kongŏp ŭi pangjo," 46.
83. Kuksa P'yŏnch'an Wiwŏnhoe, *Pukhan kwan'gye saryojip*, 539.
84. Central Statistical Board, *Statistical Returns*, 59.
85. Chosŏn Nodongdang, *Pukhan Chosŏn Nodongdang Taehoe chuyo munhŏnjip*, 97.
86. Kim Il Sung, "Uri nara esŏ sahoejuŭijŏk nongŏp hyŏpdonghwa ŭi sŭngri wa nongch'on kyŏngri ŭi kŭmhu palchŏn e taehayŏ" (On the victory of socialist agricultural cooperativization in our country and on the further development of the agricultural economy), *Rodong Sinmun*, January 6, 1959.
87. Central Statistical Board, *Statistical Returns*, 59.
88. Lee, "'Socialist Revolution,'" 19.
89. Central Statistical Board, *Statistical Returns*, 60.
90. Central Statistical Board, *Statistical Returns*, 17.
91. Central Statistical Board, *Statistical Returns*, 17.
92. Hungarian embassy to the DPRK, report, October 22, 1954, Korea Administrative Documents, box 11, 22/a, 08103/2/1954, cited in Szalontai, *Kim Il Sung in the Khrushchev Era*, 63.
93. Hungarian embassy to the People's Republic of China, report, April 22, 1954, China Administrative Documents, box 17, 22/a, 05419/1954, cited in Szalontai, *Kim Il Sung in the Khrushchev Era*, 66.

94. Hungarian embassy to the DPRK, report, May 10, 1955, Korea Top Secret Documents, box 5, 5/c, 006048/1955, cited in Szalontai, *Kim Il Sung in the Khrushchev Era*, 65.

95. Frederick C. Teiwes, *China's Road to Disaster: Mao, Central Politicians, and Provincial Leaders in the Unfolding of the Great Leap Forward, 1955–1959* (Armonk, NY: M. E. Sharpe, 1999), 199, 191.

96. Andrew Roberts, "The State of Socialism: A Note on Terminology," *Slavic Review* 63, no. 2 (2004): 349–366.

97. Karl Marx, "On the Jewish Question," in Karl Marx and Friedrich Engels, *Marx–Engels Reader*, ed. Robert Tucker (New York: Norton, 1978), 46.

98. Karl Marx, "Manifesto of the Communist Party," in Marx and Engels, *Marx–Engels Reader*, 490.

99. Chang Seki, "Chŏnhu samgaenyŏn inmin kyŏngje kyehoek ŭi yebijŏk ch'onghwa wa ch'ŏn'gubaekosipch'ilnyŏn inmin kyŏngje palchŏn kyehoek e taehayŏ" (A preliminary evaluation of the postwar Three-Year Plan and on the economic development plan of 1957), *Kŭlloja*, no. 134 (1957): 18.

100. Chang Seki, "Chŏnhu samgaenyŏn inmin kyŏngje kyehoek," 19–20.

101. Kim Sanghak, "Che ilch'a ogaenyŏn kyehoek kigan e chunggongŏp ŭl usŏnjŏgŭro palchŏnsikimyŏ kyŏnggongŏp mit nongŏp ŭl tongsi e palchŏnsikil te taehan tang ŭi chŏngch'aek" (On the party policy to first develop heavy industry and then simultaneously develop light industry and agriculture during the First Five-Year Plan), *Kŭlloja*, no. 148 (1958): 51.

102. Kim Sanghak, "Che ilch'a ogaenyŏn kyehoek," 51, 53.

103. Kim Il Sung, *Chŏjakchip*, 27:468

104. Kim Cheehyung, "Total, Thus Broken: *Chuch'e sasang* and North Korea's Terrain of Subjectivity," *Journal of Korean Studies* 17, no. 1 (2012): 75.

105. Lefebvre, "The Everyday and Everydayness," 9.

106. Kim Il Sung, *Chŏjakchip*, 15:479–480.

107. Citizens' willing support of a despotic system is a hallmark of modern dictatorship. Such an idea is captured in Lim Jie-Hyun's concept of "mass dictatorship." See Lim Jie-Hyun (Yim Chihyŏn) and Kim Yong-Woo (Kim Yongwu), eds., *Taejungdokchae* (Mass dictatorship), vol. 1: *Kangjewa tongŭi saiesŏ* (Between coercion and consent) (Seoul: Ch'aeksesang, 2004).

108. Han Kyŏnghwa, "Na nŭn irŏnsaram ŭl saranghanda: Uri chagŏpbanjang ŭl tugo" (I love such a person: About our work team leader), *Ch'ŏllima*, no. 6 (1961): 85–86. "I Love Such a Person" was a reader's column that began with the January 1961 issue after a reader, Ri Chubong, wrote a letter to the editorial board about a discussion his team had on what makes a person loved by others. This letter prompted the creation of a column printing readers' letters about people they love and admire.

109. Henri Lefebvre, "Toward a Leftist Cultural Politics: Remarks Occasioned by the Centenary of Marx's Death," in *Marxism and the Interpretation of Culture*, ed. Cary Nelson and Lawrence Grossberg (Urbana: University of Illinois Press, 1988), 80.

110. Lefebvre, "Toward a Leftist Cultural Politics," 78.

111. Kim Il Sung, *Chŏjakchip*, 8:361.

112. Khang Jeongseog, "Ilsangsaenghwal pip'an kwa salm ŭi pyŏnhyŏk: Puranhan ilsang e tŏnjinŭn puronhan munjejeki" (Criticism of everyday life and the transformation of life: A subversive question for the unstable everyday), *Pip'yŏng* 18 (2008): 94.

113. Jacques Lacan, *The Seminar of Jacques Lacan*, book 11: *Four Fundamental Concepts of Psychoanalysis* (New York: Norton, 1998), 51.

114. Slavoj Žižek, *The Sublime Object of Ideology* (London: Verso,1989), 61.

115. Žižek, *Sublime Object of Ideology*, 61.

116. Henri Lefebvre, *Critique of Everyday Life*, vol. 1: *Introduction* (London: Verso, 2008), 165.

117. Lefebvre, *Critique of Everyday Life*, 1:165.

118. The most abstract and yet the most concrete entity is Kim Il Sung. He is an everyday figure, and only in his everydayness does he complete the circle of power that must always find utility.

119. Kim Il Sung, "Pukjosŏnminjusŏn'gŏ ŭi ch'onggyŏl kwa Inmin Wiwŏnhoe tangmyŏn kwaŏp" (Results of the democratic election in northern Korea and the tasks facing the People's Committee), *Kŭlloja* 11 (1946): 26, cited in Sŏ Tongman, *Pukchosŏn sahoechuŭi*, 321.

120. Ryu Munhwa, ed., *Haebang hu sanyŏn'gan kungnaeoe chungyoilji* (Important domestic and international events in the four years since liberation) (Pyongyang: Minjujosŏnsa, 1949), 97–98, cited in Sŏ Tongman, *Pukchosŏn sahoechuŭi*, 321–322. Alexey Stakhanov (1906–1977) was a Soviet miner who became a labor hero in 1935 for his record-setting feat of mining 227 tons of coal in a single work shift. This act launched a nationwide production campaign known as the Stakhanovite Movement. Stakhanov was a celebrated figure not only in the Soviet Union and other state socialist countries but also in emerging, postcolonial countries throughout the world. The American news magazine *Time* featured him on the cover in December 1935.

121. See Ch'a Munsŏk, "Pukhan: Isip'il segi e ch'ŏllima undong?" (North Korea: The Ch'ŏllima Movement in the twenty-first century?), *T'ongil Han'guk*, no. 302 (2009): 32–35.

122. See Ch'a, "Pukhan: Isip'il segi e ch'ŏllima undong?" 32–35.

123. Pak Ch'ŏl, "Chŭngsan kyŏngjaeng undong esŏŭi myŏtkaji munje" (Several problems of the Production Increase and Competition Movement), *Kŭlloja*, no. 105 (1954): 93.

124. Pak Ch'ŏl, "Chŭngsan kyŏngjaeng," 90.

125. Han Sangdu, "Sahoejuŭi kŏnsŏl ŭl ch'okchinsikigi wihan chiptanjŏk hyŏksin undong ŭi palchŏn ŭl wihayŏ," (For the advancement of the Collective Innovation Movement in constructing socialism), *Kŭlloja*, no. 151 (1958): 54, 60.

126. Pak Ch'ŏl, "Chŭngsan kyŏngjaeng," 93.

127. Pak Ch'ŏl, "Chŭngsan kyŏngjaeng," 95. The name of the mine and the region, "Aoji," is a Manchurian word meaning "black rock."

128. Two terms are used in North Korea to mean "labor hero": *nodong yŏngung* and *noryŏk yŏngung*. *Yŏngung* is "hero," and *nodong* is either "labor" or "work." *Noryŏk* can also be translated as "labor" or "work," but it also has the sense of "effort."

129. The word *ch'ŏllima* means "thousand-*ri* horse," the name of an East Asian mythical horse capable of traveling 1,000 *ri* in a single day, which is 500 kilometers or 311 miles. A real horse can travel 128 *ri* a day (64 kilometers or 40 miles). In North Korea, because of the mass movement, the term *ch'ŏllima* has been affixed to many things, including a popular magazine founded in 1959; a typeface made to represent swiftness and forwardness; a 46-meter-high sculpture in Pyongyang with a bronze winged horse perched on top, built in 1961; and a national soccer team.

130. Kuksa P'yŏnch'an Wiwŏnhoe, *Pukhan kwan'gye saryojip*, 806.

131. Chosŏn Chigŏp Ch'ongdongmaeng (General Federation of Trade Unions of Korea), *Ch'ŏllima Kisu tokbon* (The Ch'ŏllima Riders handbook) (Pyongyang: Chigŏp Tongmaeng Ch'ulp'ansa, 1963), 13.

132. Ch'a, "Pukhan: Isip'il segi e ch'ŏllima undong?" 35. Chin Ŭngwŏn had been a prisoner of the United Nations forces during the Korean War and as the initiator of the Ch'ŏllima Work Team Movement became one of the most celebrated labor heroes in North Korea.

133. Chosŏn Chigŏp Ch'ongdongmaeng, *Ch'ŏllima Kisu tokbon*, 26.

134. Chosŏn Chigŏp Ch'ongdongmaeng, *Ch'ŏllima Kisu tokbon*, 30.

135. Pak Myŏngjun, "Inmin saenghwal hyangsang ŭl wihan tang kwa chŏngbu ŭi hwakkohan chŏngch'aek" (The firm policies of the party and government for the improvement of the people's livelihood), *Kŭlloja*, no. 154 (1958): 88.

136. Pak Myŏngjun, "Inmin saenghwal," 88.

137. Kim Tongch'ŏl, "Kŭllojadŭl sogesŏ ŭi purŭjoajŏk mit sopurŭjoajŏk chanjae ŭisik ŭi kŭkbok ŭl wihayŏ" (For the overcoming of bourgeois or petit bourgeois consciousness of workers), *Kŭlloja*, no. 116 (1955): 76.

138. Ryu Yŏngsul, "Kisul hyŏkmyŏng esŏ ŭi chungdŭng mit kisul ŭimu kyoyukche silsi ŭi ŭiŭi" (The significance of secondary and technical mandatory education in fulfilling the technological revolution), *Kŭlloja*, no. 156 (1958): 15.

139. Henri Lefebvre, *Critique of Everyday Life*, vol. 2: *Foundations for a Sociology of the Everyday* (1961; reprint, London: Verso, 2008), 185.

140. Lefebvre, *Critique of Everyday Life*, 2:188, 189.

141. Lefebvre, *Critique of Everyday Life*, 2:192.

142. Lefebvre, *Critique of Everyday Life*, 2:191, 192.

143. Lefebvre, *Critique of Everyday Life*, 2:182.

144. Lefebvre, *Critique of Everyday Life*, 2:182.

145. Sŏ Usŏk, "Pukhan ŭi chugŏsilt'ae wa chut'aekjŏngch'aek e taehan p'yŏngka" (North Korea's housing situation and evaluation of its housing policy), *Wŏlgan Pokchi Tonghyang* 24 (2000): 41.

146. Kim Jin Sun, "Sahoejuŭi kuk'ka ŭi tosigyehoek e kwanhan yŏn'gu: Pukhan ŭl chungsim ŭro" (A study on urban planning in socialist states: A case study on North Korea), PhD diss., Konkuk University, 1998, 83.

147. Kim Jin Sun, "Sahoejuŭi kuk'ka ŭi tosigyehoek," 83–84.

148. Sŏ Usŏk, "Pukhan ŭi chugŏsilt'ae," 41; Kuk'ka T'ongye Pot'ŏl (Korean Statistical Information Service), Republic of Korea, "Chut'aek pogŭpryul" (Housing supply rate), 2015, http://kosis.kr.

149. Ri Sun'gŏn and Paek Wan'gi, *Chut'aek soguyŏk kyehwek* (Housing subquarter planning) (Pyongyang: Kungnip kŏnsŏl ch'ulp'ansa, 1963), 34–35.

150. Sŏ Usŏk, "Pukhan ŭi chugŏsilt'ae," 42.

151. Sŏ Usŏk, "Pukhan ŭi chugŏsilt'ae," 41.

152. Ri and Paek, *Chut'aek soguyŏk kyehwek*, 34. *Kun* (group, 群) is to be distinguished from *kun* (district, 郡). These terms are pronounced the same, but the Chinese characters are different.

153. Kim Jin Sun, "Sahoejuŭi kuk'ka ŭi tosigyehoeke", 77.

154. Kim Jin Sun, "Sahoejuŭi kuk'ka ŭi tosigyehoeke," 77.

155. Ri and Paek, *Chut'aek soguyŏk kyehwek*, 39, 71.

156. Ri and Paek, *Chut'aek soguyŏk kyehwek*, 39.

157. Ri and Paek, *Chut'aek soguyŏk kyehwek*, 5.

158. Kim Yŏngsu, "Sahoejuŭi kŏnsŏl ŭi hyŏn tan'gye wa konghwaguk nyŏsŏng" (The current stage of socialist construction and women of the republic), *Kŭlloja*, no. 155 (1958): 61.

159. Choŭnbŏtdŭl (Good Friends), *Pukhansaramdŭri malhanŭn Pukhan iyagi* (North Korean stories told by North Korean people) (Seoul: Chŏngt'o Ch'ulp'ansa, 2000), 57.

160. Choŭnbŏtdŭl, *Pukhansaramdŭri malhanŭn Pukhan iyagi*, 56.

4. The Rhythm of Everyday Work, in Six Parts

1. *Pulgul ŭi osipnyŏndae nŭn urirŭl purŭnda* (The invincible 1950s is calling us) (documentary) (Pyongyang: Chosŏn Kirok Kwahak Yŏnghwa Chwalyŏngso, 2002).

2. Kim Pyŏnghun, "Kiltongmudŭl" (Fellow travelers), in *Pukhan munhak* (The literature of North Korea), ed. Sin Hyŏnggi, O Sŏngho, and Yi Sŏnmi (Seoul: Munhak'kwa Chisŏngsa, 2007), 627–664; all quotations come from this edition. Kim Pyŏnghun is a representative writer of this period. He was born in 1929 in the border city of Musan, North Hamgyŏng Province, and joined the People's Army after liberation. He graduated from Pyongyang Teachers' College in 1957 and twice served as the chairperson of the Korean Writers' Union. In 2006, he became the chairperson of the Federation of Literature and Arts Unions of Korea. For other major writers of North Korea and their works, see Sin, O, and Yi, *Pukhan munhak*.

3. In 1990, P'ungsan County changed its name to Kim Hyŏnggwŏn County, after Kim Il Sung's uncle. It is located in a mountainous area and is known for, among other things, a breed of hunting dog called the P'ungsan, bred to hunt big animals such as tigers.

4. See James C. Scott, *Seeing Like a State: How Certain Schemes to Improve the Human Condition Have Failed* (New Haven, CT: Yale University Press, 1998), 309–341.

5. Alf Lüdtke, "People Working: Everyday Life and German Fascism," *History Workshop Journal*, no. 50 (2000): 83, 82.

6. Lüdtke, "People Working," 90.

7. Pak Sunsŏng and Hong Min, "Pukhan ilsangsaenghwal yŏn'gu ŭi pangbŏpnonjŏk mosaek" (The methodological search for doing research on North Korea's every-day life), in *Pukhan ŭi ilsangsaenghwal segye: Oech'im kwa soksagim* (The world of everyday life in North Korea: Cries and whispers), ed. Pak Sunsŏng and Hong Min (P'aju: Hanul, 2010), 168. Formed in 2007, the Research Center on Every-day Life of North Korea conducts original research as well as housing an archive related to everyday life in North Korea.

8. Pak and Hong, "Pukhan ilsangsaenghwal," 169.

9. Kim Chonguk, "Pukhan kwallyodŭl ŭi ilsangsaenghwal segye: Hoesaek ŭi aura" (The world of everyday life of North Korea's bureaucrats: The aura of grayness), in *Pukhan ŭi ilsangsaenghwal segye*, ed. Pak and Hong, 263, 265, 265–266.

10. Henri Lefebvre, *Critique of Everyday Life*, vol. 3: *From Modernity to Modernism (Towards a Metaphilosophy of Daily Life)* (1981; reprint, London: Verso, 2008), 164.

11. In this paragraph and the next one, quotations and specific details are from Ri Kyedŭk, "Ch'ŏlchŏhan saengsan chunbi nŭn sŏlbi riyongryul chego ŭi chungyo chokŏn" (A thorough preparation is important in increasing the use rate of equip-ment), *Kŭlloja*, no. 130 (1956): 156–160. A shop (*chikchang*) is the largest production unit of a factory, headed by a chief (*chikchangjang*). Each shop is further made up of work teams or brigades (*chagŏpban*), headed by a work team leader or foreman (*chagŏpbanjang*). Located in the city of Sinŭiju in North P'yŏngan Province, Ragwŏn Machine Factory, which began production in 1941, was originally a magnesium factory of the Japanese company Toyo Metalworks.

12. See Brian Myers, *Han Sŏrya and North Korean Literature: The Failure of Socialist Real-ism in North Korea* (Ithaca, NY: Cornell University East Asia Program, 1994).

13. In August 1957, the Ministry of Education merged with the Ministry of Culture and Propaganda to form the Ministry of Education and Culture, with Han Sŏrya as minister, a position he held until September 1958. This ministry lasted until April 1960, when it was split into the Ministry of Higher Education, the Ministry of General Education, and the Ministry of Culture. Han was chairperson of the Federation of Literature and Arts Unions from 1948 to 1962. In the party leadership's view, his commitment to the party began to waver in the early 1960s. For instance, in 1960 he wrote essays praising the Korea Artista Proletaria Federa-tio, an organization of leftist writers that existed from 1925 to 1935 (before the era of Kim Il Sung), when the undeniable trend of the time was to promote a literary style based on the legacy of Kim Il Sung and his partisan faction. The most vicious criticism of Han took place in September 1962, when he was accused of lying about his family's past and of leading a life unfit for a socialist (which included having many sexual affairs). In February 1963, having been removed from the party and his posts, he was exiled to Chagang Province in the North. He died in 1976. His reputation was restored in the 1980s, and his fiction was reprinted. The place where he died is unknown, most likely where he was exiled, but his grave is now at the Patriotic Martyr's Cemetery in Pyongyang.

14. Han Sŏrya, "Uri munhak, yesul ŭl inminsŏng kwa kwallyŏnhan tangmyŏnhan myŏt kaji munje" (Several problems facing and related to the people's spirit in our literature and art), *Kŭlloja*, no. 149 (1958): 63.

15. Han Sŏrya, "Uri munhak," 60–61.

16. Charles K. Armstrong, *The North Korean Revolution, 1945–1950* (Ithaca, NY: Cornell University Press, 2003), 166–173.

17. Igor Golomstock, *Totalitarian Art in the Soviet Union, the Third Reich, Fascist Italy, and the People's Republic of China* (London: Collins Harvill, 1990), 91.

18. Myers, *Han Sŏrya*, 42.

19. Han Sŏrya, "Munye chonsŏn e issŏsŏ ŭi pandongjŏk burŭjoa sasang ŭl pandaehayŏ" (Against reactionary bourgeois ideology on the literary and artistic front), in *Munye chŏnsŏn e issŏsŏ ŭi pandongjŏk burŭjoa sasang ŭl pandaehayŏ: Charyojip* (Against reactionary bourgeois ideology on the literary and artistic front: Sourcebook), 2 vols., ed. Ŏm Toman and Kwak Chaesŏk (Pyongyang: Chosŏn Chakka Tongmaeng Ch'ulp'ansa, 1956), 1:36.

20. Myers, *Han Sŏrya*, 54.

21. Sunyoung Park, "The Colonial Origin of Korean Realism and Its Contemporary Manifestation," *Positions: East Asia Cultures Critique* 14, no. 1 (2006): 184.

22. Golomstock, *Totalitarian Art*, 84.

23. Andrei Zhdanov, "Soviet Literature—the Richest in Ideas, the Most Addvanced Literature: A Speech Delivered at the Soviet Writers' Congress, 1934," Marxists Internet Archive, http://www.marxists.org/subject/art/lit_crit/sovietwritercon gress/zhdanov.htm.

24. Leonid Heller, "A World of Prettiness: Socialist Realism and Its Aesthetic Categories," *South Atlantic Quarterly* 94, no. 3 (1995): 688–689.

25. Heller, "World of Prettiness," 688–690.

26. During the colonial period, Yun and Im had been friends in the leftist literary circle. They had joined the North Korean government in the postliberation period, Yun in 1945 and Im in 1947. At the time Yun's essay was written, in 1956, Im had been dead for three years. In 1953, during the period of persecution of former South Korean Workers' Party members, Im had been labeled an enemy and executed. Yun, however, had a respectable career in North Korea as a prominent supporter of the literary style based on the experience of Kim Il Sung and his partisan faction. On the history of North Korean literature, see Sin Hyŏnggi and O Sŏngho, *Pukhan munhaksa: Hangil hyŏngmyŏng munhak esŏ chuch'e munhak kkaji* (The history of North Korean literature: From anti-Japanese revolutionary literature to *chuch'e* literature) (Seoul: P'yŏngminsa, 2000).

27. Yun Sep'yŏng, "Munhak yusan kyesŭng e issŏsŏ kwannyŏmronjŏk hŏmujuŭi rŭl pandaehayŏ" (Against idealistic nihilism in our literary heritage), in *Munye chŏnsŏn e issŏsŏ ŭi pandongjŏk*, ed. Ŏm and Kwak, 2:161.

28. Im Hwa, "Uri oppa wa hwaro" (My older brother and the brazier) (1929), quoted in Yun Sep'yŏng, "Munhak yusan kyesŭng," 2:161.

29. Yun Sep'yŏng, "Munhak yusan kyesŭng," 2:161, 162.

30. Im Hwa, "Uri oppa wa hwaro," public domain.

31. Chŏng Sŏch'on, "Yŏngbyŏn agassi" (Young woman from Yŏngbyŏn), in *Pukhan munhak*, ed. Sin, O, and Yi, 1430. Chŏng Sŏch'on (1923–2006) was a distinguished writer with a long career, creating works both in the style of socialist realism and in line with the idealized history of Kim Il Sung and his partisan faction.

Yak Mountain is in Yŏngbyŏn County, North P'yŏngan Province, and this region is historically famous for its silk.

32. Myers, *Han Sŏrya*, 54.

33. Chŏng Ch'ŏnrye, "Pangjik'kong ch'ŏnyŏege" (To the young woman weaver), in *Pukhan munhak*, ed. Sin, O, and Yi, 1467.

34. Chŏng Kwanch'ŏl, *Chŏng Kwanch'ŏl chakp'umjip* (The art of Chŏng Kwanch'ŏl) (Pyongyang: Munhak Yesul Chonghap Ch'ulp'ansa, 1999).

35. Central Statistical Board, *Statistical Returns of the National Economy of the Democratic People's Republic of Korea, 1946–1960* (Pyongyang: Foreign Languages Publishing House, 1961), 22, 24, 28.

36. Kim Il Sung, *Kim Ilsŏng chŏjakchip* (The works of Kim Il Sung), 47 vols. (Pyongyang: Chosŏn Rodongdang Ch'ulp'ansa, 1979–1997), 11:166.

37. Kim Il Sung, Chŏjakchip, 13:361.

38. Sŏ Ch'ŏng, "Ŭijiŭi him" (The power of will), in *Ŭijiro tallyŏndwen saramdŭl* (People hardened through will), ed. Kim Tuyŏng (Pyongyang: Chigŏp Tongmaeng Ch'ulp'ansa, 1957), 158–191.

39. This shop was responsible for producing sulfuric acid, used to make a phosphate-based fertilizer. The essay has a narrative structure, but it is nonetheless based on actual events.

40. The information about the number of copies printed is given on the unnumbered last page of Kim Tuyŏng, *Ŭijiro tallyŏndwen saramdŭl*, along with other publication acknowledgments.

41. Yu Hangrim, "Chikmaeng panchang" (Union chief), in *Pukhan munhak*, ed. Sin, O, and Yi, 313–375.

42. Sin and O, *Pukhan munhaksa*, 184–185.

43. The Sŭngho Precinct Cement Factory was originally the Pyongyang Factory of Onoda Cement of Japan, formed in 1919, with the capacity to produce 43,000 tons of cement per year. See Kimura Mitsuhiko and Abe Keiji, *Chŏnjaengi mandŭn nara: Pukhan ŭi kunsa kongŏphwa* (The country made by war: The military industrialization of North Korea), trans. Ch'a Munsŏk and Pak Chŏngjin (Seoul: Mizi, 2009), 142–143.

44. Yu Hangrim, "Chikmaeng panchang," 368.

45. *Charyŏk kaengsaeng ŭi chŏngsin* (The spirit of independent rebirth) (documentary) (Seoul: Nambuk Munje Yŏn'guso, n.d. [c. late 1990s]). The film's director, producer, and precise release date are unknown. The documentary was distributed in South Korea by the South–North Research Institute.

46. Yu Hangrim, "Chikmaeng panchang," 373.

47. Kim Il Sung, Chŏjakchip, 31:105.

48. Stephen Kotkin, *Magnetic Mountain: Stalinism as Civilization* (Berkeley and Los Angeles: University of California Press, 1995), 71.

49. Central Statistical Board, *Statistical Returns*, 45, 49. The 641,000 tons of steel produced in North Korea in 1960 was about a quarter of what the Soviet Union produced in 1927–1928 and about a hundredth of what the United States produced in 1929. See Kotkin, *Magnetic Mountain*, 47, 52.

50. Central Statistical Board, *Statistical Returns*, 152.

51. Kim Ch'aek Iron and Steel Works was originally Ch'ŏngjin Iron and Steel Works built by the Japanese company Nihon Iron and Steel. It began operation in 1942. It is the largest iron and steel factory in North Korea. In 1989, it had the capacity to produce 2.4 million tons of pig iron a year. See Kimura and Abe, *Chŏnjaengi mandŭn nara*, 378.

52. Kimura and Abe, *Chŏnjaengi mandŭn nara*, 82–83.

53. Hwanghae Iron and Steel Works lies at the mouth of Taedong River, an area known as Kyŏimp'o. After Japan annexed Korea in 1910, the Mitsubishi Company purchased an iron ore mountain in the area and in 1914 began constructing Kyŏimp'o Iron and Steel Works. In 1934, a merger between several steel companies in Japan led to the formation of Nihon Iron and Steel Company, which took over the management of Kyŏimp'o. With the capacity to produce 1.1 million tons of pig iron (in 1989), Hwanghae Iron and Steel Works is the second-largest producer of pig iron after Kim Ch'aek Iron and Steel Works. See Kimura and Abe, *Chŏnjaengi mandŭn nara*, 79–82, 378.

54. Kimura and Abe, *Chŏnjaengi mandŭn nara*, 81.

55. Chosŏn Chungang T'ongsinsa (Korean Central News Agency), "Hwangahe chech'ŏlso e chunŭn ssoryŏn kisulcha tŭlŭi pangcho" (Soviet technicians providing assistance at Hwanghae Steel), *Rodong Sinmun*, March 28, 1955; *Rodong Sinmun*, "Oeguk kisulchadŭl ŭi hyŏngjejŏk pangcho" (Brotherly assistance of foreign technicians), January 13, 1955.

56. Central Statistical Board, *Statistical Returns*, 45.

57. Yun Sejung, *Yonggwangno nŭn sumshinda* (The furnace is breathing) (Pyongyang: Munye Ch'ulp'ansa, 1960). Yun Sejung (1912–1965) is considered a representative writer of the proletarian experience. He wrote *The Furnace Is Breathing* after having lived with the workers of Hwanghae Iron and Steel Works during their reconstruction effort in the late 1950s. The number of copies at first printing in 1960 was fairly small, 10,000, but the novel gained importance and popularity throughout the decade, leading to a second printing of 50,000 copies in 1974.

58. Yun Sejung, *Yonggwangno nŭn sumshinda*, 10.

59. Yun Sejung, *Yonggwangno nŭn sumshinda*, 9.

60. Yun Sejung, *Yonggwangno nŭn sumshinda*, 108.

61. Yun Sejung, *Yonggwangno nŭn sumshinda*, 123.

62. Yun Sejung, *Yonggwangno nŭn sumshinda*, 263.

63. Yun Sejung, *Yonggwangno nŭn sumshinda*, 403, 408, my emphasis.

64. This story comes from Wŏn Tomyŏng's report on the *ch'ŏllima* workers of Tŏkch'ŏn Automobile Factory, "Ch'ŏllima chikchang ŭi nanal" (The everyday of a *ch'ŏllima* shop), *Ch'ŏllima*, no. 10 (1961): 22–25.

65. Wŏn, "Ch'ŏllima chikchang," 23.

66. Filmed at and released by Chosŏn National Film Studio in 1955, *Sinhonbubu* (The newlyweds) was directed by Yun Ryonggyu, produced by Song Wŏnjun, and edited by Kim Ryŏnja. The screenplay was written by Chu Tongin, the cinematography done by O Ŭngt'ak, and the music composed by Kim Pyŏngjun. The film stars Kim Hyŏnsuk as Ŭnsil and Yu Wŏnjun as Yŏngch'ŏl. Yun Ryonggyu

was an important director in early North Korean cinema. He directed the classic *Ppalch'isan ch'ŏnyŏ* (The partisan girl) in 1954 and a North Korean version of *The Tale of Ch'unhyang* (*Ch'unhyangjŏn*) in 1959. Supporting actress Mun Yebong (1917–1999) played Yŏnhŭi in *The Newlyweds*. Mun was a seminal figure in early Korean cinema and a distinguished actress in North Korea, earning the title "people's actress" in 1982. Her career began during the colonial period, when she starred in the first sound movie made in Korea, *Ch'unhyangjŏn*, in 1932, which has yet to be fully restored. Her movie *Mi'mong* (Sweet dream, 1936) has been restored and is the oldest extant sound film in Korea. She joined the North Korean state in 1948 and starred in the first North Korean film, *Nae kohyang* (My hometown) in 1949. She also starred in Yun Ryonggyu's film *The Partisan Girl*.

67. The shots of the actual city in *The Newlyweds*—the unfinished Kim Il Sung Square, Stalin Street (now Sŭngni Street), and Mao Zedong Street (now Kaesŏnmun Square); the winding Taedong and Pot'ong Rivers; the interior of factories and a department store; the countryside viewed from gigantic steam trains—make viewing the film worthwhile.

68. Cho Pyŏngkwŏn, "Maŭl ŭi ŏmŏni" (The mother of the village), *Ch'ŏllima sidae saramdŭl* (The people of the ch'ŏllima era), vol. 4, ed. Pak Sunp'al, Ri Tonghan, and Ch'oe Ch'ansŏk (Pyongyang: Chosŏn Rodongdang Ch'ulp'ansa and Minch'ŏng Ch'ulp'ansa,1961), 103. The series *Ch'ŏllima sidae saramdŭl* was popular, each volume seeing 70,000 prints.

69. Small, impromptu markets continuously existed in North Korea's countryside, where people purchased goods not available through the distribution system or state-sanctioned stores, such as local chestnuts.

70. Cho, "Maŭl ŭi ŏmŏni," 108.

71. Cho, "Maŭl ŭi ŏmŏni," 112.

72. Chosŏn Chigŏp Ch'ongdongmaeng (General Federation of Trade Unions of Korea), *Ch'ŏllima Kisu tokbon* (The Ch'ŏllima Riders handbook) (Pyongyang: Chigŏp Tongmaeng Ch'ulp'ansa, 1963), 261–262.

73. Chosŏn Chigŏp Ch'ongdongmaeng, *Ch'ŏllima Kisu tokbon*, 294.

74. Chosŏn Chigŏp Ch'ongdongmaeng, *Ch'ŏllima Kisu tokbon*, 294.

75. Kil Hwaksil was born in 1937 in Yŏngbyŏn County, North P'yŏngan Province. She began working at the Pyongyang Spinning Factory when she was eighteen years old. By her twenties, she was a symbol of North Korea's mass movements for transforming every work team she managed into a Ch'ŏllima Work Team. At the height of her fame, she received about twenty letters a day, sometimes from places overseas, such as the Soviet Union, China, Vietnam, and Czechoslovakia. She eventually became the director of the Pyongyang Spinning Factory, and later she served as secretary of the Korean Workers' Party. The poem "Yŏngbyŏn agassi" (Young Woman from Yŏngbyŏn) by Chŏng Sŏch'on is likely about Kil Hwaksil.

76. The precursor of the Pyongyang Spinning Factory was the Pyongyang Factory of Toyo Spinning Company of Japan, which was founded by the Mitsui Corporation in 1929. Originally built by the Yamaju Spinning Company in 1926, the

Pyongyang Factory was purchased by Toyo Spinning Company in 1929 when the factory was first founded. It had the capacity to produce 50,000 tons of raw yarn a year.

77. Kil Hwaksil, *Chŏllima chagŏpbanjang ŭi sugi* (A memoir of a Chŏllima Work Team leader) (Pyongyang: Chigŏp Tongmaeng Ch'ulp'ansa).
78. Kil, *Chŏllima chagŏpbanjang ŭi sugi*, 27, 29.
79. Kil, *Chŏllima chagŏpbanjang ŭi sugi*, 31.
80. Kil, *Chŏllima chagŏpbanjang ŭi sugi*, 33.
81. Kil, *Chŏllima Chagŏpbanjang ŭi sugi*, 93, 96, 99.
82. Jacques Lacan, *The Seminar of Jacques Lacan*, book 11: *The Four Fundamental Concepts of Psychoanalysis* (New York: Norton, 1998), 103, 243.

5. Vinalon City: Industrialism as Socialist Everyday Life

1. Chunggongŏp Wiwŏnhoe (Heavy Industry Committee), *Pinallon Kongjang kŏnsŏl* (The construction of the Vinalon Factory) (Pyongyang: Kungnip Kŏnsŏl Ch'ulp'ansa, 1961), 297–300.
2. Chunggongŏp Wiwŏnhoe, *Pinallon Kongjang kŏnsŏl*, 297.
3. Wŏn Tomyŏng, "Pinallon sokdo" (Vinalon speed), *Ch'ŏllima*, no. 5 (1961): 17.
4. Chunggongŏp Wiwŏnhoe, *Pinallon Kongjang kŏnsŏl*, 300.
5. Hiromi Mizuno, *Science for the Empire: Scientific Nationalism in Modern Japan* (Stanford, CA: Stanford University Press, 2009), 60.
6. Michael Burawoy, *The Politics of Production: Factory Regimes Under Capitalism and Socialism* (London: Verso, 1985), 171.
7. Ambiguity is a characteristic of everyday life, "constituted from contradictions which have been stifled," as Lefebvre puts it (*Critique of Everyday Life*, vol. 2: *Foundations for a Sociology of the Everyday* [1961; reprint, London: Verso, 2008], 220).
8. On Noguchi and his involvement in Japan's chemical industry, see Barbara Molony, *Technology and Investment: The Prewar Japanese Chemical Industry* (Cambridge, MA: Council on East Asian Studies, Harvard University, 1990). The founding of Nihon Chisso was based on an investment by Mitsubishi and a merger of Noguchi's two existing companies: the Sogi Electric Company, founded in 1906, and the Nihon Carbide Company, founded in 1907. Nihon Chisso grew to be one of the largest nitrogenous chemical companies in Japan and one of the most notorious as a symbol of Japan's reckless postwar industrial growth. In 1973, court rulings acknowledged Nihon Chisso's responsibility in the mercury poisoning of residents at Minamata. It was discovered that from the 1930s to the 1960s, Nihon Chisso had dumped mercury waste into Minamata Bay. The poisoning, known as "Minamata disease," had led to thousands of deaths, deformities, insanity, and paralysis.
9. Molony, *Technology and Investment*, 158.
10. Kimura Mitsuhiko and Abe Keiji, *Chŏnjaengi mandŭn nara: Pukhan ŭi kunsa kongŏphwa* (The country made by war: The military industrialization of North Korea), trans. Ch'a Munsŏk and Pak Chŏngjin (Seoul: Mizi, 2009), 37, 119.

11. Charles K. Armstrong, *The North Korean Revolution, 1945–1950* (Ithaca, NY: Cornell University Press, 2003), 151.

12. Archive of the Ministry of Foreign Affairs of the Russian Federation, collection 0480, inventory 4, file 14, folder 47, cited in Kimura Mitsuhiko, "Senkyūhyaku yonjūgo gojūnen no kitachōsen sangyō shiryō" (North Korea's industrial items, 1945–1950), *Aoyama kokusai seikei ronshū* 51 (2000): 400, 403, cited in Kimura and Abe, *Chŏnjaengi mandŭn nara*, 234.

13. Morita Yoshio and Osada Kanako, *Chōsen shūsen no kiroku* (Records at the end of the war in Korea), vol. 3: *Shiryōhen* (Sources) (Tokyo: Gan'nandō Shoten 1980), 542, cited in Kimura and Abe, *Chŏnjaengi mandŭn nara*, 246.

14. The Hamhŭng Plains, fed by the fast-flowing and abundant Sŏngch'ŏn River, are the only plains in the northeastern part of North Korea. At 1,300 square kilometers (502 square miles), they are smaller than the plains in the West, but they have historically served as an important area of grain production for the mostly mountainous Hamgyŏng region.

15. Ch'a Munsŏk, "Han'guk Chŏnjaeng sigi Pukhan ŭi chŏnsi saengsanch'eje: Kongjang sogae wa chŏnsi saengsanjŏngch'aek ŭl chumgsim ŭro" (The wartime production system of North Korea during the Korean War: A look at the factory relocation project and wartime production policy), *Tongil Munje Yŏn'gu* 39 (2003): 83.

16. Central Statistical Board, *Statistical Returns of the National Economy of the Democratic People's Republic of Korea, 1946–1960* (Pyongyang: Foreign Languages Publishing House, 1961), 40–41.

17. Chang Sehun, "Kongganggujo pyŏnhwa rŭl t'onghae pon pukhan chibangdaedosi ŭi tosihwa kwajŏng" (The process of urbanization of large regional cities as seen through changes in spatial construction), in *Pukhan tosi ŭi hyŏngsŏng kwa palchŏn: Ch'ŏngjin, Sinŭiju, Hyesan* (The formation and development of cities in North Korea: A focus on Ch'ŏngjin, Sinŭiju, and Hyesan), ed. Choe Wangyu (Seoul: Hanul Academy, 2004), 36.

18. Chang Sehun, "Kongganggujo pyŏnhwa," 36.

19. Chang Sehun, "Kongganggujo pyŏnhwa," 37.

20. Kuksa P'yŏnch'an Wiwŏnhoe (National Institute of Korean History), *Pukhan kwan'gye saryojip* (Historical material on North Korea), vol. 30 (Kwachŏn: Kuksa P'yŏnch'an Wiwŏnhoe Ch'ulp'ansa, 1998), 356–386.

21. Chang Sehun, "Kongganggujo pyŏnhwa," 32, 33.

22. Rüdiger Frank, "Lessons from the Past: The First Wave of Developmental Assistance to North Korea and the German Reconstruction of Hamhŭng," *Pacific Focus* 33, no. 1 (2008): 55, 57.

23. T'ongil Yŏn'guwŏn (Korea Institute for National Unification), *Togiljiyŏk Pukhan kimil munsŏjip* (Secret documents on North Korea from the German region) (Seoul: Sunin, 2006), 75.

24. Kim Myŏn, "Pimilmunsŏro pon kudongdok ŭi Hamhŭngsi kŏnsŏlp'urojekt'ŭ: Chŏnhu sahoejuŭi tosi kŏnsŏl ŭi saeroun model" (The reconstruction project of Hamhŭng by the former East Germany as seen through secret documents: A new model of postwar socialist city construction), *Minjok 21*, no. 51 (2005): 96.

25. Kim Myŏn, "Pimilmunsŏro pon kudongdok ŭi Hamhŭngsi kŏnsŏlp'urojekt'ŭ," 97.
26. T'ongil Yŏn'guwŏn, *Togiljiyŏk Pukhan kimil munsŏjip*, 181.
27. T'ongil Yŏn'guwŏn, *Togiljiyŏk Pukhan kimil munsŏjip*, 189.
28. Kim Myŏn, "Pimilmunsŏro pon kudongdok ŭi Hamhŭngsi kŏnsŏlp'urojekt'ŭ," 98.
29. Kim Myŏn, "Pimilmunsŏro pon kudongdok ŭi Hamhŭngsi kŏnsŏlp'urojekt'ŭ," 99.
30. Yu Chŏngok, "Hamhŭng chonghap chutaek kŏnsŏlchangŭl ch'ajasŏ" (A visit to the construction site of housing complexes at Hamhŭng), *Ch'ŏllima*, no. 10 (1963): 17.
31. During my visit to Hamhŭng in May 2014, a local guide told me that Chŏngsŏng Avenue is also popularly known as "Pieck Avenue" (*p'ikŭkŏri*), but she was not sure where the name came from. I did not tell her.
32. Chŏng Yŏngch'un, "Pinallon kwa Ri Sŭnggi paksa" (Vinalon and the scientist Ri Sŭnggi), *Kwahakŭi segye*, no. 1 (1998): 68.
33. Kang Hoje, "Pinallon sinhwa ŭi chuin'gong wŏlbukgwahakcha Ri Sŭnggi" (The hero of the vinalon myth: The northbound scientist Ri Sŭnggi), *Minjok 21*, no. 103 (2009): 65.
34. On the northward movement of scientists in the postliberation period, see Kim Kŭnbae, "Wŏlbuk kwahakgisulcha wa Hŭngnam kongŏp taehak ŭi sŏllip" (Scientists and technicians who went north and the founding of the Hŭngnam College of Technology), *Asea Yŏn'gu* 40, no. 2 (1997): 95–130. In June 1946, the South Korean government announced the plan to create a single national university in Seoul instead of several specialized colleges (in Korean, *kungnip Sŏul taehakkyo sŏllipan*, or *kukdaean*, for short). Many scholars thought this plan constituted a regression of higher education in South Korea and protested against it. The scholars' protest against the plan led to moments of crises called *kukdaean p'adong*. With this situation in mind and with the plan to build Kim Il Sung University, the North Korean state launched a major campaign to recruit scientists, engineers, and technicians from South Korea. The campaign lasted until the end of the war and resulted in the northward movement of more than eighty scientists and engineers with at least a bachelor's degree.
35. Kim Kŭnbae, "Wŏlbuk kwahakgisulcha," 105.
36. Kim Kŭnbae, "Wŏlbuk kwahakgisulcha," 106.
37. Kim Kŭnbae, "Wŏlbuk kwahakgisulcha," 106.
38. Kim Kŭnbae, "Wŏlbuk kwahakgisulcha," 123. In 1990, the college name was changed to Hamhŭng College of Chemical Industry.
39. Kim Kŭnbae, "Wŏlbuk kwahakgisulcha," 126.
40. Chŏng Yŏngch'un, "Pinallon kwa Ri Sŭnggi paksa," 67.
41. Ichiro Sakurada, "The Sakurada Laboratory," in *The Commemoration Volume for the Silver Jubilee of the Institute for Chemical Fibers Research* (Kyoto: Institute for Chemical Research, 1951), 84.
42. Sakurada, "The Sakurada Laboratory," 84.
43. Ichiro Sakurada, Sŭnggi Ri, and Hiroshi Kawakami, "Japan Patent 147,958" (1941), Industrial Property Digital Library, http://www.ipdl.inpit.go.jp.
44. Sakurada, "The Sakurada Laboratory," 84–85.
45. Chŏng Yŏngch'un, "Pinallon kwa Ri Sŭnggi paksa," 68.
46. Chunggongŏp Wiwŏnhoe, *Pinallon Kongjang kŏnsŏl*, 25.

47. Chŏng Yŏngch'un, "Pinallon kwa Ri Sŭnggi paksa," 67.
48. Chŏng Yŏngch'un, "Pinallon kwa Ri Sŭnggi paksa," 67.
49. Chŏng Yŏngch'un, "Pinallon kwa Ri Sŭnggi paksa," 68.
50. Quoted in Chunggongŏp Wiwŏnhoe, *Pinallon Kongjang kŏnsŏl*, 25.
51. Kim Kŭnbae, "Wŏlbuk kwahakgisulcha," 8.
52. Sakurada, "The Sakurada Laboratory," 91.
53. Chŏng Yŏngch'un, "Pinallon kwa Ri Sŭnggi paksa," 68.
54. Ri Sŭnggi, *Hapsŏng sŏmyu pinallon yŏn'gu ronmunchip* (Collection of research papers on the synthetic fiber vinalon) (Pyongyang: Kwahakwŏn Ch'ulp'ansa, 1960), ii.
55. Chŏng Yŏngch'un, "Pinallon kwa Ri Sŭnggi paksa," 68.
56. Ri Sŭnggi, *Pinallon* (Vinalon) (Pyongyang: Kwahak Ch'ulp'ansa, 1976), i.
57. Quoted in T'ongil Yŏn'guwŏn, *Togiljiyŏk pukhan kimil munsŏjip*, 14, 15.
58. Chunggongŏp Wiwŏnhoe, *Pinallon Kongjang kŏnsŏl*, 2–3.
59. Shuichi Tsukahara and Keichi Yamada, "A Note on the Time Lag Between the Life Cycle of a Discipline and Resource Allocation in Japan," *Research Policy*, no. 11 (1982): 139.
60. Jun-ichi Hikasa, "Fibers, Poly (Vinyl Alcohol)," in *Kirk-Othmer Encyclopedia of Chemical Technology*, Wiley Online Library (Hoboken, NJ: Wiley, 2001), doi:10 .1002/0471238961.1615122508091101.a01.
61. F. L. Marten, "Vinyl Alcohol Polymers," in *Kirk-Othmer Encyclopedia of Chemical Technology*, doi:10.1002/0471238961.2209142513011820.a01.pub2.
62. George P. Jan, "Japan's Trade with Communist China," *Asian Survey* 9, no. 12 (1969): 913.
63. Calculated from Marten, "Vinyl Alcohol Polymers."
64. Hikasa, "Fibers, Poly (Vinyl Alcohol)."
65. Chosŏn Minju Nyŏsŏng Tongmaeng (Korean Democratic Women's Union), "Chuch'e sŏmyu pinallon" (Vinalon: Fiber of *chu'che*), *Chosŏn Nyŏsong*, no. 3 (1987): 36.
66. Hikasa, "Fibers, Poly (Vinyl Alcohol)."
67. Chosŏn Minju Nyŏsong Tongmaeng, "Chuch'e sŏmyu pinallon," 34; Chu Suŭng, "Pinallon taedosi" (The great Vinalon City), *Ch'ŏllima*, no. 8 (1962): 47.
68. Marten, "Vinyl Alcohol Polymers."
69. Marten, "Vinyl Alcohol Polymers."
70. Chosŏn Minju Nyŏsong Tongmaeng, "Chuch'e sŏmyu pinallon," 36.
71. Chunggongŏp Wiwŏnhoe, *Pinallon Kongjang kŏnsŏl*, 31, 107, 33.
72. Chunggongŏp Wiwŏnhoe, *Pinallon Kongjang kŏnsŏl*, 36.
73. Ri Wŏnman, "Widaehan suryŏng Kim Ilsŏng tongji ŭi hyŏnmyŏnghan ryŏngdo mite chuch'ejŏgin pinallongongŏpch'angsŏl ŭl wihan uri inmin ŭi t'ujaeng" (The struggle of our people to construct the *chuch'e*-like vinalon industry under the wise leadership of the great leader Comrade Kim Il Sung), *Ryŏksa Kwahak*, 1 (1986): 3.
74. Ri Wŏnman, "Widaehan suryŏng Kim Ilsŏng," 4.
75. Chunggongŏp Wiwŏnhoe, *Pinallon Kongjang kŏnsŏl*, 37.
76. Chunggongŏp Wiwŏnhoe, *Pinallon Kongjang kŏnsŏl*, 52.
77. Chunggongŏp Wiwŏnhoe, *Pinallon Kongjang kŏnsŏl*, 51.

78. As told in Ha Chŏnghi and Yun T'aehong, "Pinallon kongjang kŏnsŏlchang ŭi yŏngungdŭl" (The heroes of the Vinalon Factory construction site), in *Ch'ŏllima sidae saramdŭl* (The people of the ch'ŏllima era), vol. 2, ed. Sŏ Tŏksin, Im Kiju, and Choe Ch'ansŏk (Pyongyang: Chosŏn Rodongdang Ch'ulp'ansa and Chigŏp Tongmaeng Ch'ulp'ansa, 1961), 12.

79. The dates August 8 and April 1 refer to the days when Kim Il Sung visited the factory. Paektu, besides being the tallest mountain in Korea, is a source of Korea's origin myth. And Poch'ŏnbo is a border village where in June 1937 Kim Il Sung's most famous battle against Japanese imperial forces took place.

80. Ha and Yun, "Pinallon kongjang kŏnsŏlchang," 15

81. This account is from Chunggongŏp Wiwŏnhoe, *Pinallon Kongjang kŏnsŏl*, 310–311.

82. As recounted in Chunggongŏp Wiwŏnhoe, *Pinallon Kongjang kŏnsŏl*, 310–311.

83. As recounted in Chunggongŏp Wiwŏnhoe, *Pinallon Kongjang kŏnsŏl*, 292–296.

84. Susan Buck-Morss, *Dreamworld and Catastrophe: The Passing of Mass Utopia in East and West* (Cambridge, MA: MIT Press, 2000), 182.

85. Burawoy, *Politics of Production*, 163. Offering a comparison, Burawoy points out that the anarchy of the capitalist market is compensated through the direct control of labor power (the hiring and firing of workers).

86. Deborah A. Kaple, *Dream of a Red Factory: The Legacy of High Stalinism in China* (New York: Oxford University Press, 1994), 98.

87. Overachievement was equally met with intentional underachievement, so that production quotas would be kept low and the working environment more tolerable. Moreover, high levels of productivity all too often resulted in low-quality products and waste of resources.

88. Sheila Fitzpatrick, *Everyday Stalinism: Ordinary Life in Extraordinary Times, Soviet Russia in the 1930s* (Oxford: Oxford University Press, 1999), 67.

89. Quoted in Chu Suŭng, "Pinallon taedosi," 45–46.

90. Kim Ilchun, "Kiri charanghari" (We shall forever be proud), *Ch'ŏllima*, no. 3, (1963): 32.

91. Kim Ilchun, "Kiri charanghari," 31.

92. Kim Ilchun, "Kiri charanghari," 31–32.

93. Choŭnbŏtdŭl (Good Friends), *Pukhansaramdŭri malhanŭn Pukhan iyagi* (North Korean stories told by North Korean people) (Seoul: Chŏngt'o Ch'ulp'ansa, 2000), 108.

94. Choŭnbŏtdŭl, *Pukhansaramdŭri malhanŭn*, 108.

95. Stephen Kotkin, *Magnetic Mountain: Stalinism as Civilization* (Berkeley and Los Angeles: University of California Press, 1995), 66, 364.

Conclusion: The Negation of Work and Other Everyday Maneuvers

1. Kojin Karatani, *Transcritique: On Kant and Marx* (Cambridge, MA: MIT Press, 2003), 203, 275; see also chapters 5 and 7.

2. Karatani, *Transcritique*, 202.

3. Henri Lefebvre, *Critique of Everyday Life*, vol. 3: *From Modernity to Modernism (Towards a Metaphilosophy of Daily Life)* (1981; reprint, London: Verso, 2008), 167.

4. Karl Marx, "Private Property and Communism," in *Economic and Philosophic Manuscripts of 1844*, Marxists Internet Archive, http://www.marxists.org/archive /marx/works/1844/manuscripts/preface.htm.

5. Lefebvre, *Critique of Everyday Life*, 3:167.

6. Lefebvre, *Critique of Everyday Life*, 3:80.

7. Kojin Karatani, *The Structure of World History: From Modes of Production to Modes of Exchange*, trans. Michael K. Bourdaghs (Durham, NC: Duke University Press, 2014), 289, 290, 291.

8. Karatani, *Structure of World History*, 303, 304.

Bibliography

Sources from North Korea

Central Statistical Board. *Statistical Returns of the National Economy of the Democratic People's Republic of Korea, 1946–1960*. Pyongyang: Foreign Languages Publishing House, 1961.

Chang Seki. "Chŏnhu samgaenyŏn inmin kyŏngje kyehoek ŭi yebijŏk ch'onghwa wa ch'ŏn'gubaekosipch'ilnyŏn inmin kyŏngje palchŏn kyehoek e taehayŏ" (A preliminary evaluation of the postwar Three-Year Plan and on the economic development plan of 1957). *Kŭlloja*, no. 134 (1957): 18–27.

Cho Pyŏngkwŏn. "Maŭl ŭi ŏmŏni" (The mother of the village). In *Ch'ŏllima sidae saramdŭl* (The people of the *ch'ŏllima* era), vol. 4, edited by Pak Sunp'al, Ri Tonghan, and Ch'oe Ch'ansŏk, 102–121. Pyongyang: Chosŏn Rodongdang Ch'ulp'ansa and Minch'ŏng Ch'ulp'ansa, 1961.

Chŏng Kwanch'ŏl. *Chŏng Kwanch'ŏl chakp'umjip* (The art of Chŏng Kwanch'ŏl). Pyongyang: Munhak Yesul Chonghap Ch'ulp'ansa, 1999.

Chŏng Yŏngch'un. "Pinallon kwa Ri Sŭnggi paksa" (Vinalon and the scientist Ri Sŭnggi). *Kwahakŭi segye*, no. 1 (1998): 67–68.

Chosŏn Chigŏp Ch'ongdongmaeng (General Federation of Trade Unions of Korea). *Ch'ŏllima Kisu tokbon* (The Ch'ŏllima Riders handbook). Pyongyang: Chigŏp Tongmaeng Ch'ulp'ansa, 1963.

Chosŏn Chungang T'ongsinsa (Korean Central News Agency). "Che ilhoe Choguk Pogwi Pokkwŏn Ch'uch'ŏm Wiwŏnhoe kusŏng" (The first Fatherland Restoration Lottery Drawing Committee established). *Rodong Sinmun*, November 25, 1951.

———. "Hwanghae chech'ŏlso e chunŭn ssoryŏn kisulchadŭl ŭi pangcho" (Soviet technicians providing assistance at Hwanghae Steel). *Rodong Sinmun*, March 28, 1955.

Chosŏn Hwabosa (Korean Pictorial Agency). *Kim Ilsŏng chusŏk kwa onŭl ŭi Chosŏn* (Premier Kim Il Sung and North Korea today). Pyongyang: Oegukmun Chonghap Ch'ulp'ansa, 1993.

Chosŏn Minju Nyŏsŏng Tongmaeng (Korean Democratic Women's Union). "Chuch'e sŏmyu pinallon" (Vinalon: Fiber of *chu'che*). *Chosŏn Nyŏsŏng*, no. 5 (1987): 34–36.

Chosŏn Rodongdang (Korean Workers' Party). *Kukjejuŭijŏk ch'insŏn* (International friendship). Pyongyang: Chosŏn Rodongdang Ch'ulp'ansa, 1956.

Chu Suŭng. "Pinallon taedosi" (The great Vinalon City). *Ch'ŏllima*, no. 8 (1962): 44–47.

Chunggongŏp Wiwŏnhoe (Heavy Industry Committee). *Pinallon Kongjang kŏnsŏl* (The construction of the Vinalon Factory). Pyongyang: Kungnip Kŏnsŏl Ch'ulp'ansa, 1961.

Ha Chŏnghi and Yun T'aehong. "Pinallon kongjang kŏnsŏlchang ŭi yŏngungdŭl" (The heroes of the Vinalon Factory construction site). In *Ch'ŏllima sidae saramdŭl* (The people of the *ch'ŏllima* era), vol. 2, edited by Sŏ Tŏksin, Im Kiju, and Choe Ch'ansŏk, 1–34. Pyongyang: Chosŏn Rodongdang Ch'ulp'ansa and Chigŏp Tongmaeng Ch'ulp'ansa,1961.

Han Kyŏnghwa. "Na nŭn irŏnsaram ŭl saranghanda: Uri chagŏpbanjang ŭl tugo" (I love such a person: About our work team leader). *Ch'ŏllima*, no. 6 (1961): 85–86.

Han Sangdu. "Sahoejuŭi kŏnsŏl ŭl ch'okchinsikigi wihan chiptanjŏk hyŏksin undong ŭi palchŏn ŭl wihayŏ" (For the advancement of the Collective Innovation Movement in constructing socialism). *Kŭlloja*, no. 151 (1958): 54–62.

Han Sŏrya. "Munye chŏnsŏn e issŏsŏ ŭi pandongjŏk burŭjoa sasang ŭl pandaehayŏ" (Against reactionary bourgeois ideology on the literary and artistic front). In *Munye chŏnsŏn e issŏsŏ ŭi pandongjŏk burŭjoa sasang ŭl pandaehayŏ: Charyojip* (Against reactionary bourgeois ideology on the literary and artistic front: Sourcebook), 2 vols., edited by Ŏm Toman and Kwak Chaesŏk, 1:5–43. Pyongyang: Chosŏn Chakka Tongmaeng Ch'ulp'ansa, 1956.

———. "Uri munhak, yesul ŭl inminsŏng kwa kwallyŏnhan tangmyŏnhan myŏt kaji munje" (Several problems facing and related to the people's spirit in our literature and art). *Kŭlloja*, no. 149 (1958): 59–65.

Hwang Changyŏp. *Sahoe palchŏnsa* (The history of societal development). Pyongyang: Chosŏn Rodongdang Ch'ulp'ansa, 1956.

Kang Chiwŏn, "Nongŏp e taehan kongŏp ŭi pangjo" (The industrial assistance of agriculture). *Kŭlloja*, no. 128 (1956): 44–56.

Kil Hwaksil. *Ch'ŏllima chagŏpbanjang ŭi sugi* (A memoir of a Chŏllima Work Team leader). Pyongyang: Chigŏp Tongmaeng Ch'ulp'ansa, 1961.

Kim Chongyŏn. "Rodong chŏngyang saŏp esŏŭi hyŏksin ŭl wihayŏ" (For the improvement of quantitative labor tasks). *Rodong*, no. 5 (1959): 12–15.

———. "Rodong kijunhwa saŏp ŭi palchŏn" (The development in the standardization of labor). *Rodong*, no. 8 (1958): 12–17.

———. "Rodong saengsan nŭngyul ŭi piyak chŏgin changsŏng ŭl wihayŏ hyŏksinchŏk rodong kijunnyang ŭl toip haja" (Let us implement innovative work standards for the rapid growth of work-production efficiency). *Rodong*, no. 12 (1958): 19–23.

Kim Ch'unsang. "Chŏnmunhwa wa hyŏptonghwa e ŭihan chikp'o tagidae chagŏp" (Handling many fabric machines through specialization and collectivization). *Rodong*, no. 7 (1958): 39–43.

Kim Ilchun. "Kiri charanghari" (We shall forever be proud). *Ch'ŏllima*, no. 3 (1963): 31–34.

Kim Il Sung. *Kim Ilsŏng chŏjakchip* (The works of Kim Il Sung). 47 vols. Pyongyang: Chosŏn Rodongdang Ch'ulp'ansa, 1979–1997.

———. "Uri nara esŏ sahoejuŭijŏk nongŏp hyŏpdonghwa ŭi sŭngri wa nongch'on kyŏngri ŭi kŭmhu palchŏn e taehayŏ" (On the victory of socialist agricultural cooperativization in our country and on the further development of the agricultural economy). *Rodong Sinmun*, January 6, 1959.

Kim Insŏn. "Sŏnjin kisul chagŏp pangbŏp ŭl toip hayŏ sae kijunnyang ŭl ch'angjo" (The creation of new standards by adopting advanced technologies and manufacturing methods). *Rodong*, no. 12 (1958): 51–53.

Kim Pyŏngch'ŏn. "Rodong sigan riyong e taehan t'onggyejŏk punsŏk" (Statistical analysis of labor-time use). *Rodong*, no. 10 (1959): 30–34.

Kim Sanghak. "Che ilch'a ogaenyŏn kyehoek kigan e chunggongŏp ŭl usŏnjŏgŭro palchŏnsikimyŏ kyŏnggongŏp mit nongŏp ŭl tongsi e palchŏnsikil te taehan tang ŭi chŏngch'aek" (On the party policy to first develop heavy industry and then simultaneously develop light industry and agriculture during the First Five-Year Plan). *Kŭlloja*, no. 148 (1958): 46–53.

Kim Soryŏn. "Hambukdo nae tasunyŏsŏngdŭl soksok saengsanjikjang e chinch'ul" (Many women of North Hamgyŏng enter production facilities). *Rodong Sinmun*, July 27, 1950.

Kim Tongch'an. "Roryŏk poch'ung sa'ŏp ŭi palchŏn" (The development of reserve labor power). *Rodong*, no. 8 (1958): 7–12.

Kim Tongch'ŏl. "Kŭllojadŭl sogesŏ ŭi purŭjoajŏk mit sopurŭjoajŏk chanjae ŭisik ŭi kŭkbok ŭl wihayŏ" (For the overcoming of bourgeois or petit bourgeois consciousness of workers). *Kŭlloja*, no. 116 (1955): 75–88.

Kim Tubong. "Sinnyŏnsa" (New Year's address). *Rodong Sinmun*, January 1, 1953.

Kim Tuyŏng, ed. *Ŭiji ro tallyŏndwen saramdŭl* (People hardened through will). Pyongyang: Chigŏp Tongmaeng Ch'ulp'ansa, 1957.

Kim Ŭnggi. "Kiŏpso, kongjangdŭl esŏ saengsan munhwa ŭi hwangnip ŭl wihayŏ" (Toward establishing production culture in firms and factories). *Rodong*, no. 6 (1958): 4–6.

Kim Yŏngsu. "Sahoejuŭi kŏnsŏl ŭi hyŏn tan'gye wa konghwaguk nyŏsŏng" (The current stage of socialist construction and women of the republic). *Kŭlloja*, no. 155 (1958): 58–61.

Kong Chint'ae. "Kongjak kigyedŭl ŭi riyongryul chego rŭl wihan rodong sigan ŭi ch'ŭkjŏng" (Work-time measurement to improve the use rate of manufacturing machines). *Rodong*, no. 8 (1958): 40–43.

Kwŏn Tuŏn. "Ch'angjojŏk rodong ŭi him" (The strength of creative labor). *Rodong*, no. 6 (1958): 1–3.

Mun Ch'isu. "Imgŭm chedo ŭi palchŏn" (The development of the wage system). *Rodong*, no. 9 (1958): 19–26.

Ŏm Toman and Kwak Chaesŏk, eds. *Munye chŏnsŏn e issŏsŏ ŭi pandongjŏk burŭjoa sasang ŭl pandaehayŏ: Charyojip* (Against reactionary bourgeois ideology on the literary and artistic front: Sourcebook). 2 vols. Pyongyang: Chosŏn Chakka Tongmaeng Ch'ulp'ansa, 1956.

Pak Ch'angok. "Ch'ŏngubaekosipsanyŏn ch'ŏngubaekosipyuknyŏn Chosŏn Minjujuŭi Inmingonghwaguk inmingyŏngje pokgubalchŏn sam kaenyŏn kyehwek e kwanhan pogo" (A report on the Democratic People's Republic of Korea's 1954–1956 Three-Year Plan for recovery and development of the people's economy). *Kŭlloja*, no. 102 (1954): 37–66.

Pak Ch'ŏl. "Chŭngsan kyŏngjaeng undong esŏŭi myŏtkaji munje" (Several problems of the Production Increase and Competition Movement). *Kŭlloja*, no. 105 (1954): 85–99.

Pak Myŏngjun. "Inmin saenghwal hyangsang ŭl wihan tang kwa chŏngbu ŭi hwakkohan chŏngch'aek" (The firm policies of the party and government for the improvement of the people's livelihood). *Kŭlloja*, no. 154 (1958): 84–91.

Pulgul ŭi osipnyŏndae nŭn urirŭl purŭnda (The invincible 1950s is calling for us) (documentary). Pyongyang: Chosŏn Kirok Kwahak Yŏnghwa Chwalyŏngso, 2002.

Ri Chŭngok. "Roryŏk hubi yangsŏng saŏp ŭi palchŏn" (The development of training reserve labor power). *Rodong*, no. 9 (1958): 26–31.

Ri Kyedŭk. "Ch'ŏlchŏhan saengsan chunbi nŭn sŏlbi riyongryul chego ŭi chungyo chokŏn" (A thorough preparation is important in increasing the use rate of equipment). *Kŭlloja*, no. 130 (1956): 156–160.

Ri Sŭnggi. *Hapsŏng sŏmyu pinallon yŏn'gu ronmunchip* (Collection of research papers on the synthetic fiber vinalon). Pyongyang: Kwahakwŏn Ch'ulp'ansa, 1960.

———. *Pinallon* (Vinalon). Pyonyang: Kwahak Ch'ulp'ansa, 1976.

Ri Sun'gŏn, and Paek Wan'gi. *Chut'aek soguyŏk kyehwek* (Housing subquarter planning). Pyongyang: Kungnip Kŏnsŏl Ch'ulp'ansa, 1963.

Ri Wŏnman. "Widaehan suryŏng Kim Ilsŏng tongji ŭi hyŏnmyŏnghan ryŏngdo mite chuch'ejŏgin pinallongongŏpch'angsŏl ŭl wihan uri inmin ŭi t'ujaeng" (The struggle of our people to construct the *chuch'e*-like vinalon industry under the wise leadership of the great leader Comrade Kim Il Sung). *Ryŏksa Kwahak*, no. 1 (1986): 3–7.

Rodong Sinmun. "Chŏngubaekosiponyŏn inmin kyŏngje kyehoek" (People's economic plan for 1955). December 14, 1954.

———. "Chŏnsi ŭimu roryŏkdongwŏn e kwanhayŏ" (On wartime compulsory labor mobilization). July 28, 1950.

———. "Nambuk Chosŏn chikmaeng tanche rŭl t'ongil hayŏ Chosŏn Chigŏp Ch'ongdongmaeng ŭro sinbalchok" (The inauguration of the General Federation of Trade Unions of Korea by uniting the trade federations of South and North Koreas). January 24, 1951.

———. "Oeguk kisulchadŭl ŭi hyŏngjejŏk pangcho" (Brotherly assistance of foreign technicians). January 13, 1955.

Ryu Yŏngsul. "Kisul hyŏkmyŏng esŏŭi chungdŭng mit kisul ŭimu kyoyukche silsi ŭi ŭiŭi" (The significance of secondary and technical mandatory education in fulfilling the technological revolution). *Kŭlloja*, no. 156 (1958): 12–17.

Sahoegwahagwon Kyŏngjeyŏn'guso Kongŏpgyŏngjeyŏn'gusil (Industrial Economy Research Team of the Economic Research Center at the Institute for Social Science). *Sahoejuŭi kyŏngjegwalli esŏ taean ŭi saŏpch'egye* (The Taean Work System in socialist economic management). Pyongyang: Sahoegwahak Ch'ulp'ansa, 1969.

Sŏ Ch'ŏng. "Ŭiji ŭi him" (The power of will). In *Ŭiji ro tallyŏndwen saramdŭl* (People hardened through will), edited by Kim Tuyŏng, 158–191. Pyongyang: Chigŏp Tongmaeng Ch'ulp'ansa, 1957.

Wŏn Tomyŏng. "Ch'ŏllima chikchang ŭi nanal" (The everyday of a *ch'ŏllima* shop). *Ch'ŏllima*, no. 10 (1961): 22–25.

——. "Pinallon sokdo" (Vinalon speed). *Ch'ŏllima*, no. 5 (1961): 16–21.

Yang Inhyŏk. "Rodong sigan yebi ŭi chŏkbal kwa kŭ ŭi riyong pangbŏp" (The exposure of spare labor time and methods of its use). *Rodong*, no. 4 (1959): 33–36.

Yu Chŏngok. "Hamhŭng chonghap chutaek kŏnsŏlchangŭl ch'ajasŏ" (A visit to the construction site of housing complexes at Hamhŭng). *Ch'ŏllima*, no. 10 (1963): 15–17.

Yun Ryonggyu, dir. *Sinhonbubu* (The newlyweds). Pyongyang: Chosŏn Kungnip Yŏnghwa Chwalyŏngso, 1955.

Yun Sejung. *Yonggwangno nŭn sumshinda* (The furnace is breathing). Pyongyang: Munye Ch'ulp'ansa, 1960.

Yun Sep'yŏng. "Munhak yusan kyesŭng e issŏsŏ kwannyŏmronjŏk hŏmujuŭi rŭl pandaehayŏ" (Against idealistic nihilism in our literary heritage). In *Munye chŏnsŏn e issŏsŏ ŭi pandongjŏk burŭjoa sasang ŭl pandaehayŏ: Charyojip* (Against reactionary bourgeois ideology on the literary and artistic front: Sourcebook), 2 vols., edited by Ŏm Toman and Kwak Chaesŏk, 2:135–172. Pyongyang: Chosŏn Chakka Tongmaeng Ch'ulp'ansa, 1956.

Yun Ŭisŏp and Ch'a Sunhŏn. *Konghwaguk'ka esŏŭi imgŭm chojik kwa rodong ŭi kijunhwa* (The standardization of wage and labor in the republic). Pyongyang: Kungnip Ch'ulp'ansa, 1955.

Sources from South Korea

Ch'a Munsŏk. "Han'guk Chŏnjaeng sigi Pukhan ŭi chŏnsi saengsanch'eje: Kongjang sogae wa chŏnsi saengsanjŏngch'aek ŭl chumgsim ŭro" (The wartime production system of North Korea during the Korean War: A look at the factory relocation project and wartime production policy). *T'ongil Munje Yŏn'gu* 39 (2003): 77–102.

——. *Pannodong ŭi yut'op'ia* (The utopia of antilabor). Seoul: Pak Chongchŏl Ch'ulp'ansa, 2001.

——. "Pukhan: Isip'il segi e ch'ŏllima undong?" (North Korea: The Ch'ŏllima Movement in the twenty-first century?). *T'ongil Han'guk*, no. 302 (2009): 32–35.

——. "Pukhan ŭi kongjanggwallicheje wa chŏljŏnggi sŭt'allinjuŭi: Taehan ŭi saŏpch'egye e taehan saeroun haesŏk" (North Korea's factory-management system and High Stalinism: A new interpretation of the Taean Work System). *Pukhan Yŏn'gu Hakhoebo* 3, no. 2 (1999): 227–250.

Chang Sehun. "Konggangujo pyŏnhwa rŭl t'onghae pon pukhan chibangdaedosi ŭi tosihwa kwajŏng" (The process of urbanization of large regional cities as seen through changes in spatial construction). In *Pukhan tosi ŭi hyŏngsŏng kwa palchŏn: Ch'ŏngjin, Sinŭiju, Hyesan* (The formation and development of cities in North Korea: A focus on Ch'ŏngjin, Sinŭiju, and Hyesan), edited by Choe Wangyu, 21–63. Seoul: Hanul Academy, 2004.

Charyŏk kaengsaeng ŭi chŏngsin (The spirit of independent rebirth) (documentary). Seoul: Nambuk Munje Yŏn'guso, n.d. [c. late 1990s].

Chin Hŭigwan. "Pukhan ŭi kyŏngje wa kyŏngjegwalli pangsik" (North Korea's economy and economic management). In *Rodongsinmun ŭl t'onghae pon Pukhan pyŏnhwa* (Changes in North Korea as observed through *Rodong Sinmun*), edited by Ko Yuhwan, 271–316. Seoul: Sunin, 2006.

Ch'oe Chonggo. *Pukhanpŏb* (North Korean law). Seoul: Pagyŏngsa, 2001.

Chŏng Ch'ŏnrye. "Pangjik'kong ch'ŏnyŏ ege" (To the young woman weaver). In *Pukhan munhak* (The literature of North Korea), edited by Sin Hyŏnggi, O Sŏngho, and Yi Sŏnmi, 1467. Seoul: Munhak kwa Chisŏngsa, 2007.

Chŏng Ilyŏng. "Kongjang kwallich'eje rŭl t'onghae pon Pukhan sahoe ŭi pyŏnhwa: Tangbisŏ chibaein nodongja samgak kwan'gye ŭi pyŏnhwa rŭl chungsim ŭro" (Changes in North Korean society as seen through the factory-management system: Changes in the triangular relationship between the party secretary, factory director, and the worker). *T'ongil Yŏn'gu* 17, no. 1 (2013): 5–36.

Chŏng Sangdon. "Pukhan nodongjohap ŭi 'chayulsŏng' nonjaeng: Haebang ihubutŏ han'gukjŏnjaeng ijŏnkkaji" (The debate on the autonomy of North Korea's trade unions: From liberation to the Korean War). *Sahoe Kwahak Nonjip* 21, no. 1 (2003): 51–71.

Chŏng Sŏch'on. "Yŏngbyŏn agassi" (Young woman from Yŏngbyŏn). In *Pukhan munhak*, edited by Sin Hyŏnggi, O Sŏngho, and Yi Sŏnmi (The literature of North Korea), 1430–1431. Seoul: Munhak kwa Chisŏngsa, 2007.

Chosŏn Nodongdang (Korean Workers' Party). *Chosŏn Nodongdang Taehoe charyojip che ilchip* (Documents of the Korean Workers' Party Congress). Vol. 1. Seoul: Kukt'o T'ongilwŏn Ch'ulp'ansa, 1979.

——. *Pukhan Chosŏn Nodongdang Taehoe chuyo munhŏnjip* (Essential documents of North Korea's Korean Workers' Party Congress). Seoul: Tolbegae P'yŏnjipbu, 1988.

Choŭnbŏtdŭl (Good Friends). *Pukhansaramdŭri malhanŭn Pukhan iyagi* (North Korean stories told by North Korean people). Seoul: Chŏngt'o Ch'ulp'ansa, 2000.

Kang Hoje. "Pinallon sinhwa ŭi chuin'gong wŏlbukgwahakcha Ri Sŭnggi" (The hero of the vinalon myth: The defector scientist Ri Sŭnggi). *Minjok 21*, no. 103 (2009): 64–65.

Khang Jeongseog. "Ilsangsaenghwal pip'an kwa salm ŭi pyŏnhyŏk: Puranhan ilsang e tŏnjinŭn puronhan munjejeki" (Criticism of everyday life and the transformation life: A subversive question for the unstable everyday). *Pip'yŏng*, no. 18 (2008): 84–97.

Kim Chonguk. "Pukhan kwallyodŭl ŭi ilsangsaenghwal segye: Hoesaek ŭi aura" (The world of everyday life of North Korea's bureaucrats: The aura of grayness). In *Pukhan ŭi ilsangsaenghwal segye: Oech'im kwa soksagim* (The world of everyday life in North

Korea: Cries and whispers), edited by Pak Sunsŏng and Hong Min, 248–291. P'aju: Hanul, 2010.

Kim Jin Sun. "Sahoejuŭi kuk'ka ŭi tosigyehoek e kwanhan yŏn'gu: Pukhan ŭl chungsim ŭro" (A study on urban planning in socialist states: A case study on North Korea). PhD diss., Konkuk University, 1998.

Kim Kŭnbae. "Wŏlbuk kwahakgisulcha wa Hŭngnam kongŏp taehak ŭi sŏllip (Scientists and technicians who went north and the founding of the Hŭngnam College of Technology). Asea Yŏn'gu 40, no. 2 (1997): 95–130.

Kim Myŏn. "Pimilmunsŏro pon kudongdok ŭi Hamhŭngsi kŏnsŏlp'urojekt'ŭ: Chŏnhu sahoejuŭi tosi kŏnsŏl ŭi saeroun model" (The reconstruction project of Hamhŭng by the former East Germany as seen through secret documents: A new model of postwar socialist city construction). Minjok 21, no. 51 (2005): 94–99.

Kim Pyŏnghun. "Kiltongmudŭl" (Fellow travelers). In Pukhan munhak (The literature of North Korea), edited by Sin Hyŏnggi, O Sŏngho, and Yi Sŏnmi, 627–664. Seoul: Munhak kwa Chisŏngsa, 2007.

Kim Sango. "Kisa" (The engineer). In Pukhan munhak (The literature of North Korea), edited by Sin Hyŏnggi, O Sŏngho, and Yi Sŏnmi, 1223–1224. Seoul: Munhak kwa Chisŏngsa, 2007.

Kim Yŏngsŏng. "Pukhan ŭi kŏnch'uk yangsikdŭl" (North Korea's architectural styles). Kŏnch'uk 37, no. 4 (1993): 57–73.

Kimura Mitsuhiko and Abe Keiji. Chŏnjaengi mandŭn nara: Pukhan ŭi kunsa kongŏphwa (The country made by war: The military industrialization of North Korea). Translated by Ch'a Munsŏk and Pak Chŏngjin. Seoul: Mizi, 2009.

Kuk'ka T'ongye Pot'ŏl (Korean Statistical Information Service), Republic of Korea. "Chut'aek pogŭpryul" (Housing supply rate). 2015. http://kosis.kr.

Kuksa P'yŏnch'an Wiwŏnhoe (National Institute of Korean History). Pukhan kwan'gye saryojip (Historical material on North Korea). Vol. 30. Kwachŏn: Kuksa P'yŏnch'an Wiwŏnhoe Ch'ulp'ansa, 1998.

Kwŏn Hŭiyŏng. "Chosŏn Nodong Kongjehoe wa kongje" (Workers' Mutual Aid Society and kongje). Chŏngsin Munhwa Yŏn'gu 16, no. 2 (1993): 139–157.

Kwŏn Oyun. "Pukhan ŭi pyŏnhwach'ujin kanŭngseryŏk ŭrosŏ Chigŏp Ch'ongdongmaeng ŭi kŏmt'o" (A study of the General Federation of Trade Unions as a possible agent of change in North Korea). Taehan Chŏngch'ihak Hoebo 13, no. 2 (2005): 29–52.

Lankov, Andrei N. Soryŏn ŭi charyoro pon Pukhan hyŏndaechŏngch'isa (The political history of North Korea as seen through Soviet documents). Translated by Kim Kwangrin. Seoul: Orŭm, 1995.

Lim Jie-Hyun (Yim Chihyŏn) and Kim Yong-Woo (Kim Yongwu), eds. Taechungdokchae (Mass dictatorship). Vol. 1: Kangje wa tongŭi saiesŏ (Between coercion and consent). Seoul: Ch'aeksesang, 2004.

Minjujuŭi Minjok Chŏnsŏn (Democratic National United Front). Chosŏn haebang yŏn'bo (Annual report on Korea's liberation). Seoul: Minjujuŭi Minjok Chŏnsŏn Press, 1946.

On Nakchung. Pukchosŏn kihaeng (Travels to North Korea). Seoul: Chosŏn Chungang-ilbo Ch'ulp'anbu, 1948.

Paek Sŏk. "Irŭn Pom" (Early spring). In *Pukhan munhak* (The literature of North Korea), edited by Sin Hyŏnggi, O Sŏngho, and Yi Sŏnmi, 1441–1442. Seoul: Munhak kwa Chisŏngsa, 2007.

Pak Sunsŏng and Hong Min, eds. *Pukhan ŭi ilsangsaenghwal segye: Oech'im kwa soksagim* (The world of everyday life in North Korea: Cries and whispers). P'aju: Hanul, 2010.

——. "Pukhan ilsangsaenghwal yŏn'gu ŭi pangpŏpnonjŏk mosaek" (The methodological search for doing research on North Korea's everyday life). In *Pukhan ŭi ilsangsaenghwal segye: Oech'im kwa soksagim* (The world of everyday life in North Korea: Cries and whispers), edited by Pak Sunsŏng and Hong Min, 159–199. P'aju: Hanul, 2010.

Pak Yŏngja. "Yugio chŏnjaeng kwa Pukhanyŏsŏng ŭi nodongsegye: P'agoe wa pisaengsan ŭi ch'angjo wa saengsan ŭi chuch'e yŏttŏn yŏsŏng yŏn'gu" (War of June 25 and the working world of North Korean women: A study of women who were the subjects of creation and production from a war of destruction and antiproduction). *Asia Yŏsŏng Yŏn'gu* 45, no. 2 (2006): 49–84.

Sin Hyŏnggi and O Sŏngho. *Pukhan munhaksa: Hangil hyŏngmyŏng munhak esŏ chuch'e munhak kkaji* (The history of North Korean literature: From anti-Japanese revolutionary literature to *chuch'e* literature). Seoul: P'yŏngminsa, 2000.

Sin Hyŏnggi, O Sŏngho, and Yi Sŏnmi, eds. *Pukhan munhak* (The literature of North Korea). Seoul: Munhak kwa Chisŏngsa, 2007.

Sin Yongha. "Ch'ŏn'gubaekisipinyŏn Chosŏn Nodong Yŏnmaenghoe ŭi ch'angrip kwa nodong undong" (The formation of the Chosŏn Workers' League in 1922 and the labor movement). *Sahoewa Yŏksa* 15, no. 1 (1989): 55–96.

Sŏ Tongman. *Pukchosŏn sahoechuŭi ch'eje sŏngnipsa, 1945–1961* (The formation of state socialism in North Korea, 1945–1961). Seoul: Sunin, 2005.

Sŏ Usŏk. "Pukhan ŭi chugŏsilt'ae wa chut'aekjŏngch'aek e taehan p'yŏngka" (North Korea's housing situation and evaluation of its housing policy). *Wŏlgan Pokchi Tonghyang*, no. 24 (2000): 41–48.

T'ongil Yŏn'guwŏn (Korea Institute for National Unification). *Togiljiyŏk Pukhan kimil munsŏjip* (Secret documents on North Korea from the German region). Seoul: Sunin, 2006.

Wada Haruki. *Puk Chosŏn: Yugyŏkdae kuk'kaesŏ chŏnggyugun kuk'karo* (North Korea: From a guerilla state to a military state). Translated by Sŏ Tongman and Nam Kijŏng. Seoul: Dolbegae, 2002.

Yu Hangrim. "Chikmaeng panchang" (Union chief). In *Pukhan munhak* (The literature of North Korea), edited by Sin Hyŏnggi, O Sŏngho, and Yi Sŏnmi, 313–375. Seoul: Munhak kwa Chisŏngsa, 2007.

Sources in English

Agamben, Giorgio. *State of Exception*. Translated by Kevin Attell. Chicago: University of Chicago Press, 2005.

Applebaum, Herbert. *The Concept of Work: Ancient, Medieval, and Modern*. Albany: State University of New York Press, 1992.

Aristotle. *The Nichomachean Ethics.* Cambridge, MA: Harvard University Press, 1934.

Armstrong, Charles K. *The North Korean Revolution, 1945–1950.* Ithaca, NY: Cornell University Press, 2003.

Avineri, Shlomo. *The Social and Political Thought of Marx.* London: Cambridge University Press, 1968.

Barthes, Roland. *Mythologies.* New York: Hill and Wang, 1972.

Berliner, Joseph S. *Factory and Manager in the USSR.* Cambridge, MA: Harvard University Press, 1957.

Buck-Morss, Susan. *Dreamworld and Catastrophe: The Passing of Mass Utopia in East and West.* Cambridge, MA: MIT Press, 2000.

Burawoy, Michael. *The Politics of Production: Factory Regimes Under Capitalism and Socialism.* London: Verso, 1985.

Crane, Conrad C. "Raiding the Beggar's Pantry: The Search for Airpower Strategy in the Korean War." *Journal of Military History* 63, no. 4 (1999): 885–920.

Cumings, Bruce. *The Origins of the Korean War.* Vol. 2: *The Roaring of the Cataract, 1947–1950.* Princeton, NJ: Princeton University Press, 1990.

De Man, Henri. *Joy in Work.* 1927. Reprint. New York: Arno Press, 1977.

Fitzpatrick, Sheila. *Everyday Stalinism: Ordinary Life in Extraordinary Times, Soviet Russia in the 1930s.* Oxford: Oxford University Press, 1999.

Frank, Rüdiger. "Lessons from the Past: The First Wave of Developmental Assistance to North Korea and the German Reconstruction of Hamhŭng." *Pacific Focus* 33, no. 1 (2008): 46–74.

Golomstock, Igor. *Totalitarian Art in the Soviet Union, the Third Reich, Fascist Italy, and the People's Republic of China.* London: Collins Harvill, 1990.

Heller, Leonid. "A World of Prettiness: Socialist Realism and Its Aesthetic Categories." *South Atlantic Quarterly* 94, no. 3 (1995): 687–714.

Hikasa, Jun-ichi. "Fibers, Poly (Vinyl Alcohol)." In *Kirk-Othmer Encyclopedia of Chemical Technology.* Wiley Online Library. Hoboken, NJ: Wiley, 2001. doi:10.1002/0471238961.1615122508091101.a01.

Jan, George P. "Japan's Trade with Communist China." *Asian Survey* 9, no. 12 (1969): 900–913.

Kaple, Deborah A. *Dream of a Red Factory: The Legacy of High Stalinism in China.* New York: Oxford University Press, 1994.

Karatani, Kojin. *The Structure of World History: From Modes of Production to Modes of Exchange.* Translated by Michael K. Bourdaghs. Durham, NC: Duke University Press, 2014.

——. *Transcritique: On Kant and Marx.* Translated by Sabu Kohso. Cambridge, MA: MIT Press, 2003.

Khrushchev, Nikita S. "Speech to the 20th Congress of the Communist Party of the Soviet Union, 1956." Marxists Internet Archive. http://www.marxists.org/archive/khrushchev/1956/02/24.htm.

Kim, Cheehyung. "Total, Thus Broken: *Chuch'e sasang* and North Korea's Terrain of Subjectivity." *Journal of Korean Studies* 17, no. 1 (2012): 69–96.

Kim, Suzy. *Everyday Life in the North Korean Revolution, 1945–1950.* Ithaca, NY: Cornell University Press, 2013.

Kornai, János. *The Socialist System: The Political Economy of Communism*. Princeton, NJ: Princeton University Press, 1992.

Kotkin, Stephen. *Magnetic Mountain: Stalinism as Civilization*. Berkeley and Los Angeles: University of California Press, 1995.

Kuark, Yoon T. "North Korea's Industrial Development During the Post-war Period." *China Quarterly* 14 (1963): 51–64.

Kuromiya, Hiroaki. "*Edinonachalie* and the Soviet Industrial Manager, 1928–1937." *Soviet Studies* 36, no. 2 (1984): 185–204.

Lacan, Jacques. *The Seminar of Jacques Lacan*. Book 11: *The Four Fundamental Concepts of Psychoanalysis*. New York: Norton, 1998.

Lee, Chong-Sik. "The 'Socialist Revolution' in the North Korean Countryside." *Asian Survey* 2, no. 8 (1962): 9–22.

Lee, Jong Won (Yi Chongwŏn). "The Impact of the Korean War on the Korean Economy." *International Journal of Korean Studies* 5, no. 1 (2001): 97–118.

Lefebvre, Henri. *Critique of Everyday Life*. Vol. 1: *Introduction*. 1947. Reprint. London: Verso, 2008.

——. *Critique of Everyday Life*. Vol. 2: *Foundations for a Sociology of the Everyday*. 1961. Reprint. London: Verso, 2008.

——. *Critique of Everyday Life*. Vol. 3: *From Modernity to Modernism (Towards a Metaphilosophy of Daily Life)*. 1981. Reprint. London: Verso, 2008.

——. "The Everyday and Everydayness." *Yale French Studies*, no. 73 (1987): 7–11.

——. "Toward a Leftist Cultural Politics: Remarks Occasioned by the Centenary of Marx's Death." In *Marxism and the Interpretation of Culture*, edited by Cary Nelson and Lawrence Grossberg, 75–88. Urbana: University of Illinois Press, 1988.

Lenin, V. I. *Essential Works of Lenin*. New York: Dover, 1987.

——. "From the Destruction of the Old Socialist System to the Creation of the New" (April 11, 1920). Marxists Internet Archive. http://www.marxists.org/archive/lenin/works/1920/apr/11.htm.

Lüdtke, Alf. "People Working: Everyday Life and German Fascism." *History Workshop Journal*, no. 50 (2000): 74–92.

Marten, F. L. "Vinyl Alcohol Polymers." In *Kirk-Othmer Encyclopedia of Chemical Technology*. Wiley Online Library. Hoboken, NJ: Wiley, 2001. doi:10.1002/0471238961.2209142513011820.a01.pub2.

Marx, Karl. *Capital*. Vol. 1. London: Penguin, 1976.

——. *Economic and Philosophic Manuscripts of 1844*. Marxists Internet Archive. http://www.marxists.org/archive/marx/works/1844/manuscripts/preface.htm.

——. *Value, Price, and Profit*. London: ElecBooks, 1998.

Marx, Karl, and Friedrich Engels. *The Marx–Engels Reader*. Edited by Robert Tucker. New York: Norton, 1978.

McNulty, Paul J. "Adam Smith's Concept of Labor." *Journal of the History of Ideas* 34, no. 3 (1973): 345–366.

Mizuno, Hiromi. *Science for the Empire: Scientific Nationalism in Modern Japan*. Stanford, CA: Stanford University Press, 2009.

Molony, Barbara. *Technology and Investment: The Prewar Japanese Chemical Industry*. Cambridge, MA: Council on East Asian Studies, Harvard University, 1990.

Myers, Brian. *Han Sŏrya and North Korean Literature: The Failure of Socialist Realism in North Korea*. Ithaca, NY: East Asia Program, Cornell University, 1994.

Park, Hyun Ok. *The Capitalist Unconscious: From Korean Unification to Transnational Korea*. New York: Columbia University Press, 2015.

Park, Sunyoung. "The Colonial Origin of Korean Realism and Its Contemporary Manifestation." *Positions: Asia Critique* 14, no. 1 (2006): 165–192.

Polanyi, Karl. *The Great Transformation: The Political and Economic Origins of Our Time*. Boston: Beacon, 2001.

Roberts, Andrew. "The State of Socialism: A Note on Terminology." *Slavic Review* 63, no. 2 (2004): 349–366.

Rudolph, Philip. "North Korea and the Path to Socialism." *Pacific Affairs* 32, no. 2 (1959): 131–143.

Sakurada, Ichiro. "The Sakurada Laboratory." In *The Commemoration Volume for the Silver Jubilee of the Institute for Chemical Research*, 84–91. Kyoto: Institute for Chemical Research, 1951.

Sakurada, Ichiro, Sŭnggi Ri, and Hiroshi Kawakami. "Japan Patent 147,958." 1941. Industrial Property Digital Library. http://www.ipdl.inpit.go.jp.

Schurmann, Franz. *Ideology and Organization in Communist China*. Berkeley and Los Angeles: University of California Press, 1966.

Scott, James C. *Seeing Like a State: How Certain Schemes to Improve the Human Condition Have Failed*. New Haven, CT: Yale University Press, 1998.

Shabad, Theodore. "North Korea's Postwar Recovery." *Far Eastern Survey* 25, no. 6 (1956): 81–91.

Sorenson, Jay B. *The Life and Death of Soviet Trade Unionism, 1917–1928*. New York: Atherton Press, 1969.

Strong, Anna Louise. *Inside North Korea: An Eye-witness Report*. N.p.: Self-published, 1949.

Szalontai, Balázs. *Kim Il Sung in the Khrushchev Era: Soviet–DPRK Relations and the Roots of North Korean Despotism*. Stanford, CA: Stanford University Press, 2003.

Teiwes, Frederick C. *China's Road to Disaster: Mao, Central Politicians, and Provincial Leaders in the Unfolding of the Great Leap Forward, 1955–1959*. Armonk, NY: M. E. Sharpe, 1999.

Trotsky, Leon. *Problems of Everyday Life: And Other Writings on Culture and Science*. New York: Monad Press, 1973.

Tsukahara, Shuichi and Keichi Yamada. "A Note on the Time Lag Between the Life Cycle of a Discipline and Resource Allocation in Japan." *Research Policy*, no. 11 (1982): 133–140.

Vucinich, Alexander. "The Structure of Factory Control in the Soviet Union." *American Sociological Review* 15, no. 2 (1950): 179–186.

Weathersby, Kathryn. *Soviet Aims in Korea and the Origins of the Korean War, 1945–1950: New Evidence from Russian Archives*. Cold War International History Project Working Paper 8. Washington, DC: Woodrow Wilson International Center for Scholars, 1993.

Werner, Jake. "Global Fordism in 1950s Urban China." *Frontiers of History in China* 7, no. 3 (2012): 415–441.

Zhdanov, Andre. "Soviet Literature—the Richest in Ideas, the Most Advanced Literature: A Speech Delivered at the Soviet Writers' Congress, 1934." Marxists Internet Archive. http://www.marxists.org/subject/art/lit_crit/sovietwritercongress/zdhanov.htm.

Žižek, Slavoj. *The Sublime Object of Ideology.* London: Verso, 1989.

Index

markets, 48, 59, 94, 203, 228n69; capitalist, 7–8, 234n85

"market utopia," 14

Marx, Karl, 1, 10–11, 17, 98, 204; on emancipation, 97; in historical concept of work, 35–38, *36*; Smith and, 46–47

Marxism, 10–11, 212n86

mass movements, *107*, 166, 199–200, 202; competition of, 106–7; diversity of, 105–6; in everyday life, 104–9; hegemony and, 122; labor heroes and, 107–8; Mao and, 105; origin of, 105; in postwar period, 71; purpose of, 105; for Vinalon Factory, 188–89

memoir of a Ch'ŏllima Work Team leader, A (*Ch'ŏllima chagŏpbanjang ŭi sugi*), 160–63

metalworkers, 1–2; steel production, *74*, *80*, 136–37, 143–44, 227n49

Mikoyan, Anastas, 89–90

militarism, 27, 214n26. *See also* Korean War

Military Committee, 27

military recruitment, 28

mining, 31, 67, 72–73, *74*, *80*

Mining and Manufacturing Ministry, 31

Ministry of Education and Culture, 225n13

Ministry of Industry, 26, 73, *74–75*, *75*, 214n35

misrecognition, 103; conversion and, 163–64; of vinalon, 194–96

Mizuno, Hiromi, 168

modernization, 8–9, 197–98

Mun Yebong, 228n66

Myers, Brian, 133

"My Older Brother and the Brazier" (Im Hwa), 131–32

Mythologies (Barthes), 167

National Council of Chosŏn Labor Unions, 50

nationalism: danger and, 192–93; of Ri Sŭnggi, 178–79, 194. *See also* patriotism

nationalization, 24

"national/popular spirit," 130

Nazi Party, 212n86

Newlyweds, The (*Sinhonbubu*) (film), *157*, 228nn66–67; argument in, 154–55; domination in, 155–57; guilt in, 154–56; patriarchy in, 155–58; pride in, 155; reconstruction in, 153–54; subjectivity in, 155–56, 158

Nihon Chisso Hiryō Kabushiki Kaisha (Japan Nitrogenous Fertilizer Company), 170

Noguchi Jun, 170–71

North Korea: China compared to, 57–58; consolidation within, 8; Constitution of, 3, 99, 214n35; laboratories in, 176–77; science in, 176; Supreme People's Assembly of, 1–3, 32, 84–85, 91; technology in, 11–12, 115, 176

North Korean industries, 72–73

North–South Joint Conference (1948), 208n2

O Kisŏp, 51

O Myŏngsuk (fictitious character), 120–22

one-person factory management, 18, 53–55, 57–58

On Nakchung, 22–24, 208n2

Onoda Cement of Japan, 227n43

"On Wartime Labor," 27

order, 193, 221–22

"organized passivity," 70–71

Yokohama and the Silk Trade: How Eastern Japan Became the Primary Economic Region of Japan, 1843–1893, by Yasuhiro Makimura, Lexington Books, 2017

The Social Life of Inkstones: Artisans and Scholars in Early Qing China, by Dorothy Ko, University of Washington Press, 2017

Darwin, Dharma, and the Divine: Evolutionary Theory and Religion in Modern Japan, by G. Clinton Godart, University of Hawai'i Press, 2017

Dictators and Their Secret Police: Coercive Institutions and State Violence, by Sheena Chestnut Greitens, Cambridge University Press, 2016

The Cultural Revolution on Trial: Mao and the Gang of Four, by Alexander C. Cook, Cambridge University Press, 2016

Inheritance of Loss: China, Japan, and the Political Economy of Redemption After Empire, by Yukiko Koga, University of Chicago Press, 2016

Homecomings: The Belated Return of Japan's Lost Soldiers, by Yoshikuni Igarashi, Columbia University Press, 2016

Samurai to Soldier: Remaking Military Service in Nineteenth-Century Japan, by D. Colin Jaundrill, Cornell University Press, 2016

The Red Guard Generation and Political Activism in China, by Guobin Yang, Columbia University Press, 2016

Accidental Activists: Victim Movements and Government Accountability in Japan and South Korea, by Celeste L. Arrington, Cornell University Press, 2016

Ming China and Vietnam: Negotiating Borders in Early Modern Asia, by Kathlene Baldanza, Cambridge University Press, 2016

Ethnic Conflict and Protest in Tibet and Xinjiang: Unrest in China's West, edited by Ben Hillman and Gray Tuttle, Columbia University Press, 2016

One Hundred Million Philosophers: Science of Thought and the Culture of Democracy in Postwar Japan, by Adam Bronson, University of Hawai'i Press, 2016

Conflict and Commerce in Maritime East Asia: The Zheng Family and the Shaping of the Modern World, c. 1620–1720, by Xing Hang, Cambridge University Press, 2016

Chinese Law in Imperial Eyes: Sovereignty, Justice, and Transcultural Politics, by Li Chen, Columbia University Press, 2016

Imperial Genus: The Formation and Limits of the Human in Modern Korea and Japan, by Travis Workman, University of California Press, 2015

Yasukuni Shrine: History, Memory, and Japan's Unending Postwar, by Akiko Takenaka, University of Hawai'i Press, 2015

The Age of Irreverence: A New History of Laughter in China, by Christopher Rea, University of California Press, 2015

The Knowledge of Nature and the Nature of Knowledge in Early Modern Japan, by Federico Marcon, University of Chicago Press, 2015

The Fascist Effect: Japan and Italy, 1915–1952, by Reto Hofmann, Cornell University Press, 2015

Empires of Coal: Fueling China's Entry into the Modern World Order, 1860–1920, by Shellen Xiao Wu, Stanford University Press, 2015